Wireless Communications and Networks

Dr. M. Sughasiny

Dr. V. Upendran

Dr. R. Dinesh

Dr. Ankit Khare

9798886410075

First Edition: March - 2022

NOTION PRESS
India. Singapore. Malaysia.

MRP Rs. 280 /-

ISBN: 9798886410075

Notion Press Media Pvt Ltd,
Old No. 38, New No. 6, McNichols Road, Chetpet,
Chennai-600031,
Tamilnadu, India.
Email: orders@notionpress.com

AUTHOR PROFILE

 Dr. M.Sughasiny is working as Assistant Professor, PG & Research Department of Computer Science , Srimad Andavan Arts and Science College(Autonomous), Trichy. She is having 7 years of Research experience and 15 years of Teaching experience . Her Research interests are Wireless Networks, Machine Learning, Artificial Intellence and Data Analytics. She did her Ph.D from Bharathiar University, Coimbatore. Dr.Sughasiny has authored about 35+ research publications in referred international journals / National & International Conferences includes IEEE, Springer, Elsevier etc. . She has served as organizing secretary for national conference, training programme and workshops. She received Young Scientist Award for 2021 from Novel Research Academy, Puducherry, Wonder Woman Award for 2019 from Sai Charan Academy, Hyderabad and Appreciation Awards from Department of Computer Science. She acted as Editorial Board member for in-House Publication . She has participated more than 30+ Workshops, Seminars and Faculty Development Programme. She certified as Microsoft Professional 2007, EMC2 Academic Associates for Data Science, Soft Skill Trainer and International Certified Career Counseling and Coach from ISCHS, Banglore. She has filed 3 Patents and published in IPR. She served as Member Academic Council, College Committee member, Chairman/Member Board of Studies, Member for question paper setting board in various Institutes. She has supervised nearly 10+ M.Phil. and 2 Ph.D. candidates and currently guiding for 3 Research Scholars of Bharathidasan University. She has delivered 15+ lectures as Keynote Speaker, Chief Guest, invited Speaker etc. She actively contributes to society by motivating the young students to achieve by setting goals, action plans and feedback through speeches at various colleges and she has addressed nearly 5000 students.

 Dr. V. Upendran is working as a Assistant Professor and Head in PG & Research Department of Computer Science , Srimad Andavan Arts and Science College(Autonomous), Trichirappalli, Tamil Nadu, India. He is having 3 years of Research Experience and 18 years of teaching experience. His Research Interests are Wireless Networks, Machine Learning and Artificial Intelligence. He did her Ph.D from Bharathiar University, Coimbatore. Dr. Upendran has authored 16 + research publications in referred international journals, Conferences. He is a Management Representative for ISO 9001:2015 standards. He has participated more than 20 workshops, Seminars and Faculty Development Programme. He has filed 1 Patent and published in IPR. He is a Chairman in Board of Studies, Valuation and he is a Member in Academic council and varies College committee activities, Member for question paper setting in various institutes.

 Dr.R.Dinesh has been in teaching field for 17 years and currently working as a Associate Professor in ECE in Marthandam College of Engineering &Technology, India. He has received the B.E degree in Electronics and communication from Bharathidasan university, India (2000), M.E degree in Optical Communication from Anna university (2005), India and M.B.A degree from Madurai Kamaraj University, India(2010). He has completed PhD in VLSI from Sathyabama University (2021). He has published 25 technical papers in International conferences and journal in the areas of optical communication, VLSI and signal processing. His research area of interest includes, Low power VLSI, Clock Synchronization,

ADPLL, optical communication, etc. He is a life member of ISTE. He has published book in Optical Communication.

 Dr. Ankit Khare currently positioned as Assistant Professor in School of Computer Science, University of Petroleum and Energy Studies, Dehradun, Uttarakhand, India. He holds Doctorate in Computer Science from University of Petroleum and Energy Studies, Dehradun, India. He received the B.Tech. degree in Information Technology from Rajiv Gandhi Proudyogiki Vishwavidyalaya Bhopal, Madhya Pradesh, India and M. Tech. degree in computer Science & Engineering from Jaypee University of Information Technology Waknaghat, Solan, Himachal Pradesh, India. His research interests include Internet of Things, Communication Networks, Digital Signal Processing, Open Source & Open Standards, and Database Management Systems.

Contents

Chapter I
INTRODUCTION TO WIRELESS COMMUNICATION SYSTEMS

Chapter II
MOBILE RADIO PROPAGATION (LARGE-SCALE PATH LOSS)

Chapter III
MOBILE RADIO PROPAGATION: SMALL –SCALE FADING AND MULTIPATH

Chapter IV
WI-FI AND THE IEEE 802.11 WIRELESS LAN STANDARDS

Chapter V
MOBILE DATA NETWORKS

PREFACE

Wireless Communications Systems starts by explaining the fundamentals needed to understand, design, and deploy wireless communications systems. The authors, a noted expert on the topic, explores the basic concepts of signals, modulation, antennas, and propagation with a MATLAB emphasis. The book emphasizes practical applications and concepts needed by wireless engineers.

The authors introduce applications of wireless communications and includes information on satellite communications, radio frequency identification, and offers an overview with practical insights into the topic of multiple input multiple output (MIMO). The book also explains the security and health effects of wireless systems concerns on users and designers. Designed as a practical resource, the text contains a range of examples and pictures that illustrate many different aspects of wireless technology. The book relies on MATLAB for most of the computations and graphics. Written for students of engineering and physics and practicing engineers and scientists, Wireless Communications Systems covers the fundamentals of wireless engineering in a clear and concise manner and contains many illustrative examples.

Authors

Chapter - I

Introduction to Wireless Communication Systems

The ability to communicate with people on the move has evolved remarkably since Guglielmo Marconi first demonstrated radio's ability to provide continuous contact with ships sailing the English Channel in 1897. Since then new wireless communications methods and services have been enthusiastically adopted by people throughout the world. Particularly during the past ten years, the mobile radio communications industry has grown by orders of magnitude, fueled by digital and RF circuit fabrication improvements, new large-scale circuit integration, and other miniaturization technologies which make portable radio equipment smaller, cheaper, and more reliable. Digital switching techniques have facilitated the large scale deployment of affordable, easy-to-use radio communication networks.

1.1 EVOLUTION OF MOBILE RADIO COMMUNICATIONS

The ability to provide wireless communications to an entire population was not even conceived until Bell Laboratories developed the cellular concept in the 1960s and 1970s. With the development of highly reliable, miniature, solid-state radio frequency hardware in the 1970s, the wireless communications era was born.

The following market penetration data show how wireless communications in the consumer sector has grown in popularity. Figure 1.1 illustrates how mobile telephony has penetrated our daily lives compared with other popular inventions of the 20th century. Figure 1.1 shows that the first 35 years of mobile telephony saw little market penetration due to high cost and the technological challenges involved, but however, in the past decade, wireless communications has been accepted by consumers at rates comparable to television and the video cassette recorder.

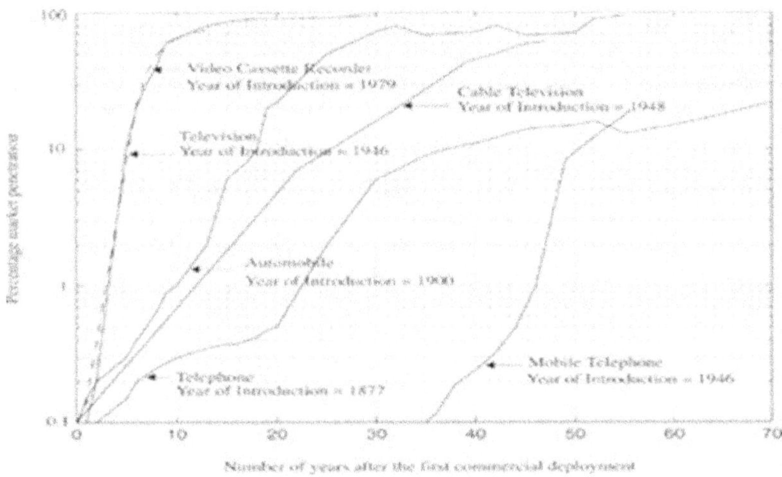

Figure 1.1. The growth of mobile telephony as compared with other popular inventions of the 20th century.

By 1934, 194 municipal police radio systems and 58 state police stations had adopted amplitude modulation (AM) mobile communication systems for public safety in the U.S. In 1935, Edwin Armstrong demonstrated frequency modulation (FM) for the first time, and since the late 1930s, FM has been the primary modulation technique used for mobile communication systems throughout the world. With the boom in CB radio and cordless appliances such as garage door openers and telephones, the number of users of mobile and portable radio in 1995 was about 100 million, or 37% of the U.S. population.

The number of worldwide cellular telephone users grew from 25,000 in 1984 to about 25 million in 1993, and since then subscription-based wireless services have been experiencing customer growth rates well in excess of 50% per year. At the beginning of the 21st century, over 1% of the worldwide wireless subscriber population had already abandoned wired telephone service for home use, and had begun to rely solely on their cellular service provider for telephone access.

1.2 MOBILE RADIOTELEPHONY IN THE U.S.

In 1946, the first public mobile telephone service was introduced in twenty-five major American cities. Each system used a single, high-powered transmitter and large tower in order to cover distances of over 50 km in a particular market. During the 1950s and 1960s, AT&T Bell Laboratories and other telecommunications companies throughout the world developed the theory and techniques of cellular radiotelephony—the concept of breaking a coverage zone (market) into small cells, each of which reuse portions of the spectrum to increase spectrum usage at the expense of greater system infrastructure. AT&T proposed the concept of a cellular mobile system to the FCC in 1968, although technology was not available to implement cellular telephony until the late 1970s. In 1983, the FCC finally allocated 666 duplex channels (40 MHz of spectrum in the 800 MHz band, each channel having a one-way bandwidth of 30 kHz for a total spectrum occupancy of 60 kHz for each duplex channel) for the U.S. Advanced Mobile Phone System (AMPS).

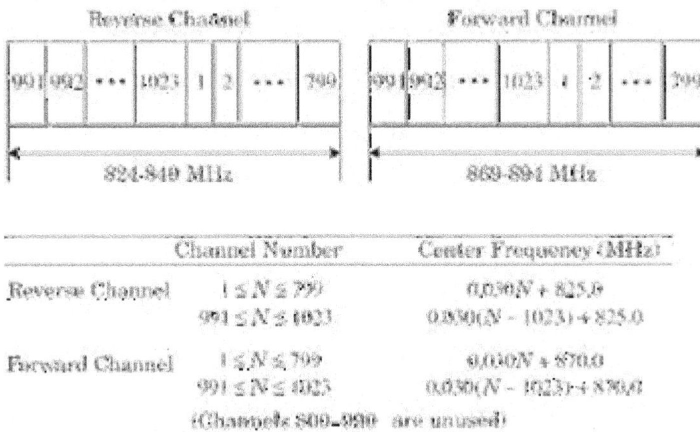

Figure 1.2. Frequency spectrum allocation for the U.S. cellular radio service

In late 1991, the first US Digital Cellular (USDC) system hardware was installed in major U.S. cities. The USDC standard (Electronic Industry Association Interim Standard IS-54 and later IS-136) allowed cellular operators to replace gracefully some single-user analog channels with digital channels which support three users in the same 30 kHz bandwidth. In this way, U.S. carriers gradually phased out AMPS as more users accepted digital phones.

A cellular system based on code division multiple access (CDMA) has been developed by Qualcomm, Inc. and standardized by the Telecommunications Industry Association (TIA) as an Interim Standard (IS-95). This system supports a variable number of users in 1.25 MHz wide channels using direct sequence spread spectrum. CDMA systems can operate at much larger interference levels because of their inherent interference resistance properties. The ability of CDMA to operate with a much smaller signal -to-noise ratio (SNR) than conventional narrowband

FM techniques allows CDMA systems to use the same set of frequencies in every cell, which provides a large improvement in capacity.

Personal Communication Service (PCS) licenses in the 1800/1900 MHz band were auctioned by the U.S. Government to wireless providers in early 1995, and these have spawned new wireless services that complement, as well as compete with, cellular and SMR.

1.3 MOBILE RADIO SYSTEMS AROUND THE WORLD

Many mobile radio standards have been developed for wireless systems throughout the world, and more standards are likely to emerge. Tables 1.1 through 1.3 list the most common paging, cordless, cellular, and personal communications standards used in North America, Europe, and Japan.

Table 1.1. Major Mobile Radio Standards in North America

Standard	Type	Year Introduction	o Multiple Access	Frequency Band	Modulation	Channel Bandwidth
AMPS	Cellular	1983	FDMA	824-894 MHz	FM	30 kHz
NAMPS	Cellular	1992	FDMA	824-894 MHz	FM	10 kHz
USDC	Cellular	1991	TDMA	824-894 MHz	$\pi/4$-DQPSK	30 kHz
CDPD	Cellular	1993	FH/ Packet	824-894 MHz	GMSK	30 kHz
IS-95	Cellular/PCS	1993	CDMA	824-894 MHz 1.8 2.0 GHz	QPSK/BPSK	1.25 MHz
GSC	Paging	1970s	Simplex	Several	FSK	12.5 kHz
POCSAG	Paging	1970s	Simplex	Several	FSK	12.5 kHz
FLEX	Paging	1993	Simplex	Several	4-FSK	15 kHz
DCS-1900 (GSM)	PCS	1994	TDMA	1.85-1.99 GHz	GMSK	200 kHz
PACS	Cordless/PCS	1994	TDMA/FDMA	1.85-1.99 GHz	$\pi/4$-DQPSK	300 kHz
MIRS	SMR/PCS	1994	TDMA	Several	16-QAM	25 kHz
iDen	SMR/PCS	1995	TDMA	Several	16-QAM	25 kHz

Table 1.2. Major Mobile Radio Standards in Europe

Standard	Type	Year Introduction	o Multiple Access	Frequency Band	Modulation	Channel Bandwidth
ETACS	Cellular	1985	FDMA	900 MHz	FM	25 kHz
NMT-450	Cellular	1981	FDMA	450-470 MHz	FM	25 kHz
NMT-900	Cellular	1986	FDMA	890-960 MHz	FM	12.5 kHz
GSM	Cellular/PCS	1990	TDMA	890-960 MHz	GMSK	200 kHz
C-450	Cellular	1985	FDMA	450-465 MHz	FM	20 kHz/10 kHz

Table 1.3. Major Mobile Radio Standards in Japan

Standard	Type	Year of Introduction	Multiple Access	Frequency Band	Modulation	Channel Bandwidth
JTACS	Cellular	1988	FDMA	860-925 MHz	FM	25 kHz
PDC	Cellular	1993	TDMA	810-1501 MHz	$\pi/4$-DQPSK	25 kHz
NTT	Cellular	1979	FDMA	400/800 MHz	FM	25 kHz
NTACS	Cellular	1993	FDMA	843-925 MHz	FM	12.5 kHz
NTT	Paging	1979	FDMA	280 MHz	FSK	12.5 kHz
NEC	Paging	1979	FDMA	Several	FSK	10 kHz
PHS	Cordless	1993	TDMA	1895-1907 MHz	$\pi/4$-DQPSK	300 kHz

The world's first cellular system was implemented by the Nippon Telephone and Telegraph company (NTT) in Japan. The system, deployed in 1979, uses 600 FM duplex channels (25 kHz for each one-way link) in the 800 MHz band. In Europe, the Nordic Mobile Telephone system (NMT 450) was developed in 1981 for the 450 MHz band and uses 25 kHz channels. The European Total Access Cellular System (ETACS) was deployed in 1985 and is virtually identical to the U.S. AMPS system, except that the smaller bandwidth channels result in a slight degradation of signal-to-noise ratio (SNR) and coverage range. In Germany, a cellular standard called C-450 was introduced in 1985. The first generation European cellular systems are generally incompatible with one another because of the different frequencies and communication protocols used. These systems are now being replaced by the Pan European digital cellular standard GSM (Global System for Mobile) which was first deployed in 1990 in a new 900 MHz band which all of Europe dedicated for cellular telephone service. The GSM standard has gained worldwide acceptance as the first universal digital cellular system with modern network features extended to each mobile user, and is the leading digital air interface for PCS services above 1800 MHz throughout the world. In Japan, the Pacific Digital Cellular (PDC) standard provides digital cellular coverage using a system similar to North America's USDC.

Examples of Wireless Communication Systems

Most people are familiar with a number of mobile radio communication systems used in everyday life. Garage door openers, remote controllers for home entertainment equipment, cordless telephones, hand-held walkie-talkies, pagers (also called paging receivers or "beepers"), and cellular telephones are all examples of mobile radio communication systems. However, the cost, complexity, performance, and types of services offered by each of these mobile systems are vastly different.

Table 1.4. Wireless Communications System Definitions

Base Station	A fixed station in a mobile radio system used for radio communication with mobile stations Base stations are located at the center or on the edge of a coverage region and consist o radio channels and transmitter and receiver antennas mounted on a tower.
Control Channel	Radio channel used for transmission of call setup, call request, call initiation, and other beacon or control purposes.
Forward Channel	Radio channel used for transmission of information from the base station to the mobile.
Full Duplex Systems	Communication systems which allow simultaneous two-way communication. Transmission and reception is typically on two different channels (FDD) although new cordless/PCS systems are using TDD.
Half Duplex Systems	Communication systems which allow two-way communication by using the same radio channel for both transmission and reception. At any given time, the user can only either transmit or receive information.
Handoff	The process of transferring a mobile station from one channel or base station to another.
Mobile Station	A station in the cellular radio service intended for use while in motion at unspecified locations. Mobile stations may be hand-held personal units (portables) or installed in vehicles (mobiles).
Mobile Switching Center	Switching center which coordinates the routing of calls in a large service area. In a cellular radio system, the MSC connects the cellular base stations and the mobiles to the PSTN. AnMSC is also called a mobile telephone switching office (MTSO).
Page	A brief message which is broadcast over the entire service area, usually in a simulcast fashionby many base stations at the same time.

Mobile radio transmission systems may be classified as simplex, half-duplex or full-duplex. In simplex systems, communication is possible in only one direction. Paging systems, in which messages are received but not acknowledged, are simplex systems. Half- duplex radio systems allow two-way communication, but use the same radio channel for both transmission and reception. This means that at any given time, a user can only transmit or receive information. Constraints like "push-to- talk" and "release-to-listen" are fundamental features of half-duplex systems. Full duplex systems, on the other hand, allow simultaneous radio transmission and reception between a subscriber and a base station, by providing two simultaneous but separate channels (frequency division duplex, or FDD) or adjacent time slots on a single radio channel (time division duplex, or TDD) for communication to and from the user.

In FDD, a pair of simplex channels with a fixed and known frequency separation is used to define a specific radio channel in the system. The channel used to convey traffic to the mobile user from a base station is called the forward channel, while the channel used to carry traffic from the mobile user to a base station is called the reverse channel. In the U.S. AMPS standard, the reverse channel has a frequency which is exactly 45 MHz lower than that of the forward channel. Full duplex mobile radio systems provide many of the capabilities of the standard telephone, with the added convenience of mobility. Full duplex and half-duplex systems use transceivers for radio communication. FDD is used exclusively in analog mobile radio systems.

Time division duplexing (TDD) uses the fact that it is possible to share a single radio channel in time, so that a portion of the time is used to transmit from the base station to the mobile, and the remaining time is used to transmit from the mobile to the base station. If the data transmission rate in the channel is much greater than the end-user's data rate, it is possible to store information bursts and provide the appearance of full duplex operation to a user, even though there are not two simultaneous radio transmissions at any instant. TDD is only possible with digital transmission formats and digital modulation, and is very sensitive to timing. It is for this reason that TDD has only recently been used, and only for indoor or small area wireless applications where the physical coverage distances (and thus the radio propagation time delay) are much smaller than the many kilometers used in conventional cellular telephone systems.

1.4 PAGING SYSTEMS

Paging systems are communication systems that send brief messages to a subscriber. Depending on the type of service, the message may be either a numeric message, an alphanumeric message, or a voice message. Paging systems are typically used to notify a subscriber of the need to call a particular telephone number or travel to a known location to receive further instructions. In modern paging systems, news headlines, stock quotations, and faxes may be sent. A message is sent to a paging subscriber via the paging system access number (usually a toll-free telephone number) with a telephone keypad or modem. The issued message is called a page. The paging system then transmits the page throughout the service area using base stations which broadcast the page on a radio carrier.

Paging systems vary widely in their complexity and coverage area. While simple paging systems may cover a limited range of 2 to 5 km, or may even be confined to within individual buildings, wide area paging systems can provide worldwide coverage. Though paging receivers are simple and inexpensive, the transmission system required is quite sophisticated. Wide area paging systems consist of a network of telephone lines, many base station transmitters, and large radio towers that simultaneously broadcast a page from each base station (this is called simulcasting). Simulcast transmitters may be located within the same service area or in different cities or countries. Paging systems are designed to provide reliable communication to subscribers wherever they are; whether inside a building, driving on a highway, or flying in an airplane. This necessitates large transmitter powers (on the order of kilowatts) and low data rates (a couple of thousand bits per second) for maximum coverage from each base station. Figure 1.3 shows a diagram of a wide area paging system.

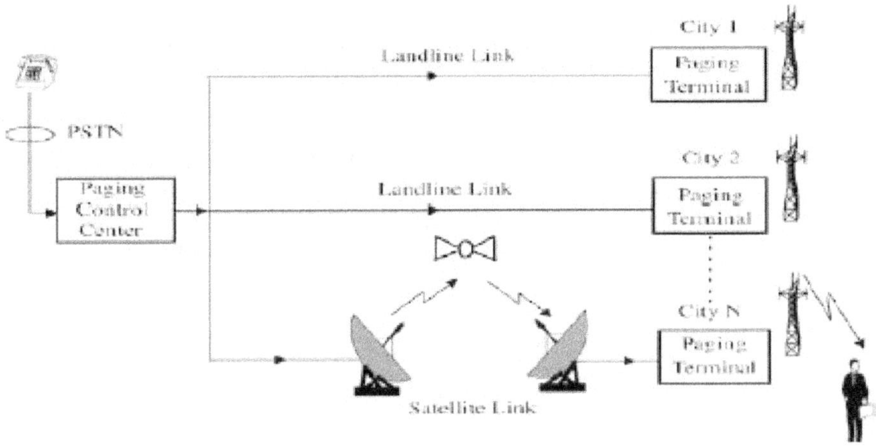

Figure 1.3. A wide area paging system. The paging control center dispatches pages received from the PSTN throughout several cities at the same time.

Paging systems are designed to provide ultra-reliable coverage, even inside buildings. Buildings can attenuate radio signals by 20 or 30 dB, making the choice of base station locations difficult for the paging companies. For this reason, paging transmitters are usually located on tall buildings in the center of a city, and simulcasting is used in conjunction with additional base stations located on the perimeter of the city to flood the entire area. Small RF bandwidths are used to maximize the signal-to-noise ratio at each paging receiver, so low data rates (6400 bps or less) are used.

1.5 CORDLESS TELEPHONE SYSTEMS

Cordless telephone systems are full duplex communication systems that use radio to connect a portable handset to a dedicated base station, which is then connected to a dedicated telephone line with a specific telephone number on the public switched telephone network (PSTN). In first generation cordless telephone systems (manufactured in the 1980s), the portable unit communicates only to the dedicated base unit and only over distances of a few tens of meters.

Early cordless telephones operate solely as extension telephones to a transceiver connected to a subscriber line on the PSTN and are primarily for in-home use.

Second generation cordless telephones have recently been introduced which allow subscribers to use their handsets at many outdoor locations within urban centers such as London or Hong Kong. Modern cordless telephones are sometimes combined with paging receivers so that a subscriber may first be paged and then respond to the page using the cordless telephone. Cordless telephone systems provide the user with limited range and mobility, as it is usually not possible to maintain a call if the user travels outside the range of the base station. Typical second generation base stations provide coverage ranges up to a few hundred meters. Figure 1.4 illustrates a cordless telephone system.

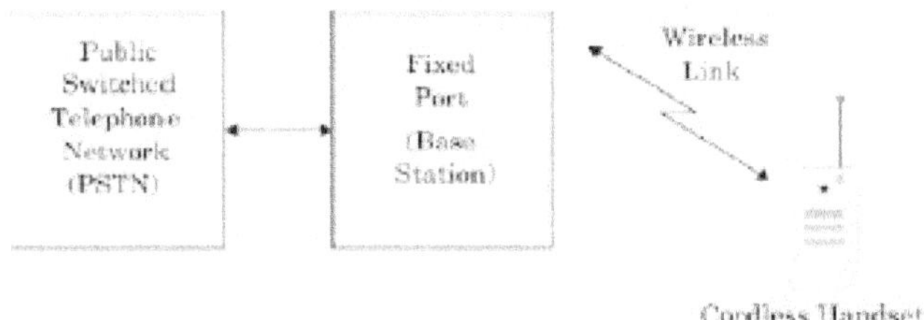

Figure 1.4. A cordless telephone system.

1.6 CELLULAR TELEPHONE SYSTEMS

A cellular telephone system provides a wireless connection to the PSTN for any user location within the radio range of the system. Cellular systems accommodate a large number of users over a large geographic area, within a limited frequency spectrum. Cellular radio systems provide high quality service that is often comparable to that of the landline telephone systems. High capacity is achieved by limiting the coverage of each base station transmitter to a small geographic area called a cell so that the same radio channels may be reused by another base station located some distance away. A sophisticated switching technique called a handoff enables a call to proceed uninterrupted when the user moves from one cell to another.

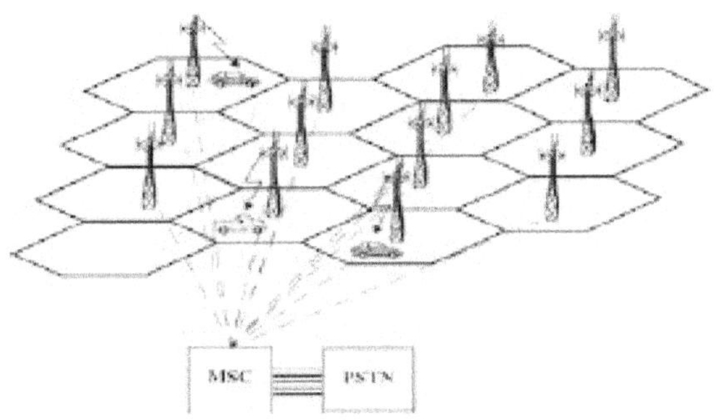

Figure 1.5 shows a basic cellular system which consists of mobile stations, base stations and a mobile switching center (MSC). The mobile switching center is sometimes called a mobile telephone switching office (MTSO), since it is responsible for connecting all mobiles to the PSTN in a cellular system. Each mobile communicates via radio with one of the base stations and may be handed-off to any number of base stations throughout the duration of a call. The mobile station contains a transceiver, an antenna, and control circuitry, and may be mounted in a vehicle or used as a portable hand -held unit. The base stations consist of several transmitters and receivers which simultaneously handle full duplex communications and generally have towers which support several transmitting and receiving antennas. The base station serves as a bridge between all mobile users in the cell and connects the simultaneous mobile calls via telephone lines or microwave links to the MSC. The MSC coordinates the activities of all of the base stations and connects the entire cellular system to the PSTN. A typical MSC handles 100,000 cellular subscribers and 5,000 simultaneous conversations at a time, and accommodates all billing and system maintenance functions, as well. In large cities, several MSCs are used by a single carrier.

Communication between the base station and the mobiles is defined by a standard common air interface (CAI) that specifies four different channels. The channels used for voice transmission from the base station to mobiles are called forward voice channels (FVC), and the channels used for voice transmission from mobiles to the base station are called reverse voice channels (RVC). The two channels responsible for initiating mobile calls are the forward control channels (FCC) and reverse control channels (RCC). Control channels are often called setup channels because they are only involved in setting up a call and moving it to an unused voice channel. Control channels transmit and receive data messages that carry call initiation and service requests, and are monitored by mobiles when they do not have a call in progress. Forward control channels also serve as beacons which continually broadcast all of the traffic requests for all mobiles in the system.

Cellular systems rely on the frequency reuse concept, which requires that the forward control channels (FCCs) in neighboring cells be different. By defining a relatively small number of FCCs as part of the common air interface, cellular phones can be manufactured by many companies which can rapidly scan all of the possible FCCs to determine the strongest channel at any time. Once finding the strongest signal, the cellular phone receiver stays "camped" to the particular FCC. By broadcasting the same setup data on all FCCs at the same time, the MSC is able to signal all subscribers within the cellular system and can be certain that any mobile will be signaled when it receives a call via the PSTN.

How a Cellular Telephone Call is Made?

When a cellular phone is turned on, but is not yet engaged in a call, it first scans the group of forward control channels to determine the one with the strongest signal, and then monitors that control channel until the signal drops below a usable level. At this point, it again scans the control channels in search of the strongest base station signal. When a telephone call is placed to a mobile user, the MSC dispatches the request to all base stations in the cellular system. The mobile identification number (MIN), which is the subscriber's telephone number, is then broadcast as a paging message over all of the forward control channels throughout the cellular system. The mobile receives the paging message sent by the base station which it monitors, and responds by identifying itself over the reverse control channel. The base station relays the acknowledgment sent by the mobile and informs the MSC of the handshake. Then, the MSC instructs the base station to move the call to an unused voice channel within the cell (typically, between ten to sixty voice channels and just one control channel are used in each cell's base station). At this point, the base station signals the mobile to change frequencies to an unused forward and reverse voice channel pair, at which point another data message (called an alert) is transmitted over the forward voice channel to instruct the mobile telephone to ring, thereby instructing the mobile user to answer the phone. Figure 1.6 shows the sequence of events involved with connecting a call to a mobile user in a cellular telephone system. All of these events occur within a few seconds and are not noticeable by the user.

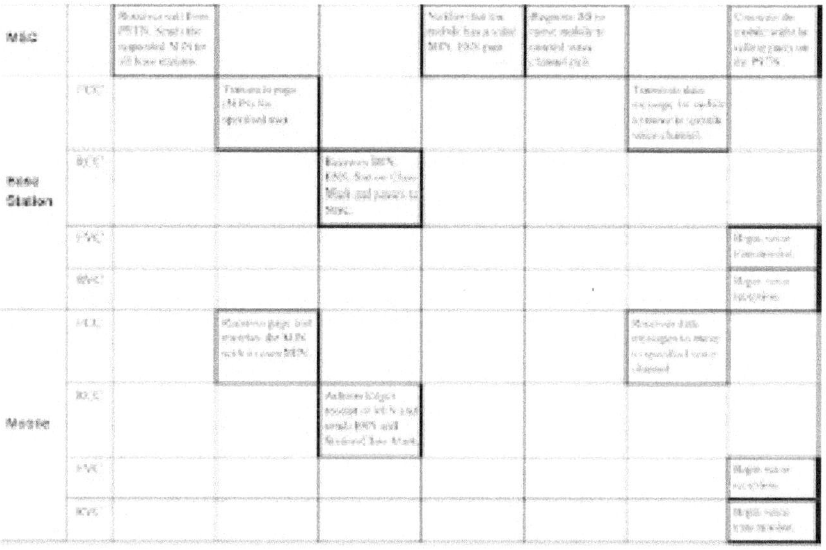

Figure 1.6. Timing diagram illustrating how a call to a mobile user initiated by a landline subscriber is established.

Once a call is in progress, the MSC adjusts the transmitted power of the mobile and changes the channel of the mobile unit and base stations in order to maintain call quality as the subscriber moves in and out of range of each base station. This is called a handoff. Special control signaling is applied to the voice channels so that the mobile unit may be controlled by the base station and the MSC while a call is in progress.

When a mobile originates a call, a call initiation request is sent on the reverse control channel. With this request the mobile unit transmits its telephone number (MIN), electronic serial number (ESN), and the telephone number of the called party. The mobile also transmits a station class mark (SCM) which indicates what the maximum transmitter power level is for the particular user. The cell base station receives this data and sends it to the MSC. The MSC validates the request, makes connection to the called party through the PSTN, and instructs the base station and mobile user to move to an unused forward and reverse voice channel pair to allow the conversation to begin. Figure 1.7 shows the sequence of events involved with connecting a call which is initiated by a mobile user in a cellular system.

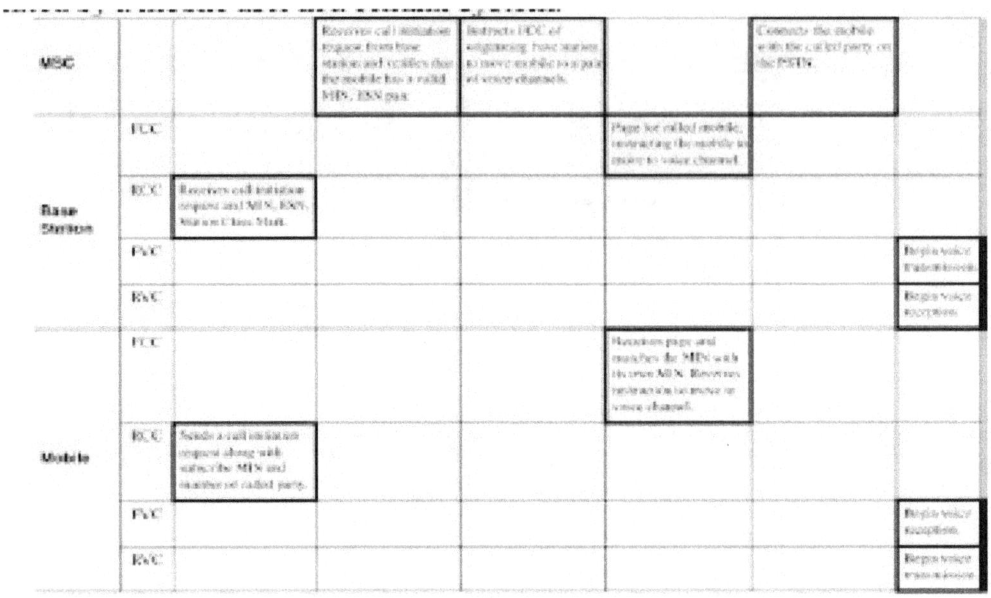

MSC			Receives call initiation request from base station and verifies that the mobile has a valid MIN, ESN pair.	Instructs BSC of originating base station to move mobile to a pair of voice channels.		Connects the mobile with the called party on the PSTN.
Base Station	FCC				Pages the called mobile, instructing the mobile to move to voice channel	
	RCC	Receives call initiation request and MIN, ESN, Station Class Mark.				
	FVC					Begin voice transmission
	RVC					Begin voice reception
Mobile	FCC				Receives page and matches the MIN with its own MIN. Receives instruction to move to voice channel.	
	RCC	Sends a call initiation request along with subscriber MIN and number of called party.				
	FVC					Begin voice reception
	RVC					Begin voice transmission

Figure 1.7. Timing diagram illustrating how a call initiated by a mobile is established.

All cellular systems provide a service called roaming. This allows subscribers to operate in service areas other than the one from which service is subscribed. When a mobile enters a city or geographic area that is different from its home service area, it is registered as a roamer in the new service area. If a particular roamer has roaming authorization for billing purposes, the MSC registers the subscriber as a valid roamer. Once registered, roaming mobiles are allowed to receive and place calls from that area, and billing is routed automatically to the subscriber's home service provider.

Comparison of Common Wireless Communication Systems

Tables 1.5 and 1.6 illustrate the types of service, level of infrastructure, cost, and complexity required for the subscriber segment and base station segment of each of the five mobile or portable radio systems discussed earlier in this chapter. For comparison purposes, common household wireless remote devices are shown in the table. It is important to note that each of the five mobile radio systems given in Tables 1.5 and 1.6 use a fixed base station, and for good reason. Virtually all mobile radio communication systems strive to connect a moving terminal to a fixed distribution system of some sort and attempt to look invisible to the distribution system.

Table 1.5. Comparison of Mobile Communication Systems—Mobile Station

Service	Coverage Range	Required Infrastructure	Complexity	Hardware Cost	Carrier Frequency	Functionality
TV Remote Control	Low	Low	Low	Low	Infrared	Transmitter
Garage Door Opener	Low	Low	Low	Low	< 100 MHz	Transmitter
Paging System	High	High	Low	Low	< 1 GHz	Receiver
Cordless Phone	Low	Low	Moderate	Low	< 1 GHz	Transceiver
Cellular Phone	High	High	High	Moderate	< 2 GHz	Transceiver

Table 1.6. Comparison of Mobile Communication Systems—Base Station

Service	Coverage Range	Required Infrastructure	Complexity	Hardware Cost	Carrier Frequency	Functionality
TV Remote Control	Low	Low	Low	Low	Infrared	Receiver
Garage Door Opener	Low	Low	Low	Low	< 100 MHz	Receiver
Paging System	High	High	High	High	< 1 GHz	Transmitter
Cordless Phone	Low	Low	Low	Moderate	< 1 GHz	Transceiver
Cellular Phone	High	High	High	High	< 2 GHz	Transceiver

Notice that the expectations vary widely among the services, and the infrastructure costs are dependent upon the required coverage area. For the case of low power, hand- held cellular phones, a large number of base stations are required to insure that any phone is in close range to a base station within a city. If base stations were not within close range, a great deal of transmitter power would be required of the phone, thus limiting the battery life and rendering the service useless for hand-held users.

1.7 TRENDS IN CELLULAR RADIO AND PERSONAL COMMUNICATIONS

Since 1989, there has been enormous activity throughout the world to develop personal wireless systems that combine the network intelligence of today's PSTN with modern digital signal processing and RF technology. The concept, called Personal Communication Services (PCS), originated in the United Kingdom when three companies were given spectrum in the 1800 MHz range to develop Personal Communication Networks (PCN) throughout Great Britain. PCN was seen by the U.K. as a means of improving its international competitiveness in the wireless field while developing new wireless systems and services for citizens.

Indoor wireless networking products are rapidly emerging and promise to become a major part of the telecommunications infrastructure within the next decade. An international standards body, IEEE 802.11, is developing standards for wireless access between computers inside buildings. The

European Telecommunications Standard Institute (ETSI) is also developing the 20 Mbps HIPERLAN standard for indoor wireless networks. Products have emerged that allow users to link their phone with their computer within an office environment, as well as in a public setting, such as an airport or train station.

A worldwide standard, the Future Public Land Mobile Telephone System (FPLMTS)— renamed International Mobile Telecommunication 2000 (IMT -2000) in mid-1995—has been formulated by the International Telecommunications Union (ITU) which is the standards body for the United Nations, with headquarters in Geneva, Switzerland. FPLMTS (now IMT-2000) is a third generation universal, multi-function, globally compatible digital mobile radio system that will integrate paging, cordless, and cellular systems, as well as low earth orbit (LEO) satellites, into one universal mobile system.

In emerging nations, where existing telephone service is almost nonexistent, fixed cellular telephone systems are being installed at a rapid rate. This is due to the fact that developing nations are finding it is quicker and more affordable to install cellular telephone systems for fixed home use, rather than install wires in neighbourhoods which have not yet received telephone connections to the PSTN.

1.8 MODERN WIRELESS COMMUNICATION SYSTEMS

Since the mid 1990s, the cellular communications industry has witnessed explosive growth. Wireless communications networks have become much more pervasive than anyone could have imagined when the cellular concept was first developed in the 1960s and 1970s. The widespread adoption of wireless communications was accelerated in the mid 1990s, when governments throughout the world provided increased competition and new radio spectrum licenses for personal communications services (PCS) in the 1800–2000 MHz frequency bands.

The rapid worldwide growth in cellular telephone subscribers has demonstrated conclusively that wireless communications is a robust, viable voice and data transport mechanism. New standards and technologies are being implemented to allow wireless networks to replace fiber optic or copper lines between fixed points several kilometers apart (fixed wireless access). Similarly, wireless networks have been increasingly used as a replacement for wires within homes, buildings, and office settings through the deployment of wireless local area networks (WLANs). The evolving Bluetooth modem standard promises to replace troublesome appliance communication cords with invisible wireless connections within a person's personal workspace. Used primarily within buildings, WLANs and Bluetooth use low power levels and generally do not require a license for spectrum use.

1.9 SECOND GENERATION (2G) CELLULAR NETWORKS

Most of today's ubiquitous cellular networks use what is commonly called second generation or 2G technologies which conform to the second generation cellular standards. Unlike first generation cellular systems that relied exclusively on FDMA/FDD and analog FM, second generation standards use digital modulation formats and TDMA/FDD and CDMA/FDD multiple access techniques.

The most popular second generation standards include three TDMA standards and one CDMA standard: (a) Global System Mobile (GSM), which supports eight time slotted users for each 200 kHz radio channel and has been deployed widely by service providers in Europe, Asia, Australia, South America, and some parts of the US (in the PCS spectrum band only); (b) Interim Standard 136 (IS-136), also known as North American Digital Cellular (NADC), which supports three time slotted users for each 30 kHz radio channel and is a popular choice for carriers in North America, South America, and Australia (in both the cellular and PCS bands); (c) Pacific Digital Cellular (PDC), a Japanese TDMA standard that is similar to IS-136 with more than 50 million users; and (d) the popular 2G CDMA standard Interim Standard 95 Code Division Multiple Access (IS-95), also known as cdmaOne, which supports up to 64 users that are orthogonally coded and simultaneously transmitted on each 1.25 MHz channel. CDMA is widely deployed by carriers in North America (in both cellular and PCS bands), as well as in Korea, Japan, China, South America, and Australia.

In many countries, 2G wireless networks are designed and deployed for conventional mobile telephone service, as a high capacity replacement for, or in competition with, existing older first generation cellular telephone systems. Modern cellular systems are also being installed to provide fixed (non-mobile) telephone service to residences and businesses in developing nations—this is particularly cost effective for providing plain old telephone service (POTS) in countries that have poor telecommunications infrastructure and are unable to afford the installation of copper wire to all homes.

Table 2.1. Key Specifications of Leading 2G Technologies (adapted from [Lib99])

	cdmaOne, IS-95,ANSI J STD-008	GSM, DCS-1900,ANSI J-STD 007	NADC, IS-54/IS-136,ANSI J STD-011, PDC
Uplink Frequencies	824-849 MHz (US Cellular) 1850-1910 MHz (US PCS)	890-915 MHz (Europe) 1850-1910 MHz (US PCS)	800 MHz, 1500 MHz (Japan) 1850-1910 MHz (US PCS)
Downlink Frequencies	869-894 MHz (US Cellular) 1930-1990 MHz (US PCS)	935-960 MHz (Europe) 1930-1990 MHz (US PCS)	869-894 MHz (US Cellular) 1930-1990 MHz (US PCS) 800 MHz, 1500 MHz (Japan)
Duplexing	FDD	FDD	FDD
Multiple Access Technology	CDMA	TDMA	TDMA
Modulation	BPSK with Quadrature Spreading	GMSK with $BT = 0.3$	$\pi/4$ DQPSK
Carrier Separation	1.25 MHz	200 kHz	30 kHz (IS-136) (25 kHz for PDC)
Channel Data Rate	1.2288 Mchips/sec	270.833 kbps	48.6 kbps (IS-136) (42 kbps for PDC)
Voice channels per carrier	64	8	3
Speech Coding	Code Excited Linea Prediction (CELP) @ 13 kbps, Enhanced Variable Rate Codec (EVRC @ 8 kbps	Residual Pulse Excited Long Term Prediction (RPE-LTP) @ 13 kbps	Vector Sum Excited Linea Predictive Coder (VSELP) @ 7.95 kbps

Since the mid 1990s, the 2G digital standards have been widely deployed by wireless carriers for cellular and PCS, even though these standards were designed before the widespread use of the Internet. Consequently, 2G technologies use circuit-switched data modems that limit data users to a single circuit-switched voice channel.

In an effort to retrofit the 2G standards for compatibility with increased throughput data rates that are required to support modern Internet applications, new data-centric standards have been developed that can be overlaid upon existing 2G technologies. These new standards represent 2.5G technology and allow existing 2G equipment to be modified and supplemented with new base station add-ons and subscriber unit software upgrades to support higher data rate transmissions for web browsing, e-mail traffic, mobile commerce (m-commerce), and location-based mobile services. The 2.5G technologies also support a popular new web browsing format language, called Wireless Applications Protocol (WAP), that allows standard web pages to be viewed in a compressed format specifically designed for small, portable hand held wireless devices, a wide range of 2.5G standards have been developed to allow each of the major 2G technologies (GSM, CDMA, and IS- to be upgraded incrementally for faster Internet data rates. Figure 2.3 illustrates the various 2.5G and 3G upgrade paths for the major 2G technologies.

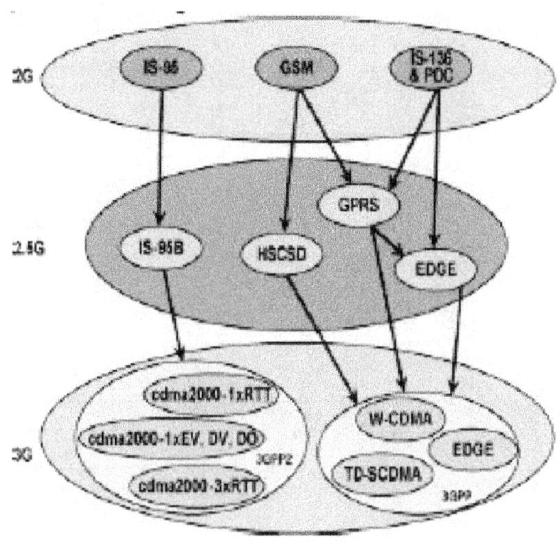

Figure 2.3. Various upgrade paths for 2G technologies.

Table 2.2 describes the required changes to the network infrastructure (e.g., the base station and the switch) and the subscriber terminals (e.g., the handset) for the various upgrade options for 2.5G and 3G. The technical features of each 2.5G upgrade path are described below.

Table 2.2. Current and Emerging 2.5G and 3G Data Communication Standards

Wireless Data Technologies	Channel BW	Duplex	Infrastructure change	Requires New Spectrum	Requires New Handsets
HSCSD	200 KHz	FDD	Requires software upgrade a base station.	No	Yes New HSCSD handsets provide 57.6 Kbps on HSCSD networks, and 9.6 Kbps on GSM networks with dua mode phones. GSM-only phones will not work in HSCSD networks.
GPRS	200 KHz	FDD	Requires new packet overla including routers an gateways.	No	Yes New GPRS handsets work on GPRS networks at 171.2 Kbps, 9.6 Kbpson GSM networks with dual mode phones. GSM-only phones will no work in GPRS networks.
EDGE	200 KHz	FDD	Requires new transceiver a base station. Also, software upgrades to the base statior controller and base station.	No	Yes New handsets work on EDGEnetworks at 384 Kbps, GPRSnetworks at 144 Kbps, and GSMnetworks at 9.6 Kbps with tri mode phones. GSM and GPRS-onlyphones will not work in EDGE networks.

Wireless Data Technologies	Channel BW	Duplex	Infrastructure change	Requires New Spectrum	Requires New Handsets
W-CDMA	5 MHz	FDD	Requires completely new base stations.	Yes	Yes New W-CDMA handsets will work on W-CDMA at 2 Mbps, EDGE networks at 384 Kbps, GPRS networks at 144 Kbps, GSM networks at 9.6 Kbps. Older handsets will not work in W CDMA.
IS-95B	1.25 MHz	FDD	Requires new software inbase station controller.	No	Yes New handsets will work on IS-95B at 64 Kbps and IS-95A at 14.4 Kbps. CdmaOne phones can work in IS-95B at 14.4 Kbps.
cdma2000 1xRTT	1.25 MHz	FDD	Requires new software inbackbone and new channecards at base station. Alsoneed to build a new packe service node.	No	Yes New handsets will work on 1xRTT at 144 Kbps, IS-95B at 64 Kbps, IS 95A at 14.4 Kbps. Older handsets can work in 1xRTT but at lower speeds.
cdma2000 IxEV (DO and DV)	1.25 MHz	FDD	Requires software and digita car upgrade on 1xRTT networks.	No	Yes New handsets will work on 1xEV at 2.4 Mbps, 1xRTT at 144 Kbps IS-95B at 64 Kbps, IS-95A at 14.4 Kbps. Older handsets can work in 1xEV but at lower speeds.
cdma2000 3xRTT	3.75 MHz	FDD	Requires backbone modifications and new channel card at base station.	Maybe	Yes New handsets will work on 95A a 14.4 Kbps, 95B at 64 Kbps, 1xRTT at 144 Kbps, 3xRTT at 2 Mbps Older handsets can work in 3X bu at lower speeds.

1.10 EVOLUTION FOR 2.5G TDMA STANDARDS

Three different upgrade paths have been developed for GSM carriers, and two of these solutions also support IS-136. The three TDMA upgrade options include: (a) High Speed Circuit Switched Data (HSCSD); (b) General Packet Radio Service (GPRS); and (c) Enhanced Data Rates for GSM Evolution (EDGE). These options provide significant improvements in Internet access speed over today's GSM and IS-136 technology and support the creation of new Internet-ready cell phones.

HSCSD for 2.5G GSM

As the name implies, High Speed Circuit Switched Data is a circuit switched technique that allows a single mobile subscriber to use consecutive user time slots in the GSM standard. That is, instead of limiting each user to only one specific time slot in the GSM TDMA standard, HSCSD allows individual data users to commandeer consecutive time slots in order to obtain higher speed data access on the GSM network. HSCSD relaxes the error control coding algorithms originally specified in the GSM standard for data transmissions and increases the available application data rate to 14,400 bps, as compared to the original 9,600 bps in the GSM specification. HSCSD is ideal for dedicated streaming Internet access or real-time interactive web sessions and simply requires the service provider to implement a software change at existing GSM base stations.

GPRS for 2.5G GSM and IS-136

General Packet Radio Service is a packet-based data network, which is well suited for non-real time Internet usage, including the retrieval of email, faxes, and asymmetric web browsing, where the user downloads much more data than it uploads on the Internet. Unlike HSCSD, which dedicates circuit switched channels to specific users, GPRS supports multi-user network sharing of individual radio channels and time slots. Similar to the Cellular Digital Packet Data (CDPD) standard developed for the North American AMPS systems in the early 1990s, the GPRS standard provides a packet network on dedicated GSM or IS-136 radio channels. GPRS retains the original modulation formats specified in the original 2G TDMA standards, but uses a completely redefined air interface in order to better handle packet data access.

As is the case for any packet network, the data throughput experienced by an individual GPRS user decreases substantially as more users attempt to use the network or as propagation conditions become poor for particular users. It is worth noting that GPRS was originally designed to provide a packet data access overlay solely for GSM networks, but at the request of North American IS - 136 operators (see UWC-136 Air Interface in Table 2.3), GPRS was extended to include both TDMA standards.

Table 2.3. Leading IMT-2000 Candidate Standards as of 1998 (adapted from [Lib99])

Air Interface	Mode of Operation	Duplexing Method	Key Features
cdma2000 US TIA TR45.5	Multi-Carrier and Direc Spreading DS-CDMA a N = 1.2288 Mcps with N = 1, 3, 6, 9, 12	FDD and TDD Modes	Backward compatibility withIS-95A and IS-95B. Downlinkcan be implemented usingeither Multi-Carrier or DirecSpreading. Uplink cansupport a simultaneouscombination of Multi-Carrie or Direct Spreading Auxiliary carriers to help with downlink channe estimation in forward link beamforming.
UTRA (UMTS Terrestria Radio Access) ETSSMG2	DS_CDMA at Rates of N × 0.960 Mcps with N = 4, 8 16	FDD and TDD Modes	Wideband DS_CDMA System. Backward compatibility with GSM/DCS-1900. Up to 2.048 Mbps on Downlink in FDD Mode. Minimum forward channebandwidth of 5 GHz. The collection of proposedstandards represented hereeach exhibit unique featuresbut support a common set o chip rates, 10 ms framestructure, with 16 slots pe frame. Connection-dedicated pilo bits assist in downlink beamforming.
W-CDMA/NA (Wideband CDMA North America) USA T1P1-ATIS			
W-CDMA/Japan (Wideband CDMA Japan ARIB			
CDMA II South Korea TTA			
WIMS/W-CDMA USA TIA TR46.1			
CDMA I South Korea TTA	DS-CDMA at N × 0.9216 Mcps with N = 1, 4, 16	FDD and TDD Modes	Up to 512 kbps per spreadingcode, code aggregation up to 2.048 Mbps.
UWC-136 (Universal Wireless Communications Consortium) USA TIATR 45.3	TDMA - Up to 722.2 kbp (Outdoor/Vehicular), Upto 5.2 Mbps (Indoo Office)	FDD (Outdoor/Vehicular), TDD (Indoor Office)	Backward compatibility and upgrade path for both IS-136 and GSM. Fits into existing IS-136 and GSM. Explicit plans to suppor adaptive antenna technology.
TD-SCDMA China Academy of Telecommunication Technology (CATT)	DS-CDMA 1.1136 Mcps	TDD	RF channel bit rate up to 2.227 Mbps. Use of smart antenna technology is fundamenta (but not strictly required) in TDSCMA.
DECT ETSI Project (EP DECT	1150-3456 kbps TDMA	TDD	Enhanced version of 2G DECT technology.

EDGE for 2.5G GSM and IS-136

Enhanced Data rates for GSM (or Global) Evolution is a more advanced upgrade to the GSM standard, and requires the addition of new hardware and software at existing base stations. EDGE introduces a new digital

 modulation format, 8-PSK (octal phase shift keying), which is used in addition to GSM's standard GMSK modulation. EDGE allows for nine different (autonomously and rapidly selectable) air interface formats, known as multiple modulation and coding schemes (MCS), with varying degrees of error control protection. Each MCS state may use either GMSK (low data rate) or 8-PSK (high data rate) modulation for network access, depending on the instantaneous demands of the network and the operating conditions. Because of the higher data rates and relaxed error control covering in many of the selectable air interface formats, the coverage range is smaller in EDGE than in HSDRC or GPRS. EDGE is sometimes referred to as Enhanced GPRS, or EGPRS.

IS-95B for 2.5G CDMA

Unlike the several GSM and IS-136 evolutionary paths to high speed data access, CDMA (often called cdmaOne) has a single upgrade path for eventual 3G operation. The interim data solution for CDMA is called IS-95B. Like GPRS, IS-95B is already being deployed worldwide, and provides high speed packet and circuit switched data access on a common CDMA radio channel by dedicating multiple orthogonal user channels (Walsh functions) for specific users and specific purposes. Each IS-95 CDMA radio channel supports up to 64 different user channels.

The 2.5G CDMA solution, IS-95B, supports medium data rate (MDR) service by allowing a dedicated user to command up to eight different user Walsh codes simultaneously and in parallel for an instantaneous throughput of 115.2 kbps per user (8×14.4 kbps). IS-95B also specifies hard handoff procedures that allow subscriber units to search different radio channels in the network without instruction from the switch so that subscriber units can rapidly tune to different base stations to maintain link quality.

1.11 THIRD GENERATION (3G) WIRELESS NETWORKS

3G systems promise unparalleled wireless access in ways that have never been possible before. Multi-megabit Internet access, communications using Voice over Internet Protocol (VoIP), voice-activated calls, unparalleled network capacity, and ubiquitous "always-on" acc ess are just some of the advantages being touted by 3G developers. Companies developing 3G equipment envision users having the ability to receive live music, conduct interactive web sessions, and have simultaneous voice and data access with multiple parties at the same time using a single mobile handset, whether driving, walking, or standing still in an office setting.

The eventual 3G evolution for CDMA systems leads to cdma2000. Several variants of CDMA 2000 are currently being developed, but they all are based on the fundamentals of IS-95 and IS-95B technologies. The eventual 3G evolution for GSM, IS-136, and PDC systems leads to Wideband CDMA (W-CDMA), also called Universal Mobile Telecommunications Service (UMTS). W-CDMA is based on the network fundamentals of GSM, as well as the merged versions of GSM and IS-136 through EDGE.

3G W-CDMA (UMTS)

The Universal Mobile Telecommunications System (UMTS) is a visionary air interface standard that has evolved since late 1996 under the auspices of the European Telecommunications Standards Institute (ETSI). European carriers, manufacturers, and government regulators collectively developed the early versions of UMTS as a competitive open air-interface standard for third generation wireless telecommunications.

UMTS, or W-CDMA, assures backward compatibility with the second generation GSM, IS-136, and PDC TDMA technologies, as well as all 2.5G TDMA technologies. The network structure and bit level packaging of GSM data is retained by W-CDMA, with additional capacity and bandwidth provided by a new CDMA air interface. The 3G W-CDMA air interface standard had been designed for "always-on" packet-based wireless service, so that computers, entertainment devices, and telephones may all share the same wireless network and be connected to the Internet, anytime, anywhere. W -CDMA requires a minimum spectrum allocation of 5 MHz, which is an important distinction from the other G standards. With W-CDMA data rates from as low as 8 kbps to as high as 2 Mbps will be carried simultaneously on a single W-CDMA 5 MHz radio channel, and each channel will be able to support between 100 and 350 simultaneous voice calls at once, depending on antenna sectoring, propagation conditions, user velocity, and antenna polarizations. W-CDMA employs variable/selectable direct sequence spread spectrum chip rates that can exceed 16 Megachips per second per user.

3G cdma2000

The cdma2000 vision provides a seamless and evolutionary high data rate upgrade path for current users of 2G and 2.5G CDMA technology, using a building block approach that centers on the original 2G CDMA channel bandwidth of 1.25 MHz per radio channel.

The first 3G CDMA air interface, cdma2000 1xRTT, implies that a single 1.25 MHz radio channel is used (the initials RTT stand for Radio Transmission Technology). The ultimate 3G solution for CDMA relies upon multicarrier techniques that gang adjacent cdmaOne radio channels together for increased bandwidth. The cdma2000 3xRTT standard uses three adjacent 1.25 MHz radio channels that are used together to provide packet data throughput speeds in excess of 2 Mbps per user, depending upon cell loading, vehicle speed, and propagation conditions.

3G TD-SCDMA

The China Academy of Telecommunications Technology (CATT) and Siemens Corporation jointly submitted an IMT-2000 3G standard proposal in 1998, based on Time Division - Synchronous Code Division Multiple Access (TD-SCDMA). This proposal was adopted by ITU as one of the 3G options in late 1999.

TD-SCDMA relies on the existing core GSM infrastructure and allows a 3G network to evolve through the addition of high data rate equipment at each GSM base station. TD-SCDMA combines TDMA and TDD techniques to provide a data-only overlay in an existing GSM network. By using TDD, different time slots within a single frame on a single carrier frequency are used to provide both forward channel and reverse channel transmissions. For the case of asynchronous traffic demand, such as when a user downloads a file, the forward link will require more bandwidth than the reverse link, and thus more time slots will be dedicated to providing forward link traffic than for providing reverse link traffic. TD-SCDMA proponents claim that the TDD feature allows this 3G standard to be very easily and inexpensively added to existing GSM systems.

1.12 WIRELESS LOCAL LOOP (WLL) AND LMDS

Fixed wireless equipment is extremely well suited for rapidly deploying a broadband connection in many instances, and this approach is steadily becoming more popular for providing "last mile" broadband local loop access, as well as for emergency or redundant point-to-point or point-to-multipoint private networks.

Modern fixed wireless systems are usually assigned microwave or millimeter radio frequencies in the 28 GHz band and higher, which is greater than ten times the carrier frequency of 3G terrestrial cellular telephone networks. At these higher frequencies, the wavelengths are extremely small, which in turn allows very high gain directional antennas to be fabricated in small physical form factors. Microwave wireless links can be used to create a wireless local loop (WLL) such as the one shown in Figure 2.4.

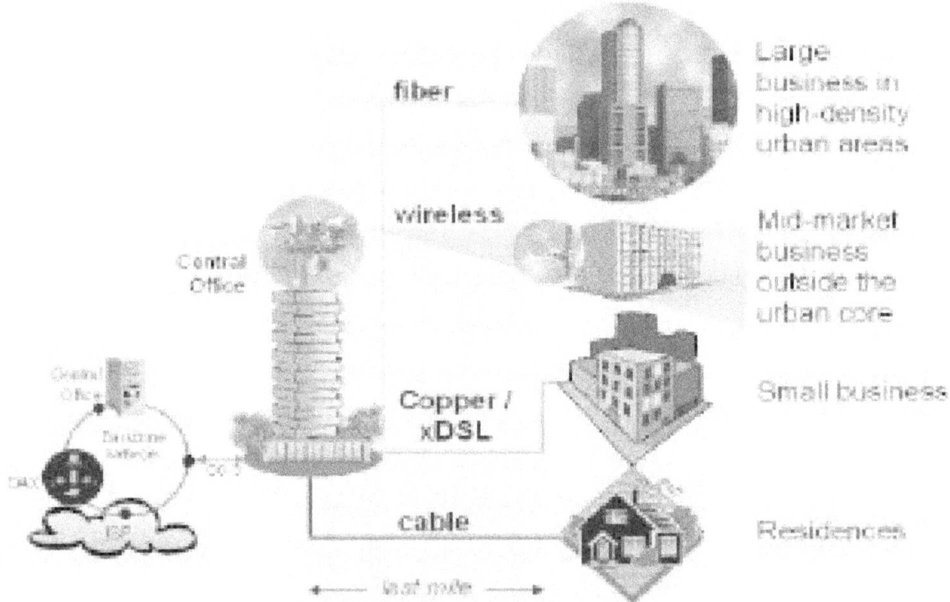

Figure 2.4. Example of the emerging applications and markets for broadband services.

The local loop can be thought of as the "last mile" of the telecommunication network that resides between the central office (CO) and the individual homes and businesses in close proximity to the CO.

Governments throughout the world have realized that WLL could greatly improve the efficiency of their citizens while stimulating competition that could lead to improved telecommunications services. A vast array of new services and applications have been proposed and are in the early stages of commercialization. These services include the concept of Local Multipoint Distribution Service (LMDS), which provides broadband telecommunications access in the local exchange.

Governments throughout the world have realized that WLL could greatly improve the efficiency of their citizens while stimulating competition that could lead to improved telecommunications services. A vast array of new services and applications have been proposed and are in the early stages of commercialization. These services include the concept of Local Multipoint Distribution Service (LMDS), which provides broadband telecommunications access in the local exchange.

In 1998, 1300 MHz of unused spectrum in the 27–31 GHz band was auctioned by the US government to support LMDS. Similar auctions have been held in other countries around the world.

One of the most promising applications for LMDS is in a local exchange carrier (LEC) network. Figure 2.7 shows a typical network configuration, where the LEC owns a very wide bandwidth asynchronous transfer mode (ATM) or Synchronous Optical Network (SONET) backbone switch, capable of connecting hundreds of megabits per second of traffic with the Internet, the PSTN, or to its own private network. As long as a LOS path exists, LMDS will allow LECs to install wireless equipment on the premises of customers for rapid broadband connectivity without having to lease or install its own cables to the customers.

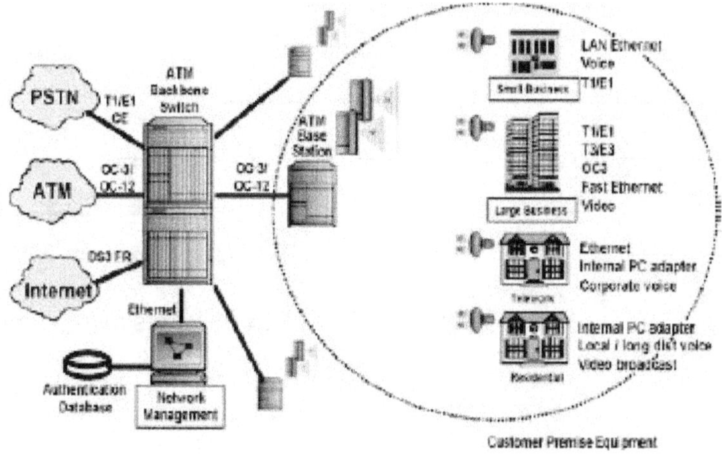

Figure 2.7. A wireless Competitive Local Exchange Carrier (CLEC) using Asynchronous Transfer Mode (ATM) distribution.

1.13 WIRELESS LOCAL AREA NETWORKS (WLANS)

In 1997 the FCC allocated 300 MHz of unlicensed spectrum in the Industrial Scientific and Medical (ISM) bands of 5.150–5.350 GHz and 5.725–5.825 GHz for the express purpose of supporting low-power license-free spread spectrum data communication. This allocation is called the Unlicensed National Information Infrastructure (UNII) band.

The IEEE 802.11 Wireless LAN working group was founded in 1987 to begin standardization of spread spectrum WLANs for use in the ISM bands. Figure 2.10 illustrates the evolution of IEEE 802.11 Wireless LAN standards, which also include infrared communications. Figure 2.10 shows how both frequency hopping and direct sequence approaches were used in the original IEEE 802.11 standard (2 Mbps user throughput), but as of late 2001 only direct sequence spread spectrum (DS-SS) modems had thus far been standardized for high rate (11 Mbps) user data rates within IEEE 802.11.

The DS-SS IEEE 802.11b standard has been named Wi-Fi by the Wireless Ethernet Compatibility Alliance (WECA), a group that promotes adoption of 802.11b DS-SS WLAN equipment and interoperability between vendors. IEEE 802.11g is developing Complimentary Code Keying Orthogonal Frequency Division Multiplexing (CCK-OFDM) standards in both the 2.4 GHz (802.11b) and 5 GHz (802.11a) bands, and will support roaming capabilities and dual-band use for public WLAN networks, while supporting backward compatibility with 802.11b technology.

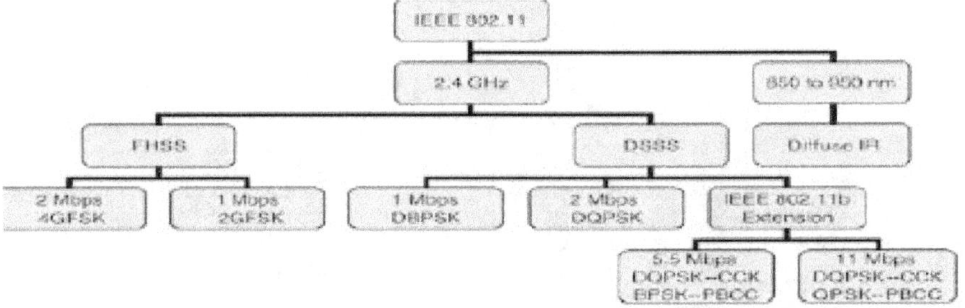

Figure 2.10. Overview of the IEEE 802.11 Wireless LAN standard.

The frequency-hopping spread spectrum (FH-SS) proponents of IEEE 802.11 have formed the HomeRF standard that supports frequency hopping equipment. It is worth noting that both DS and FH types of WLANs must operate in the same unlicensed bands that contain cordless phones, baby monitors, Bluetooth devices, and other WLAN users.

Table 2.4. IEEE 802.11b Channels for Both DS-SS and FH-SS WLAN Standards

Country	Frequency Range Available	DSSS Channels Available	FHSS Channels Available
United States	2.4 to 2.4835 GHz	1 through 11	2 through 80
Canada	2.4 to 2.4835 GHz	1 through 11	2 through 80
Japan	2.4 to 2.497 GHz	1 through 14	2 through 95
France	2.4465 to 2.4835 GHz	10 through 13	48 through 82
Spain	2.445 to 2.4835 GHz	10 through 11	47 through 73

Figure 2.12 illustrates the unique WLAN channels that are specified in the IEEE 802.11b standard for the 2400–2483.5 MHz band. All WLANs are manufactured to operate on any one of the specified channels and are assigned to a particular channel by the network operator when the WLAN system is first installed. The channelization scheme used by the network installer becomes very important for a high density WLAN installation, since neighboring access points must be separated from one another in frequency to avoid interference and significantly degraded performance.

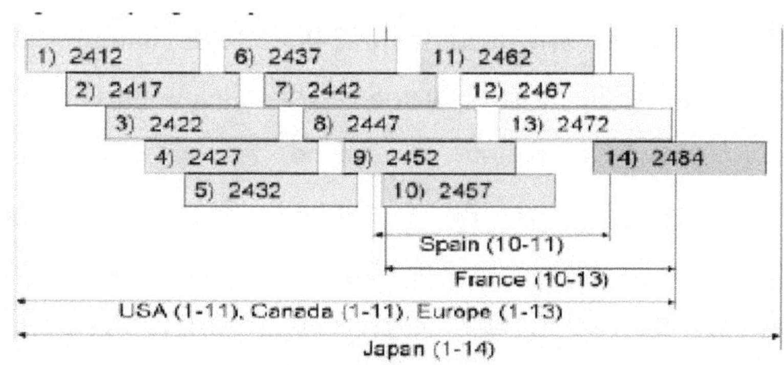

Figure 2.12. Channelization scheme for IEEE 802.11b throughout the world.

In Europe in the mid 1990s, the High Performance Radio Local Area Network (HIPERLAN) standard was developed to provide a similar capability to IEEE 802.11. HIPERLAN was intended to provide individual wireless LANs for computer communications and used the 5.2 GHz and the 17.1 GHz frequency bands. HIPERLAN provides asynchronous user data rates of between 1 to 20 Mbps, as well as time bounded messaging at rates of 64 kbps to 2.048 Mbps. HIPERLAN was designed to operate up to vehicle speeds of 35 km/hr, and typically provided 20 Mbps throughput at 50 m range.

In 1997, Europe's ETSI established a standardization committee for Broadband Radio Access Networks (BRANs). The goal of BRAN is to develop a family of broadband WLAN-type protocols that allow user interoperability, covering both short range (e.g., WLAN) and long range (e.g., fixed wireless) networking. HIPERLAN/2 has emerged as the next generation European WLAN standard and will provide up to 54 Mbps of user data to a variety of networks, including the ATM backbone, IP based networks, and the UMTS core.

1.14 BLUETOOTH AND PERSONAL AREA NETWORKS (PANS)

Bluetooth is an open standard that has been embraced by over 1,000 manufacturers of electronic appliances. It provides an ad-hoc approach for enabling various devices to communicate with one another within a nominal 10 meter range. Named after King Harald Bluetooth, the 10th century Viking who united Denmark and Norway, the Bluetooth standard aims to unify the connectivity chores of appliances within the personal workspace of an individual.

Bluetooth operates in the 2.4 GHz ISM Band (2400–2483.5 MHz) and uses a frequency hopping TDD scheme for each radio channel. Each Bluetooth radio channel has a 1 MHz bandwidth and hops at a rate of approximately 1600 hops per second. Transmissions are performed in 625 microsecond slots with a single packet transmitted over a single slot. For long data transmissions, particular users may occupy multiple slots using the same transmission frequency, thus slowing the instantaneous hopping rate to below 1600 hops/second. The frequency hopping scheme of each Bluetooth user is determined from a cyclic code of length $2^{27} - 1$, and each user has a channel symbol rate of 1 Mbps using GFSK modulation. The standard has been designed to support operation in very high interference levels and relies on a number of forward error control (FEC) coding and automatic repeat request (ARQ) schemes to support a raw channel bit error rate (BER) of about 10^{-3}.

Different countries have allocated various channels for Bluetooth operation. In the US and most of Europe, the FHSS 2.4 GHz ISM band is available for Bluetooth use. A detailed list of states is defined in the Bluetooth standard to support a wide range of applications, appliances, and potential uses of the Personal Area Network. Audio, text, data, and even video is contemplated in the Bluetooth standard [Tra01]. Figure 2.17 provides a depiction of the Bluetooth concept where a gateway to the Internet via IEEE 802.11b is shown as a conceptual possibility.

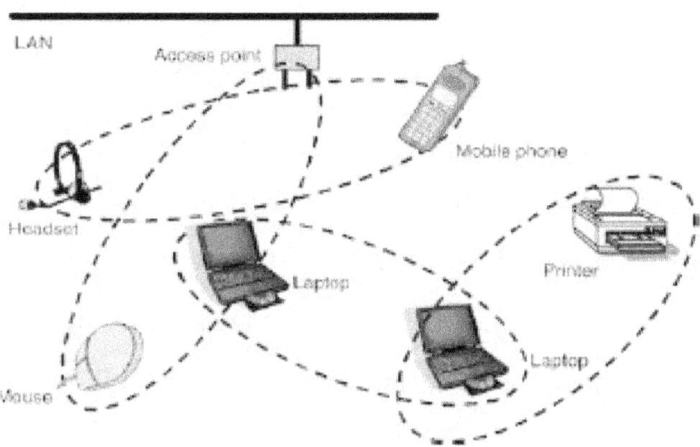

Figure 2.17. Example of a Personal Area Network (PAN) as provided by the Bluetooth standard.

The IEEE 802.15 standards committee has been formed to provide an international forum for developing Bluetooth and other PANs that interconnect pocket PCs, personal digital assistants (PDAs), cellphones, light projectors, and other appliances [Bra00]. With the rapid proliferation of wearable computers, such as PDAs, cellphones, smart cards, and position location devices, PANs may provide the connection to an entire new era of remote retrieval and monitoring of the world around us.

Chapter - II

Mobile Radio Propagation (Large-Scale Path Loss)

2.1 INTRODUCTION

There are two basic ways of transmitting an electro-magnetic (EM) signal, through a guided medium or through an unguided medium. Guided mediums such as coaxial cables and fiber optic cables, are far less hostile toward the information carrying EM signal than the wireless or the unguided medium. It presents challenges and conditions which are unique for this kind of transmissions. A signal, as it travels through the wireless channel, undergoes many kinds of propagation effects such as reflection, diffraction and scattering, due to the presence of buildings, mountains and other such obstructions. Reflection occurs when the EM waves impinge on objects which are much greater than the wavelength of the traveling wave. Diffraction is a phenomena occurring when the wave interacts with a surface having sharp irregularities. Scattering occurs when the medium through the wave is traveling contains objects which are much smaller than the wavelength of the EM wave. These varied phenomena's lead to large scale and small scale propagation losses. Due to the inherent randomness associated with such channels they are best described with the help of statistical models. Models which predict the mean signal strength for arbitrary transmitter receiver distances are termed as large scale propagation models. These are termed so because they predict the average signal strength for large Tx-Rx separations, typically for hundreds of kilometers.

2.2 FREE SPACE PROPAGATION MODEL

The free space propagation model is used to predict received signal strength when the transmitter and receiver have a clear, unobstructed line-of-sight path between them. Satellite communication systems and microwave line-of-sight radio links typically undergo free space propagation. As with most large- scale radio wave propagation models, the free space model predicts that received power decays as a function of the T-R separation distance raised to some power (i.e. a power law function). The free space power received by a receiver antenna which is separated from a radiating transmitter antenna by a distance d, is given by the Friis free space equation

$$Pr(d)= PtGtGr\lambda 2/(4\pi d)2$$

Where Pt is the transmitted power, Pr (d) is the received power which is a function of the T-R separation, Gt is the transmitter antenna gain, Gr is the receiver antenna gain, d is the T-R separation distance in meters and λ is the wavelength in meters. The gain of an antenna is related to its effective aperture, Ae by,

$$G = 4\pi Ae/\lambda 2$$

The effective aperture Ae is related to the physical size of the antenna, and λ is related to the carrier frequency by,

$$EIRP = PtGt$$

$$\lambda = c/f = 2\pi c/\omega c$$

where f is the carrier frequency in Hertz, ωc is the carrier frequency in radians per second and c is the speed of light given in meters/s. An isotropic radiator is an ideal antenna which radiates power with unit gain uniformly in all directions, and is often used to reference antenna gains in wireless systems. The effective isotropic radiated power (EIRP) is defined as it represents the maximum radiated power available from a transmitter in the direction of maximum antenna gain, as compared to an isotropic radiator. In practice, effective radiated power (ERP) is used instead of EIRP to denote the maximum radiated power as compared to a half-wave dipole antenna (instead of an isotropic antenna).

The path loss, which represents signal attenuation as a positive quantity measured in dB, is defined as the difference (in dB) between the effective transmitted power and the received power, and may or may not include the effect of the antenna gains. The path loss for the free space model when antenna gains are included is given by

$$PL \text{ (dB)} = 10\log (Pt/Pr) = -10\log [GtGr\lambda 2/(4\pi d)2]$$

When antenna gains are excluded, the antennas are assumed to have unity gain, and path loss is given by PL (dB) = 10log (Pt/Pr) = -10log[$\lambda 2/(4\pi d)2$]. The Friis free space model is only a valid predictor for Pr for values of d which are in the far-field of the transmitting antenna. The far-field or Fraunhofer region of a transmitting antenna is defined as the region beyond the far-field distance df, which is related to the largest linear dimension of the transmitter antenna aperture and the carrier wavelength. The Fraunhofer distance is given by

$$df = 2D2/\lambda$$

Where D is the largest physical linear dimension of the antenna. The far-fieldregion df must satisfy

$$df \gg D$$

What will be the far-field distance for a Base station antenna with Largest dimension D=0.5m Frequency of operation fc=900MHz

Sol:

$$\lambda = c/f = 3*10^8/900*10^6) = 0.33m$$

$$df = 2D^2/\lambda = 2(0.5)^2/0.33 = 1.5m$$

If a transmitter produces 50 watts of power, express the transmit power in units of (a) dBm, and(b) dBW If 50 watts is applied to a unity gain antenna with a 900 MHz carrier frequency, find the received power in dBm at a free space distance of 100 m from the antenna. What is Pr(10 km) ? Assume unity gain for the receiver antenna.

Given:

Transmitter power, P_t = 50 W.

Carrier frequency, f_c = 900 MHz

Using equation (3.9),

(a) Transmitter power,

$$P_t(dBm) = 10\log[P_t(mW)/(1\ mW)]$$
$$= 10\log[50 \times 10^1] = 47.0\ dBm.$$

(b) Transmitter power,

$$P_t(dBW) = 10\log[P_t(W)/(1\ W)]$$
$$= 10\log[50] = 17.0\ dBW.$$

The received power can be determined using equation (3.1).

$$P_r = \frac{P_t G_t G_r \lambda^2}{(4\pi)^2 d^2 L} = \frac{50\,(1)\,(1)\,(1/3)^2}{(4\pi)^2 (100)^2 (1)} = 3.5 \times 10^{-6}\ W = 3.5 \times 10^{-3}\ mW$$

$$P_r(dBm) = 10\log P_r(mW) = 10\log\left(3.5 \times 10^{-3}\ mW\right) = -24.5\ dBm.$$

The received power at 10 km can be expressed in terms of dBm using equation (3.9), where d_0 = 100 m and d = 10 km

$$P_r(10\ km) = P_r(100) + 20\log\left[\frac{100}{10000}\right] = -24.5\ dBm - 40\ dB$$
$$= -64.5\ dBm.$$

2.3 THREE BASIC PROPAGATION MECHANISMS

Reflection, Diffraction and Scattering is the three basic propagation mechanisms which impact propagation in a mobile communication system. Reflection occurs when a propagating electromagnetic wave impinges upon an object which has very large dimensions when compared to the wavelength of the propagating wave. Reflections occur from the surface of the earth and from buildings and walls. Diffraction occurs when the radio path between the transmitter and receiver is obstructed by a surface that has sharp irregularities (edges). The secondary waves resulting from the obstructing surface are present throughout the space and even behind the obstacle, giving rise to a bending of waves around the obstacle, even when a line-of-sight path does not exist between transmitter and receiver. At high frequencies, diffraction, like reflection depends on the geometry of the object, as well as the amplitude, phase, and polarization of the incident wave at the point of diffraction.

Scattering occurs when the medium through which the wave travels consists of objects with dimensions that are small compared to the wavelength, and where the number of obstacles per unit volume is large. Scattered waves are produced by rough surfaces, small objects, or by other irregularities in the channel. In practice, foliage, street signs, and lamp posts induce scattering in a mobile communications system.

Reflection

When a radio wave propagating in one medium impinges upon another medium having different electrical properties, the wave is partially reflected and partially transmitted. If the plane wave is incident on a perfect dielectric, part of the energy is transmitted into the second medium and part of the energy is reflected back into the first medium, and there is no loss of energy in absorption. If the second medium is a perfect conductor, then all incident energy is reflected back into the first medium without loss of energy. The electric field intensity of the reflected and transmitted waves may be related to the incident wave in the medium of origin through the Fresnel reflection coefficient (Γ). The reflection coefficient is a function of the material properties, and generally depends on the wave polarization, angle of incidence, and the frequency of the propagating wave.

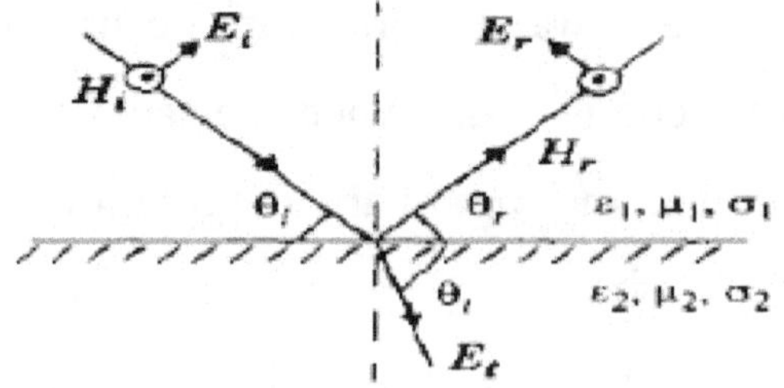

(a) E-field in the plane of incidence

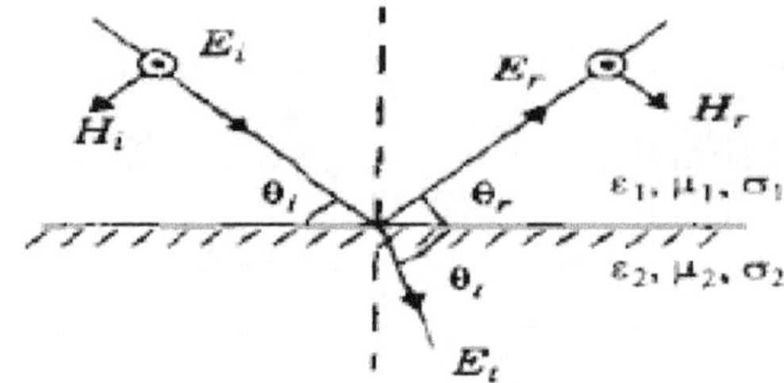

(b) E-field normal to the plane of incidence

Reflection from Dielectrics:

Figure 3.4 shows an electromagnetic wave incident at an angle θi with the plane of the boundary between two dielectric media. As shown in the figure, part of the energy is reflected back to the first media at an angle θr, and part of the energy is transmitted (refracted) into the second media at an angle θt. The nature of reflection varies with the direction of polarization of the E-field. The behavior for arbitrary directions of polarization can be studied by considering the two distinct cases shown in Figure

The plane of incidence is defined as the plane containing the incident, reflected, and transmitted rays. In Figure 3.4a, the E—field polarization is parallel with the plane of incidence (that is, the E-field has a vertical polarization, or normal component, with respect to the reflecting surface) and in Figure 3.4b, the E-field polarization is perpendicular to the plane of incidence (that is, the incident E-field is pointing out of the page towards the reader, and is perpendicular to the page and parallel to the reflecting surface).

Because of superposition, only two orthogonal polarizations need be considered to solve general reflection problems. The reflection coefficients for the two cases of parallel and perpendicular E-field polarization at the boundary of two dielectrics are given by

$$\Gamma_{\parallel} = \frac{E_r}{E_i} = \frac{\eta_2 \sin\theta_t - \eta_1 \sin\theta_i}{\eta_2 \sin\theta_t + \eta_1 \sin\theta_i} \qquad \text{(E-field in plane of incidence)}$$

$$\Gamma_{\perp} = \frac{E_r}{E_i} = \frac{\eta_2 \sin\theta_i - \eta_1 \sin\theta_t}{\eta_2 \sin\theta_i + \eta_1 \sin\theta_t} \qquad \text{(E-field not in plane of incidence)}$$

Where η is the intrinsic impedance of the respective medium.

Where ε is the permittivity of the respective medium.

Brewster Angle:

$$\Gamma_{\parallel} = \frac{-\varepsilon_r \sin\theta_i + \sqrt{\varepsilon_r - \cos^2\theta_i}}{\varepsilon_r \sin\theta_i + \sqrt{\varepsilon_r - \cos^2\theta_i}}$$

$$\Gamma_{\perp} = \frac{\sin\theta_i - \sqrt{\varepsilon_r - \cos^2\theta_i}}{\sin\theta_i + \sqrt{\varepsilon_r - \cos^2\theta_i}}$$

The Brewster angle is the angle at which no reflection occurs in the medium of origin. It occurs when the incident angle BB is such that the reflection coefficient $\Gamma\parallel$ is equal to zero. The Brewster angle is given by the value of θB which satisfies

Sin (θB) = √(ε1)/√(ε1+ε2)

For the case when the first medium is free space and the second medium has a relative permittivity εr, above equation can be expressed as

Sin(θB) = √(εr-1)/√(εr2-1) Note that the Brewster angle occurs only for vertical (i.e. parallel) polarization.

Reflection from Perfect Conductors:
Since electromagnetic energy cannot pass through a perfect conductor a plane wave incident on a conductor has all of its energy reflected. As the electric field at the surface of the conductor must be equal to zero at all times in order to obey Maxwell's equations, the reflected wave must be equal in magnitude to the incident wave. For the case when E-field polarization is in the plane of incidence, the boundary conditions require that θi =θr and Ei = Er (E-field in plane of incidence)

Similarly, for the case when the E-field is horizontally polarized, the boundary conditions require that θi =θr and Ei = - Er (E-field not in plane of incidence)

2.4 GROUND REFLECTION (2-RAY) MODEL:

In a mobile radio channel, a single direct path between the base station and a mobile is seldom the only physical means for propagation, and hence the free space propagation model is in most cases inaccurate when used alone. The 2-ray ground reflection model shown in Figure 3.7 is a useful propagation model that is based on geometric optics, and considers both the direct path and a ground reflected propagation path between transmitter and receiver. This model has been found to be reasonably accurate for predicting the large-scale signal strength over distances of several kilometers for mobile radio systems that use tall towers (heights which exceed 50 m), as well as for line of-sight, microcell channels in urban environments.

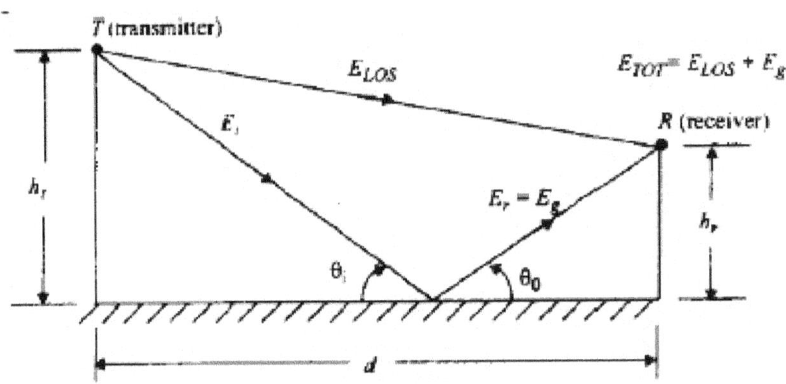

Figure 3.7
Two-ray ground reflection model.

Referring to Figure 3.7, ht is the height of the transmitter and hr is the height of the receiver. If Eo is the free space E-field (in units of V/m) at a reference distance do from the transmitter, then for d > do , the free space propagating E—field is given by Two propagating waves arrive at the receiver: the direct wave that travels a distance d'; and the reflected wave that travels a distance d". The electric field ETOT(d, t) can be expressed as the sum of equations for distances d' and d" (i.e. direct wave and reflected wave).

Diffraction:

Diffraction allows radio signals to propagate around the curved surface of the earth, beyond the horizon, and to propagate behind obstructions. Although the received field strength decreases rapidly as a receiver moves deeper into the obstructed (shadowed) region, the diffraction field still exists and often has sufficient strength to produce a useful signal.

The phenomenon of diffraction can be explained by Huygens's principle, which states that all points on a wave front can be considered as point sources for the production of secondary wavelets, and that these wavelets combine to produce a new wave front in the direction of propagation. Diffraction is caused by the propagation of secondary wavelets into a shadowed region. The field strength of a diffracted wave in the shadowed region is the vector sum of the electric field components of all the secondary wavelets in the space around the obstacle.

2.5 FRESNEL ZONE GEOMETRY:

Fresnel zones represent successive regions where secondary waves have a path length from the TX to the RX which are $n\lambda/2$ greater in path length than of the LOS path. The plane below illustrates successive Fresnel zones.

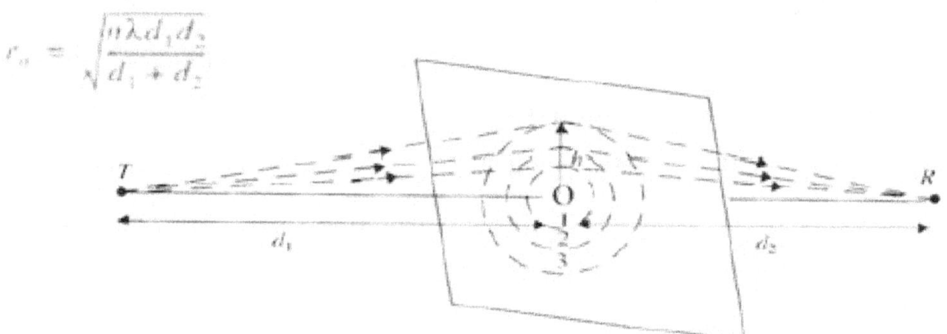

Figure 4.11   Concentric circles which define the boundaries of successive Fresnel zones.

$$\Delta = \frac{h^2}{2} \frac{(d_1 + d_2)}{d_1 d_2}$$

The corresponding phase difference is given by

$$\phi = \frac{2\pi\Delta}{\lambda} = \frac{2\pi}{\lambda} \frac{h^2}{2} \frac{(d_1 + d_2)}{d_1 d_2}$$

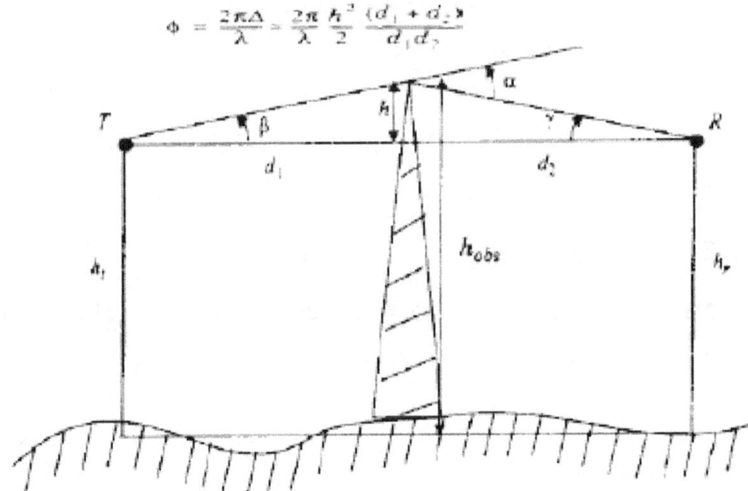

(a) Knife-edge diffraction geometry. The point T denotes the transmitter and R denotes the receiver, with an infinite knife-edge obstruction blocking the line-of-sight path.

Consider a transmitter and receiver separated in free space as shown in Figure 3.10a. Let an obstructing screen of effective height h with infinite width (going into and out of the paper,) be placed between them at a distance d1 from the transmitter and d2 from the receiver. It is apparent that the wave propagating from the transmitter to the receiver via the top of the screen travels a longer distance than if a direct line- of-sight path (through the screen) existed. Assuming h << d1, d2 and h >>λ , then the difference between the direct path and the diffracted path, called the excess path length (Δ) , can be obtained from the geometry of Figure as

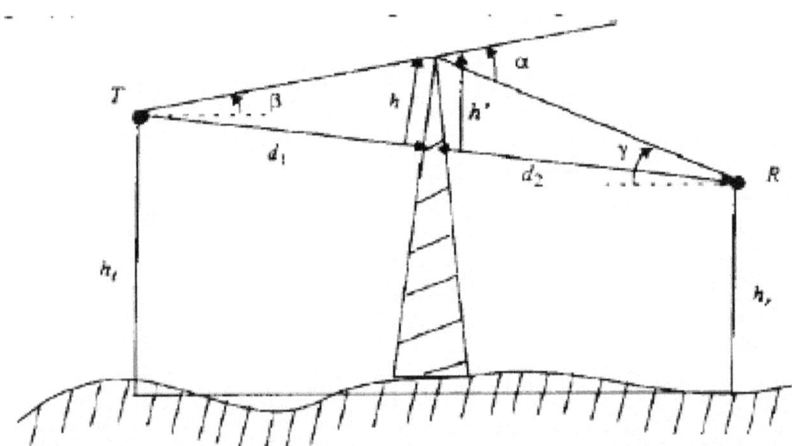

(b) Knife-edge diffraction geometry when the transmitter and receiver are not at the same height. Note that if α and β are small and $h << d_1$ and d_2, then h and h' are virtually identical and the geometry may be redrawn as shown in Figure 3.10c.

2.6 KNIFE-EDGE DIFFRACTION MODEL:

Estimating the signal attenuation caused by diffraction of radio waves over hills and buildings is essential in predicting the field strength in a given service area. Generally, it is impossible to make very precise estimates of the diffraction losses, and in practice prediction is a process of theoretical approximation modified by necessary empirical corrections. Though the calculation of diffraction losses over complex and irregular terrain is a mathematically difficult problem, expressions for diffraction losses for many simple cases have been derived. As a starting point, the limiting case of propagation over a knife-edge gives good insight into the order of magnitude of diffraction loss.

When shadowing is caused by a single object such as a hill or mountain, the attenuation caused by diffraction can be estimated by treating the obstruction as a diffracting knife edge. This is the simplest of diffraction models, and the diffraction loss in this case can be readily estimated using the classical Fresnel solution for the field behind a knife edge (also called a half-plane).

Multiple Knife-edge Diffraction:

In many practical situations, especially in hilly terrain, the propagation path may consist of more than one obstruction, in which case the total diffraction loss due to all of the obstacles must be computed. Burlington suggested that the series of obstacles be replaced by a single equivalent obstacle so that the path loss can be obtained using single knife-edge diffraction models. This method, illustrated in Figure 3.15, oversimplifies the calculations and often provides very optimistic estimates of the received signal strength. In a more rigorous treatment, Millington et. al. gave a wave-theory solution for the field behind two knife edges in series. This solution is very useful and can be applied easily for predicting diffraction losses due to two knife edges. However, extending this to more than two knife edges becomes a formidable mathematical problem. Many models that are mathematically less complicated have been developed to estimate the diffraction losses due to multiple obstructions.

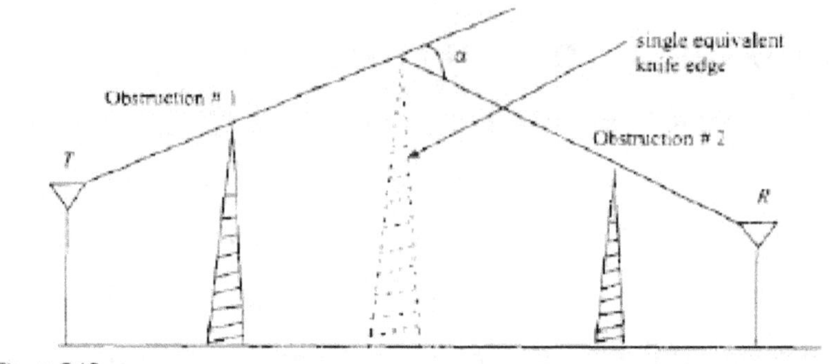

Figure 3.15
Bullington's construction of an equivalent knife edge [From [Bul47] © IEEE]

Scattering:

The actual received signal in a mobile radio environment is often stronger than what is predicted by reflection and diffraction models alone. This is because when a radio wave impinges on a rough surface, the reflected energy is spread out (diffused) in all directions due to scattering. Objects such as lamp posts and trees tend to scatter energy in all directions, thereby providing additional radio energy at a receiver. Flat surfaces that have much larger dimension than a wavelength may be modeled as reflective surfaces. However, the roughness of such surfaces often induces propagation effects different from the specular reflection described earlier in this chapter.

Rayleigh criterion: used for testing surface roughness A surface is considered smooth if its min to max protuberance (bumps) h is less than critical height $h_c = \lambda/8 \sin\Theta_i$

Scattering path loss factor ρ_s is given by $\rho_s = \exp[-8[(\pi*\sigma_h *\sin\Theta_i)/ \lambda] 2]$

Where h is surface height and σ_h is standard deviation of surface height about mean surface height. For rough surface, the flat surface reflection coefficient is multiplied by scattering loss factor ρ_s to account for diminished electricfield.

Reflected E-fields for h> hc for rough surface can be calculatedas $\Gamma_{rough} = \rho_s \Gamma$

A surface is considered smooth if it's minimum to maximum protuberance h is less than hc, and is considered rough if the protuberance is greater than hc. For rough surfaces, the flat surface reflection coefficient needs to be multiplied by a scattering loss factor, ρ_s to account for the diminished reflected field.

2.7 OUTDOOR PROPAGATION MODELS

Based on the coverage area, the Outdoor propagation environment may be divided into three categories

1. Propagation in Macro cells
2. Propagation in Micro cells

Outdoor radio transmission takes place over an irregular terrain. The terrain profile must be taken into consideration for estimating the path loss.

e.g. trees buildings and hills must be taken into consideration

Longley-Ryce Model:

The Longley-Ryce model is applicable to point-to-point communication systems in the frequency range from 40 MHz to 100 GHz, over different kinds of terrain. The median transmission loss is predicted using the path geometry of the terrain profile and the refractivity of the troposphere. Geometric optics techniques (primarily the 2-ray ground reflection model) are used to predict signal strengths within the radio horizon. Diffraction losses over isolated obstacles are estimated using the Fresnel-Kirchoff knife- edge models. Forward scatter theory is used to make troposcatter predictions over long distances.

The Longley-Ryce method operates in two modes. When a detailed terrain path profile is available, the path-specific parameters can be easily determined and the prediction is called a point-to-point mode prediction. On the other hand, if the terrain path profile is not available, the Longley-Ryce method provides techniques to estimate the path-specific parameters, and such a prediction is called an area mode prediction.

Okumura Model:

Okumura`s model is one of the most widely used models for signal prediction in urban areas. This model is applicable for frequencies in the range 150 MHz to 1920 MHz (although it is typically extrapolated up to 3000 MHz) and distances of 1 km to 100 km. It can be used for base station antenna heights ranging from 30 m to 1000 m. Okumura developed a set of curves giving the median attenuation relative to free space (Amu), in an urban area over a quasi-smooth terrain with a base station effective antenna height (hte) of 200 m and a mobile antenna height (hre) of 3 m. These curves were developed from extensive measurements using vertical omni-directional antennas at both the base and mobile, and are plotted as a function of frequency in the range 100 MHz to 1920 MHz and as a function of distance from the base station in the range 1 km to 100 km. To determine path loss using Okumura`s model, the free space path loss between the points of interest is first determined, and then the value of Amu(f, d) (as read from the curves) is added to it along with correction factors to account for the type of terrain. The model can be expressed as

$$L50(dB) = LF + Amu(f, d) - G(te) - G(re) - GAREA$$

where L50 is the 50th percentile (i.e., median) value of propagation path loss, LF is the free space propagation loss, Amu is the median attenuation relative to free space, G(hte) is the base station antenna height gain factor, G(hre) is the mobile antenna height gain factor, and G A R E A is the gain due to the type of environment. Note that the antenna height gains are strictly a function of height and have nothing to do with antenna patterns.

$$G(h_{te}) = 20\log\left(\frac{h_{te}}{200}\right) \qquad 1000 \text{ m} > h_{te} > 30 \text{ m}$$

$$G(h_{re}) = 10\log\left(\frac{h_{re}}{3}\right) \qquad h_{re} \leq 3 \text{ m}$$

$$G(h_{re}) = 20\log\left(\frac{h_{re}}{3}\right) \qquad 10 \text{ m} > h_{re} > 3 \text{ m}$$

Hata Model:

The Hata model [Hat90] is an empirical formulation of the graphical path loss data provided by Okumura, and is valid from 150 MHz to 1500 MHz. Hata presented the urban area propagation loss as a standard formula and supplied correction equations for application to other situations. The standard formula for median path loss in urban areas is given by L50(urban)(dB) = 69.55 + 26.16logfc -13.82loghte-a(hre) + (44.9 - 6.55loghte)logd where fc is the frequency (in MHz) from 150 MHz to 1500 MHz, hte is the effective transmitter (base station) antenna height (in meters) ranging from 30 m to 200 m, hre is the effective receiver (mobile) antenna height (in meters) ranging from 1 m to 10 m, d is the T-R separation distance (in km), and a(hre) is the correction factor for effective mobile antenna height which is a function of the size of the coverage area. For a small to medium sized city, the mobile antenna correction factor is given by

a(hre) = (1.11ogfc - 0.7)hre - (1.56logfc - 0.8) dB

for a large city, it is given by

a(hre) = 8.29(log1.54hre)2 -1.1 dB for fc <= 300 MHz a(hre) = 3.2(log11.75hre)2 —4.97 dB for fc>= 300 MHz

To obtain the path loss in a suburban area the standard Hata formula in equations are modified as L50(dB) = L50(urban)-2[log(fc/28)]2-5.4

and for path loss in open rural areas, the formula is modified as L50(dB) = L50(urban) – 4.78(logfc)2 + 18.33logfc - 40.94

PCS Extension to Hata Model

The European Co-operative for Scientific and Technical research (EURO-COST) formed the COST-231 working committee to develop an extended version of the Hata model. COST-231 proposed the following formula to extend Hata's model to 2 GHz. The proposed model for path loss is [EUR91]

$$L_{50}(urban) = 46.3 + 33.9\log f_c - 13.82\log h_{te} - a(h_{re}) \qquad (3.87)$$
$$+ (44.9 - 6.55\log h_{te})\log d + C_M$$

where $a(h_{re})$ is defined in equations (3.83), (3.84.a), and (3.84.b) and

$$C_M = \begin{cases} 0 \text{ dB} & \text{for medium sized city and suburban areas} \\ 3 \text{ dB} & \text{for metropolitan centers} \end{cases} \qquad (3.88)$$

The COST-231 extension of the Hata model is restricted to the following range of parameters:

f : 1500 MHz to 2000 MHz
h_{te} : 30 m to 200 m
h_{re} : 1 m to 10 m
d : 1 km to 20 km

Walfisch and Bertoni Model

A model developed by Walfisch and Bertoni [Wal88] considers the impact of rooftops and building height by using diffraction to predict average signal strength at street level. The model considers the path loss, S, to be a product of three factors.

$$S = P_0 Q^2 P_1 \qquad (3.89)$$

where P_0 represents free space path loss between isotropic antennas given by

$$P_0 = \left(\frac{\lambda}{4\pi R}\right)^2 \qquad (3.90)$$

The factor Q^2 gives the reduction in the rooftop signal due to the row of buildings which immediately shadow the receiver at street level. The P_1 term is based upon diffraction and determines the signal loss from the rooftop to the street.

In dB, the path loss is given by

$$S\,(\text{dB}) \;=\; L_0 + L_{rts} + L_{ms} \tag{3.91}$$

where L_0 represents free space loss, L_{rts} represents the "rooftop-to-street diffraction and scatter loss", and L_{ms} denotes multiscreen diffraction loss due to the rows of buildings [Xia92]. Figure 3.25 illustrates the geometry used in the Walfisch Bertoni model [Wal88], [Mac93]. This model is being considered for use by ITU-R in the IMT-2000 standards activities.

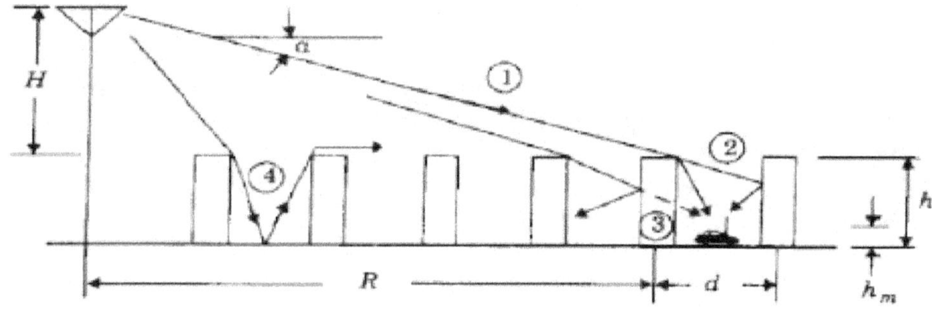

Figure 3.25
Propagation geometry for model proposed by Walfisch and Bertoni [From [Wal88] © IEEE]

Wideband PCS Microcell Model

Work by Feuerstein, et.al. in 1991 used a 20 MHz pulsed transmitter at 1900 MHz to measure path loss, outage, and delay spread in typical microcellular systems in San Francisco and Oakland. Using base station antenna heights of 3.7 m, 8.5 m, and 13.3 m, and a mobile receiver with an antenna height of 1.7 m above ground, statistics for path loss, multipath, and coverage area were developed from extensive measurements in line-of-sight (LOS) and obstructed (OBS) environments [Feu94]. This work revealed that a 2-ray ground reflection model (shown in Figure 3.7) is a good estimate for path loss in LOS microcells, and a simple log-distance path loss model holds well for OBS microcell environments.

For a flat earth ground reflection model, the distance d_f at which the first Fresnel zone just becomes obstructed by the ground (first Fresnel zone clearance) is given by

$$d_f = \frac{1}{\lambda}\sqrt{(\Sigma^2 - \Delta^2)^2 - 2(\Sigma^2 + \Delta^2)\left(\frac{\lambda}{2}\right)^2 + \left(\frac{\lambda}{2}\right)^4} \qquad (3.92.a)$$

$$= \frac{1}{\lambda}\sqrt{16 h_t^2 h_r^2 - \lambda^2 (h_t^2 + h_r^2) + \frac{\lambda^4}{16}}$$

For LOS cases, a double regression path loss model that uses a regression breakpoint at the first Fresnel zone clearance was shown to fit well to measurements. The model assumes omnidirectional vertical antennas and predicts average path loss as

$$PL(d) = \begin{cases} 10n_1 \log(d) + p_1 & \text{for } 1 < d < d_f \\ 10n_2 \log(d/d_f) + 10n_1 \log d_f + p_1 & \text{for } d > d_f \end{cases} \qquad (3.92.b)$$

where p_1 is equal to $\overline{PL}(d_0)$ (the path loss in decibels at the reference distance of $d_0 = 1$ m), d is in meters and n_1, n_2 are path loss exponents which are a function of transmitter height, as given in Figure 3.26. It can easily be shown that at 1900 MHz, $p_1 = 38.0$ dB.

For the OBS case, the path loss was found to fit the standard log-distance path loss law of equation (3.69.a)

$$PL(d)\,[dB] = 10n \log(d) + p_1 \qquad (3.92.c)$$

3.8 INDOOR PROPAGATION MODELS

With the advent of Personal Communication Systems (PCS), there is a great deal of interest in characterizing radio propagation inside buildings. The indoor radio channel differs from the traditional mobile radio channel in two aspects - the distances covered are much smaller, and the variability of the environment is much greater for a much smaller range of T-R separation distances. It has been observed that propagation within buildings is strongly influenced by specific features such as the layout of the building, the construction materials, and the building type. This section outlines models for path loss within buildings.

Indoor radio propagation is dominated by the same mechanisms as outdoor: reflection, diffraction, and scattering. However, conditions are much more variable. For example, signal levels vary greatly depending on whether interior doors are open or closed inside a building. Where antennas are mounted also impacts large-scale propagation. Antennas mounted at desk level in a partitioned office receive vastly different signals than those mounted on the ceiling. Also, the smaller propagation distances make it more difficult to insure far-field radiation for all receiver locations and types of antennas.

Partition Losses (same floor):

Buildings have a wide variety of partitions and obstacles which form the internal and external structure. Houses typically use a wood frame partition with plaster board to form internal walls and have wood or non-reinforced concrete between floors. Office buildings, on the other hand, often have large open areas (open plan) which are constructed by using moveable office partitions so that the space may be reconfigured easily, and use metal reinforced concrete between floors. Partitions that are formed as part of the building structure are called hard partitions, and partitions that may be moved and which do not span to the ceiling are called soft partitions. Partitions vary widely in their physical and electrical characteristics, making it difficult to apply general models to specific indoor installations.

Partition Losses between Floors:

The losses between floors of a building are determined by the external dimensions and materials of the building, as well as the type of construction used to create the floors and the external surroundings. Even the number of windows in a building and the presence of tinting (which attenuates radio energy) can impact the loss between floors. It can be seen that for all three buildings, the attenuation between one floors of the building is greater than the incremental attenuation caused by each additional floor. After about five or six floor separations, very little additional path loss is experienced.

Log-distance Path Loss Model:

According to this model the received power at distance d is given by,

$$PL \, (dB) \; = \; PL \, (d_0) \, + \, 10n \log\left(\frac{d}{d_0}\right) + X_\sigma$$

The value of n varies with propagation environments. The value of n is 2 for free space. The value of n varies from 4 to 6 for obstruction of building, and 3 to 5 for urban scenarios. The important factor is to select the correct reference distance d0. For large cell area it is 1 Km, while for micro-cell system it varies from 10m-1m.

Ericsson multiple breakpoint model:

It was obtained by measurements in a multiple floor office building. It has 4 breakpoints and considers both an upper and lower bound on path loss. It assumes that there is 30dB attenuation at d0 = 1m which is accurate for f = 900MHz & unity gain antennas.

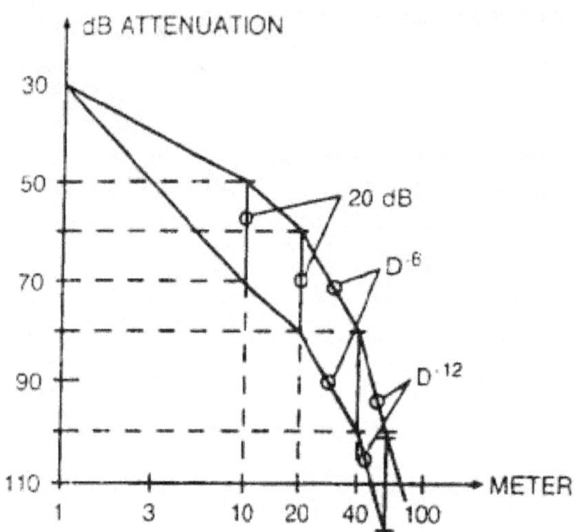

Attenuation Factor Model:

The attenuation factor model incorporates a special path loss exponent and a floor attenuation factor to provide an estimate of indoor path loss. NSF is the path loss exponent for a same floor measurement and FAF is a floor attenuation factor based on the number of floors between transmitter and receiver.

2.9 RAY TRACING AND SITE SPECIFIC MODELLING

In physics, ray tracing is a method for calculating the path of waves or particles through a system with regions of varying propagation velocity, absorption characteristics, and reflecting surfaces. Under these circumstances, wave fronts may bend, change direction, or reflect off surfaces, complicating analysis. Ray tracing solves the problem by repeatedly advancing idealized narrow beams called rays through the medium by discrete amounts. Simple problems can be analyzed by propagating a few rays using simple arithmetic. More detailed analysis can be performed by using a computer to propagate many rays.

When applied to problems of electromagnetic radiation, ray tracing often relies on approximate solutions to Maxwell's equations that are valid as long as the light waves propagate through and around objects whose dimensions are much greater than the light's wavelength. Ray theory does not describe phenomena such as interference and diffraction, which require wave theory (involving the phase of the wave).

Chapter - III

Mobile Radio Propagation: Small –Scale Fading and Multipath

3.1 INTRODUCTION

The focus of this chapter is to identify the parameters that distort the information signal as it penetrates the propagation medium. The corruptive elements are in the form of multipath delay, signal fading and distortion due to time dispersion. The multipath components can add constructively or destructively depending on the carrier frequency and delay differences. The over all effect is that received signal level fluctuates with time, which leads a phenomenon called 'fading'. Fading refers to the time variation of received signal power caused by changes in the transmission medium or traveling paths. In a mobile environment, where one is moving relative to the other, the relative location of various obstacles changes over time which leads to path loss and fading.

3.2 SMALL-SCALE FADING

Small scale fading is used to described the rapid fluctuations of the amplitudes, phases, or multipath delays of a radio signal over a short period of time or travel distance so that the large scale path loss effects may be ignored. These rapid changes occur because the signal is received at receiver from many directions. Depending on the different paths the signals take, each signal may have a different phase and cancel each other. However, if these changes are too fast, such as driving on a highway, through a city, the signal level fluctuates rapidly and increases fading on that channel.

3.3 FACTORS AFFECTING SMALL-SCALE FADING

Following factors in the radio propagation channel may affect small scale fading:

1. Speed of the mobile
2. Speed of surround objects
3. Bandwidth of the transmitted signal
4. Multipath propagation
5. Dopper shift

3.4 REASONS OF SIGNAL FADING

There are three basic reasons of fading of wireless signals

1. Absorption

2. Free-space loss

3. Multipath propagation

3.4.1 Absorption

Absorption simply describes how a radio signal is absorbed by objects. When a radio wave strikes on object, there is possibility that it can be absorbed. Radio frequencies can be absorbed by buildings, trees or hills. It is usually seen that the objects made from organic materials tend to absorb more RF signal than the objects made from inorganic materials. Absorption can be compensated by using higher gain antennas and higher power levels in order to cover the same geographic area. The greater the amount of absorption of an RF signal, the higher the fading and the less geographic area covered.

3.4.2 Free-Space Loss

It is also known as path-loss It describes the attenuation of a radio signal over a given distance. It is directly proportional to the radio frequency. As the frequency of a radio signal increases, free space path loss also increases.

3.4.3 Multipath Propagation

In multipath propagation, multiple signal paths are established between the base station and the user terminal (mobile phone).

The fading due to multipath propagation is known as 'Multipath fading' or 'Rayleigh fading'. One signal path arrives at an antenna (either mobile or base station) as a direct signal, while other signals are multipath or indirect signals. Indirect signal generated due to reflection; refraction or diffraction of signals from any or all objects lie in the path of transmitting antenna and receiving antenna. These indirect signals can add to or subtract from the direct signal arriving at the antenna This depends on whether or not the indirect signals are in-phase or out-of-phase with the direct signal.

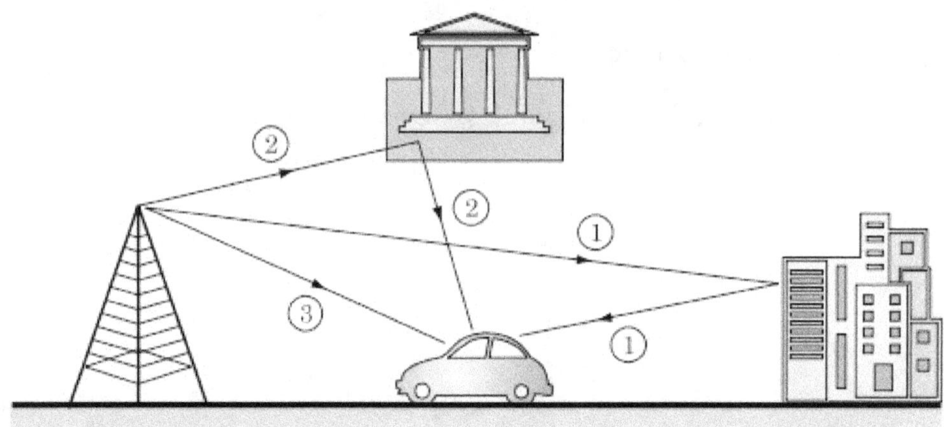

If the signals are in-phase then overall signal strength increases and if the signals are out-of-phase then over all signal strength decreases.

- Reflection occurs when the surface is large relative to the wavelength of the signal.
- Diffraction occurs at the edge of the surface that is large compared to the wavelength of radio wave.
- An incoming signal scattered into several weaker outgoing signals if the size of an obstacle is on the order of the wavelength of the signal or less.

3.5 DOPPLER SHIFT IN MULTIPATH RECEPTION

If the mobile and base station have relative motion between them then there is an apparent shift in frequency of each multipath wave. The shift in received signal frequency due to motion is called the doppler shift. Doppler shift is directly proportional to the velocity and direction of motion of the mobile with respect to the direction of arrival of received multipath wave. If a mobile unit takes Δt time to travel from point A to point B with a constant velocity 'v' then the doppler shift (fd) is

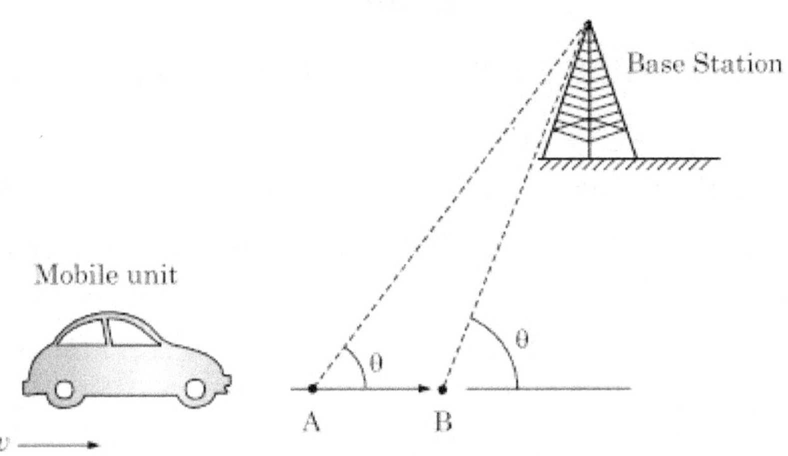

θ is assumed same for point A and B since the source (i.e. base station) is assumed to be very far away from Mobile unit.

Chapter – IV

WI-FI AND THE IEEE 802.11 WIRELESS LAN STANDARDS

The most prominent specification for wireless LANs (WLANs) was developed by theIEEE 802.11 working group. We look first at the overall architecture of IEEE 802 standards and then at the specifics of IEEE 802.11

4.1 IEEE 802 architecture

The architecture of a LAN is best described in terms of a layering of protocols that organize the basic functions of a LAN. This section opens with a description of the standardized protocol architecture for LANs, which encompasses physical, medium access control, and logical link control layers. We then look in more detail at medium access control and logical link control.

Protocol Architecture

Protocols defined specifically for LAN and MAN (metropolitan area network) transmission address issues relating to the transmission of blocks of data over the network. In OSI terms, higher-layer protocols (layer 3 or 4 and above) are independent of network architecture and are applicable to LANs, MANs, and WANs. Thus, a discussion of LAN protocols is concerned principally with lower layers of the OSI model. Figure 14.1 relates the LAN protocols to the OSI architecture (Figure 4.3).This architecture was developed by the IEEE 802 committee and has been adopted by all organizations working on the specification of LAN standards. It is generally referred to as the IEEE 802 reference model.! Working from the bottom up, the lowest layer of the IEEE 802 reference model corresponds to the physical layer of the OSI model and includes such functions as

- Encoding/decoding of signals (e.g., PSK, QAM, etc.)
- Preamble generation/removal (for synchronization)
- Bit transmission reception

In addition, the physical layer of the 802 model includes a specification of the transmission medium and the topology. Generally, this is considered "below" the lowest layer of the OSI model. However, the choice of transmission medium and topology is critical in LAN design, and so a specification of the medium is included. For some of the IEEE 802 standards, the physical layer is further subdivided into sublayers. In the case of IEEE 802.11, two sublayers are defined:

Physical layer convergence procedure (PLCP): Defines a method of mapping802.11 MAC layer protocol data units (MPDUs) into a framing format suitable for sending and receiving user data and management information between two or more stations using the associated PMD sublayer Physical medium dependent sublayer (PMD): Defines the characteristics of, and method of transmitting and receiving, user data through a wireless medium between two or more stations

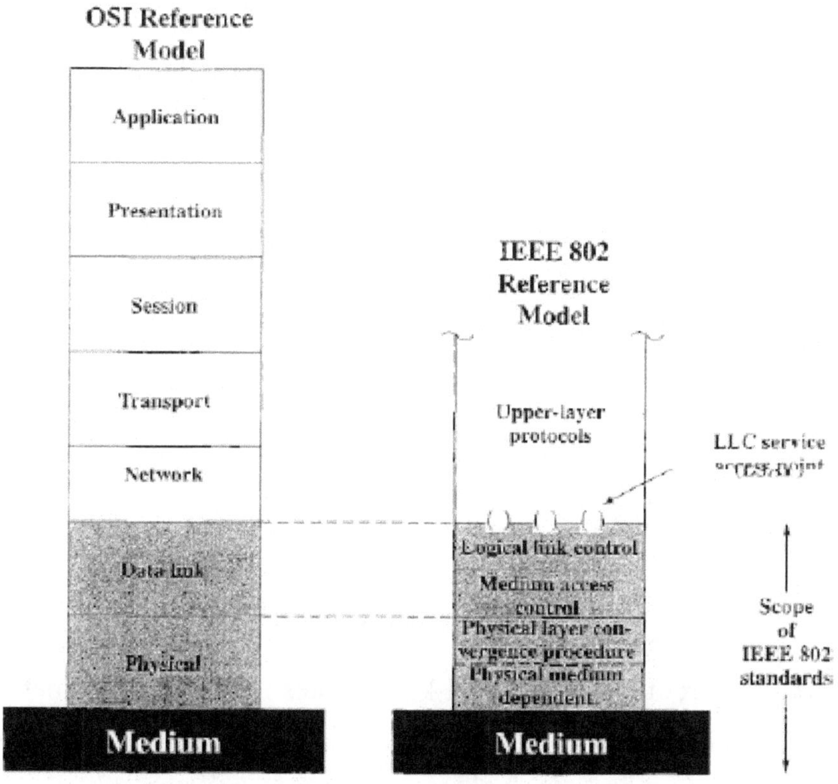

Figure 14.1   IEEE 802 Protocol Layers Compared to OSI Model

Above the physical layer are the functions associated with providing service to LAN users. These include

- On transmission, assemble data into a frame with address and error detection fields.
- On reception, disassemble frame, and perform address recognition and error detection.
- Govern access to the LAN transmission medium.

- Provide an interface to higher layers and perform flow and error control.

These are functions typically associated with OSI layer 2. The set of functions in the last bullet item is grouped into a logical link control (LLC) layer. The functions in the first three bullet items are treated as a separate layer, called medium access control (MAC). The separation is done for the following reasons:

The logic required to manage access to a shared-access medium is not found in traditional layer 2 data link control.

For the same LLC, several MAC options may be provided.

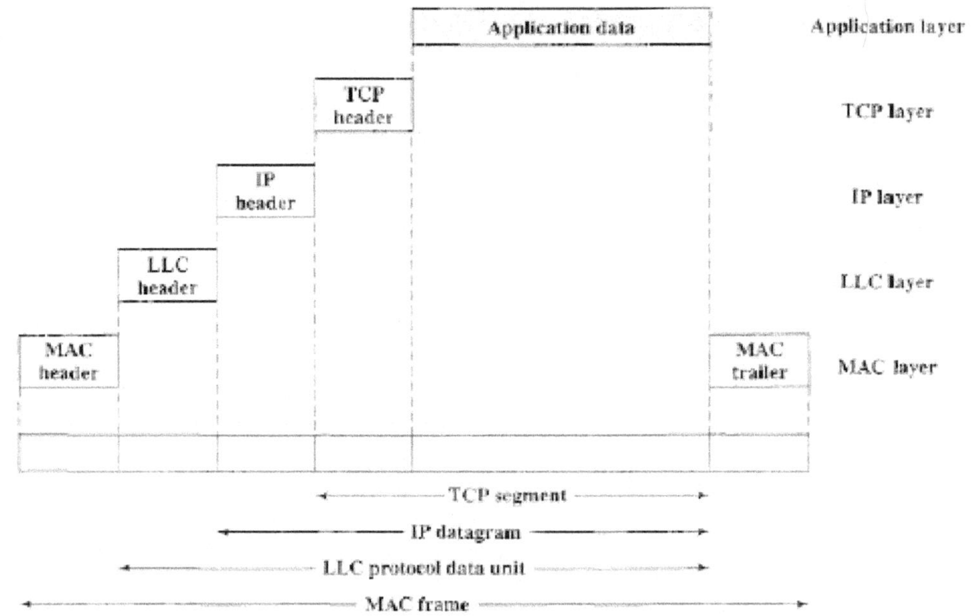

Figure 14.2   IEEE 802 Protocols in Context

Figure 14.2, which reproduces Figure 11.14, illustrates the relationship between the levels of the architecture. Higher-level data are passed down to LLC, which appends control information as a header, creating an LLC protocol data unit (PDU). This control information is used in the operation of the LLC protocol.The entire LLC PDU is then passed down to the MAC layer, which appends control information at the front and back of the packet, forming a MAC frame. Again, the control information in the frame is needed for the operation of the MAC protocol. For context, the figure also shows the use of TCP/IP and an application layer above the LAN protocols.

4.2 MAC frame format

The MAC layer receives a block of data from the LLC layer and is responsible for performing functions related to medium access and for transmitting the data. As with other protocol layers, MAC implements these functions making use of a protocol data unit at its layer. In this case, the PDU is referred to as a MAC frame. The exact format of the MAC frame differs somewhat for the various MAC protocols in use. In general, all of the MAC frames have a format similar to that of Figure 14.3. The fields of this frame are as follows:

- MAC Control: This field contains any protocol control information needed for the functioning of the MAC protocol. For example, a priority level could be indicated here.

Destination MAC Address: The destination physical attachment point on the LAN for this frame.

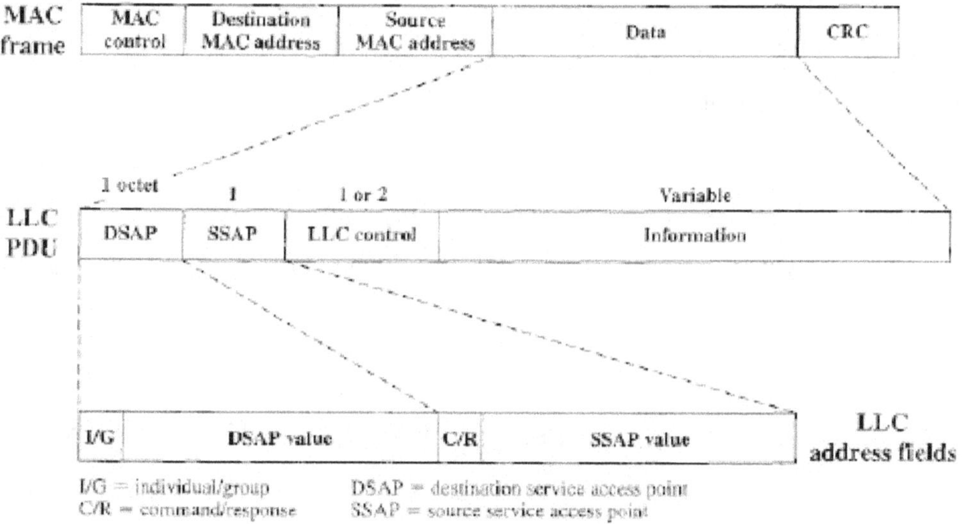

Figure 14.3   LLC PDU in a Generic MAC Frame Format

- Source MAC Address: The source physical attachment point on the LAN for this frame.
- Data: The body of the MAC frame. This may be LLC data from the next higher layer or control information relevant to the operation of the MAC protocol.

- CRC: The cyclic redundancy check field (also known as the frame checksequence, PCS, field). This is an error-detecting code, as described in Section8.1. The CRC is used in virtually all data link protocols, such as HDLC(Appendix C).

In most data link control protocols, the data link protocol entity is responsible notonly for detecting errors using the CRC but for recovering from those errors by retransmittingdamaged frames. In the LAN protocol architecture, these two functions are splitbetween the MAC and LLC layers. The MAC layer is responsible for detecting errorsand discarding any frames that are in error. The LLC layer optionally keeps track ofwhich frames have beensuccessfully received and retransmits unsuccessful frames.1 octet 1 lor 2LLC

4.3 Logical Link Control

The LLC layer for LANs is similar in many respects to other link layers in common use. Like all link layers, LLC is concerned with the transmission of a link-level PDUbetween two stations, without the necessity of an intermediate switching node. LLChas two characteristics not shared by most other link control protocols:

It must support the multiaccess, shared-medium nature of the link (this differs from a multidrop line in that there is no primary node). It is relieved of some details of link access by the MAC layer.

Addressing in LLC involves specifying the source and destination LLC users. Typically, a user is a higher-layer protocol or a network management function in the station. These LLC user addresses are referred to as service access points (SAPs), in keeping with OSI terminology for the user of a protocol layer.We look first at the services that LLC provides to a higher-level user, and then at the LLC protocol. LLC Services LLC specifies the mechanisms for addressing stations across the medium and for controlling the exchange of data between two users. The operation and format of this standard is based on HDLC. LLC provides three alternative services for attached devices:

It Unacknowledged connectionless service: This is a datagram-style service. It is a very simpleservice that does not involve any flow- and error-control mechanisms. Thus, the delivery of data is not guaranteed. However, in most devices, there will be some higher layer of software that deals with reliability issues. Connection-mode service: This service is similar to that offered by HDLC. A logical connection is set up between two users exchanging data, and flow control and error control are provided. Acknowledged connectionless service: This is a cross between the previous two services. It provides that datagrams are to be acknowledged, but no prior logical connection is set up. Typically, a vendor will provide these services as options that the customer can select when purchasing the equipment. Alternatively, the customer can purchase equipment that provides two or all three services and select a specific service based on application.

The unacknowledged connectionless service requires minimum logic and is useful in two contexts. First, it will often be the case that higher layers of software will provide the necessary reliability and flow-control mechanism, and it is efficient to avoid duplicating them. For example, TCP could provide the mechanisms needed to ensure that data are delivered reliably. Second, there are instances in which the overhead of connection establishment and maintenance is unjustified or even counterproductive (for example, data collection activities that involve the periodic sampling of data sources, such as sensors and automatic self-test reports from security equipment or network components). In a monitoring application, the loss of an occasional data unit would not cause distress, as the next report should arrive shortly. Thus, in most cases, the unacknowledged connectionless service is the preferred option.

The connection-mode service could be used in very simple devices, such as remote sensors, that have little software operating above this level. In these cases, it would provide the flow control and reliability mechanisms normally implemented at higher layers of the communications software. The acknowledged connectionless service is useful in several contexts. With the connection-mode service, the logical link control software must maintain some sort of table for each active connection, to keep track of the status of that connection. If the user needs guaranteed delivery but there is a large number of destinations for data, then the connection-mode service may be impractical because of the large number of tables required. An example is a process control or automated factory environment.

Where a central site may need to communicate with a large number of processors and programmable controllers. Another use of this is the handling of important and time critical alarm or emergency control signals in a factory. Because of their importance, an acknowledgment is needed so that the sender can be assured that the signal got through. Because of the urgency of the signal, the user might not want to take the time first to establish a logical connection and then send the data.

- LLC Protocol The basic LLC protocol is modeled after HDLC and has similar functions and formats. The differences between the two protocols can be summarized as follows:
- LLC makes use of the asynchronous balanced mode of operation of HDLC, to support connection-mode LLC service; this is referred to as type 2 operation. The other HDLC modes are not employed.
- LLC supports an unacknowledged connectionless service using the unnumbered information PDU; this is known as type 1 operation.
- LLC supports an acknowledged connectionless service by using two new unnumbered PDUs; this is known as type 3 operation.
- LLC permits multiplexing by the use of LLC service access points (LSAPs).

All three LLC protocols employ the same PDU format (Figure 14.3), which consists of four fields. The DSAP and SSAP fields each contain a 7-bit address, which specify the destination and source users of LLC, respectively. One bit of the DSAP indicates whether the DSAP is an individual or group address. One bit of the SSAP indicates whether the PDU is a command or response PDU. The format of the LLC control field is identical to that of HDLC (Figure C.1, Appendix C), using extended (7-bit) sequence numbers.

For type 1 operation, which supports the unacknowledged connectionless service, the unnumbered information (UI) PDU is used to transfer user data. There is no acknowledgment, flow control, or error control. However, there is error detection and discard at the MAC level. Two other PDU types, XID and TEST, are used to support management functions associated with all three types of operation. Both PDU types are used in the following fashion. An LLC entity may issue a command (C/R bit = 0) XID or TEST. The receiving LLC entity issues a corresponding XID or TEST in response. The XID PDU is used to exchange two types of information: types of operation supported and window size. The TEST PDU is used to conduct a loopback test of the transmission path between two LLC entities. Upon receipt of a TEST command PDU, the addressed LLC entity issues a TEST response PDU as soon as possible.

With type 2 operation, a data link connection is established between two LLC SAPs prior to data exchange. Connection establishment is attempted by the type 2 protocol in response to a request from a user. The LLC entity issues a SABME PDU2 to request a logical connection with the other LLC entity. If the connection is accepted by the LLC user designated by the DSAP, then the destination LLc entity returns an unnumbered acknowledgment (UA) PDU. The connection is henceforth uniquely identified by the pair of user SAPs. If the destination LLC user rejects the connection request, its LLC entity returns a disconnected mode (DM) PDU.Once the connection is established, data are exchanged using information PDUs, as in HDLC. Information PDUs include send and receive sequence numbers, for sequencing and flow control. The supervisory PDUs are used, as in HDLC, for flow control and error control. Either LLC entity can terminate a logical LLC connection by issuing a disconnect (DISC) PDU.

With type 3 operation, each transmitted PDU is acknowledged. A new (not found in HDLC) unnumbered PDU, the acknowledged connectionless (AC) information PDU, is defined. User data are sent in AC command PDUs and must be acknowledged using an AC response PDU. To guard against lost PDUs, a I- bit sequence number is used. The sender alternates the use of 0 and 1 in its AC command PDU, and the receiver responds with an AC PDU with the opposite number of the corresponding command. Only one PDU in each direction may be outstanding at any time.

4.4 IEEE 802.11 ARCHITECTURE AND SERVICES

In 1990, the IEEE 802 Committee formed a new working group, IEEE 802.11, specifically devoted to wireless LANs, with a charter to develop a MAC protocol and physical medium specification. The initial interest was in developing a wireless LAN operating in the ISM (industrial, scientific, and medical) band. Since that time, the demand for WLANs, at different frequencies and data rates, has exploded. Keeping pace with this demand, the IEEE 802.11 working group has issued an ever-expanding list of standards (Table 14.1). Table 14.2 briefly defines key terms used in the IEEE 802.11 standard.

The Wi-Fi Alliance

The first 802.11 standard to gain broad industry acceptance was 802.11b. Although 802.11b products are all based on the same standard, there is always a concern whether products from different vendors will successfully interoperate. To meet this concern, the Wireless Ethernet Compatibility Alliance (WECA), an industry consortium, was formed in 1999. This organization, subsequently renamed the Wi-Fi (Wireless Fidelity) Alliance, created a test suite to certify interoperability for 802.11b products. As of 2004, products from over 120 vendors have been certified. The term used for certified 802.11b products is Wi-Fi. Wi-Fi certification has been extended to 802.11g products, and 57 vendors have so far been qualified. The Wi-Fi Alliance has also developed a certification process for 802.11a products, called Wi-PiS. So far, 32 vendors have qualified for Wi-PiS certification. The Wi-Pi Alliance is concerned with a range of market areas for WLANs, including enterprise, home, and hot spots.

Table 14.1   IEEE 802.11 Standards

Standard	Date	Scope
IEEE 802.11	1997	Medium access control (MAC): One common MAC for WLAN applications
		Physical layer: Infrared at 1 and 2 Mbps
		Physical layer: 2.4-GHz FHSS at 1 and 2 Mbps
		Physical layer: 2.4-GHz DSSS at 1 and 2 Mbps
IEEE 802.11a	1999	Physical layer: 5-GHz OFDM at rates from 6 to 54 Mbps
IEEE 802.11b	1999	Physical layer: 2.4-GHz DSSS at 5.5 and 11 Mbps
IEEE 802.11c	2003	Bridge operation at 802.11 MAC layer
IEEE 802.11d	2001	Physical layer: Extend operation of 802.11 WLANs to new regulatory domains (countries)
IEEE 802.11e	Ongoing	MAC: Enhance to improve quality of service and enhance security mechanisms
IEEE 802.11f	Ongoing	Recommended practices for multivendor access point interoperability
IEEE 802.11g	2003	Physical layer: Extend 802.11b to data rates >20 Mbps
IEEE 802.11h	Ongoing	Physical/MAC: Enhance IEEE 802.11a to add indoor and outdoor channel selection and to improve spectrum and transmit power management
IEEE 802.11i	Ongoing	MAC: Enhance security and authentication mechanisms
IEEE 802.11j	Ongoing	Physical: Enhance IEEE 802.11a to conform to Japanese requirements
IEEE 802.11k	Ongoing	Radio resource measurement enhancements to provide interface to higher layers for radio and network measurements
IEEE 802.11m	Ongoing	Maintenance of IEEE 802.11-1999 standard with technical and editorial corrections
IEEE 802.11n	Ongoing	Physical/MAC: Enhancements to enable higher throughput

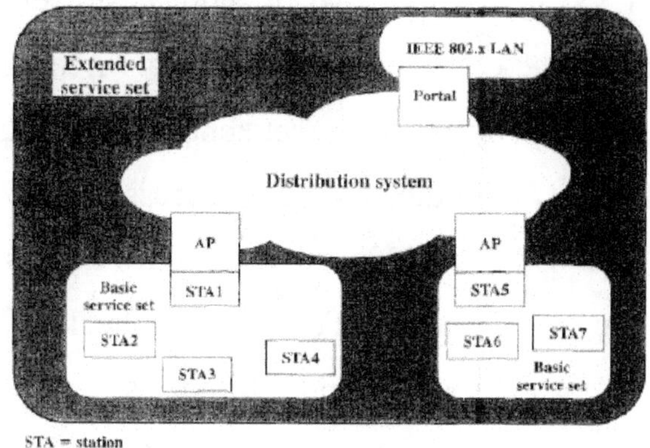

Figure 14.4   IEEE 802.11 Architecture

4.5 IEEE 802.11 Architecture

Figure 14.4 illustrates the model developed by the 802.11 working group. The smallest building block of a wireless LAN is a basic service set (BSS), which consists of some number of stations executing the same MAC protocol and competing for access to the same shared wireless medium. A BSS may be isolated or it may connect to a backbone distribution system (DS) through an access point (AP). The AP functions as a bridge and a relay point. In a BSS, client stations do not communicate directly with one another. Rather, if one station in the BSS wants to communicate with another station in the same BSS, the MAC frame is first sent from the originating station to the AP, and then from the AP to the destination station. Similarly, a MAC frame from a station in the BSS to a remote station is sent from the local station to the AP and then relayed by the AP over the DS on its way to the destination station. The BSS generally corresponds to what is referred to as a cell in the literature. The DS can be a switch, a wired network, or a wireless network.

When all the stations in the BSS are mobile stations, with no connection to other BSSs, the BSS is called an independent BSS (IBSS). An IBSS is typically an ad hoc network. In an IBSS, the stations all communicate directly, and no AP is involved. A simple configuration is shown in Figure 14.4, in which each station belongs to a single BSS; that is, each station is within wireless range only of other stations within the same BSS. It is also possible for two BSSs to overlap geographically, so that a single station could participate in more than one BSS. Further, the association between a station and a BSS is dynamic. Stations may turn off, come within range, and go out of range.

An extended service set (ESS) consists of two or more basic service sets interconnected by a distribution system. Typically, the distribution system is a wired backbone LAN but can be any communications network. The extended service set appears as a single logical LAN to the logical link control (LLC) level. Figure 14.4 indicates that an access point (AP) is implemented as part of a station; the AP is the logic within a station that provides access to the DS by providing DS services in addition to acting as a station. To integrate the IEEE 802.11 architecture with a traditional wired LAN, a portal is used. The portal logic is implemented in a device, such as a bridge or router, that is part of the wired LAN and that is attached to the DS.

4.6 IEEE 802.11 Services

IEEE 802.11 defines nine services that need to be provided by the wireless LAN to provide functionality equivalent to that which is inherent to wired LANs. Table 14.3 lists the services and indicates two ways of categorizing them.

The service provider can be either the station or the distribution system (DS). Station services are implemented in every 802.11 station, including access point (AP) stations. Distribution services are provided between basic service sets (BSSs); these services may be implemented in an AP or in another special purpose device attached to the distribution system.

Three of the services are used to control IEEE 802.11 LAN access and confidentiality. Six of the services are used to support delivery of MAC service data units (MSDUs) between stations. The MSDU is the block of data passed down from the MAC user to the MAC layer; typically, this is a LLC PDU If the MSDU is too large to be transmitted in a single MAC frame, it may be fragmented and transmitted in a series of MAC frames. Fragmentation is discussed in Section 14.3.

Following the IEEE 802.11 document, we next discuss the services in an order designed to clarify the operation of an IEEE 802.11 ESS network. MSDU delivery, which is the basic service, has already been mentioned.

Table 14.3   IEEE 802.11 Services

Service	Provider	Used to Support
Association	Distribution system	MSDU delivery
Authentication	Station	LAN access and security
Deauthentication	Station	LAN access and security
Disassociation	Distribution system	MSDU delivery
Distribution	Distribution system	MSDU delivery
Integration	Distribution system	MSDU delivery
MSDU delivery	Station	MSDU delivery
Privacy	Station	LAN access and security
Reassocation	Distribution system	MSDU delivery

Distribution of messages within a DS the two services involved with a distribution of messages within a DS are distribution and integration. Distribution is the primary service used by stations to exchange MAC frames when the frame must traverse the DS to get from a station in one BSS to a station in another BSS. For example, suppose a frame is to be sent from station 2 (STA 2) to STA 7 in Figure 14.4.The frame is sent from STA 2 to STA 1, which is the AP for this BSS.The AP gives the frame to the DS, which has the job of directing the frame to the AP associated with STA 5 in the target BSS. STA 5 receives the frame and forwards it to STA 7. How the message is transported through the DS is beyond the scope of the IEEE 802.11 standard. If the two stations that are communicating are within the same BSS, then the distribution service logically goes through the single AP of that BSS.

The integration service enables transfer of data between a station on an IEEE 802.11 LAN and a station on an integrated IEEE 802.x LAN. The term integrated refers to a wired LAN that is physically connected to the DS and whose stations may be logically connected to an IEEE 802.11 LAN via the integration service. The integration service takes care of any address translation and media conversion logic required for the exchange of data.

Association-H..elated Services The primary purpose of the MAC layer is to transfer MSDUs between MAC entities; this purpose is fulfilled by the distribution service. For that service to function, it requires information about stations within the ESS, which is provided by the association-related services. Before the distribution service can deliver data to or accept data from a station, that station must be associated. Before looking at the concept of association, we need to describe the concept of mobility. The standard defines three transition types based on mobility:

$ No transition: A station of this type is either stationary or moves only within the direct communication range of the communicating stations of a single BSS.

BSS transition: This is defined as a station movement from one BSS to another BSS within the same ESS. In this case, delivery of data to the station requires that the addressing capability be able to recognize the new location of the station.

ESS transition: This is defined as a station movement from a BSS in one ESS to a BSS within another ESS. This case is supported only in the sense that the station can move. Maintenance of upper-layer connections supported by 802.11 cannot be guaranteed. In fact, disruption of service is likely to occur. To deliver a message within a DS, the distribution service needs to know where the destination station is located. Specifically, the DS needs to know the identity of the AP to which the message should be delivered in order for that message to reach the destination station. To meet this requirement, a station must maintain an association with the AP within its current BSS. Three services relate to this requirement:

- Association: Establishes an initial association between a station and an AP Before a station can transmit or receive frames on a wireless LAN, its identity and address must be known. For this purpose, a station must establish an association with an AP within a particular BSS. The AP can then communicate this information to other APs within the ESS to facilitate routing and delivery of addressed frames.
- Re-association: Enables an established association to be transferred from one AP to another, allowing a mobile station to move from one BSS to another.
- Disassociation: A notification from either a station or an AP that an existing association is terminated. A station should give this notification before leaving an ESS or shutting down. However, the MAC management facility protects itself against stations that disappear without notification.

- Access and Privacy: Services There are two characteristics of a wired LAN that are not inherent in a wireless LAN.

In order to transmit over a wired LAN, a station must be physically connected to the LAN. On the other hand, with a wireless LAN, any station within radio range of the other devices on the LAN can transmit. In a sense, there is a form of authentication with a wired LAN, in that it requires some positive and presumably observable action to connect a station to a wired LAN.

Similarly, in order to receive a· transmission from a station that is part of a wired LAN, the receiving station must also be attached to the wired LAN. On the other hand, with a wireless LAN, any station within radio range can receive. Thus, a wired LAN provides a degree of privacy, limiting reception of data to stations connected to the LAN.

IEEE 802.11 defines three services that provide a wireless LAN with these two features:

- Authentication: Used to establish the identity of stations to each other. In a wired LAN, it is generally assumed that access to a physical connection conveys authority to connect to the LAN. This is not a valid assumption for a wireless LAN, in which connectivity is achieved simply by having an attached antenna that is properly tuned. The authentication service is used by stations to establish their identity with stations they wish to communicate with. IEEE 802.11 supports several authentication schemes and allows for expansion of the functionality of these schemes. The standard does not mandate any particular authentication scheme, which could range from relatively unsecure handshaking to public key encryption schemes. However, IEEE 802.11 requires mutually acceptable, successful authentication before station can establish an association with an AP.
- DE authentication: This service is invoked whenever an existing authentication to be terminated.
- Privacy: Used to prevent the contents of messages from being read by other than the intended recipient. The standard provides for the optional use of encryption to assure privacy.

4.7 IEEE 802.11 MEDIUM ACCESS CONTROL

The IEEE 802.11 MAC layer covers three functional areas: reliable data delivery, medium access control, and security. This section covers the first two topics.

Reliable Data Delivery

As with any wireless network, a wireless LAN using the IEEE 802.11 physical and MAC layers is subject to considerable unreliability. Noise, interference, and other propagation effects result in the loss of a significant number of frames. Even with error-correction codes, a number of MAC frames may not successfully be received. This situation can be dealt with by reliability mechanisms at a higher layer, such as TCP.

However, timers used for retransmission at higher layers are typically on the order of seconds. It is therefore more efficient to deal with errors at the MAC level. For this purpose, IEEE 802.11 includes a frame exchange protocol. When a station receives a data frame from another station, it returns an acknowledgment (ACK) frame to the source station. This exchange is treated as an atomic unit, not to be interrupted by a transmission from any other station. If the source does not receive an ACK within a short period of time, either because its data frame was damaged or because the returning ACK was damaged, the source retransmits the frame.

Thus, the basic data transfer mechanism in IEEE 802.11 involves an exchange of two frames. To further enhance reliability, a four-frame exchange may be used. In this scheme, a source first issues a request to send (RTS) frame to the destination. The destination then responds with a clear to send (CTS).After receiving the CTS, the source transmits the data frame, and the destination responds with an ACK.The RTS alerts all stations that are within reception range of the source that an exchange is under way; these stations refrain from transmission in order to avoid a collision between two frames transmitted at the same time. Similarly, the CTS alerts all stations that are within reception range of the destination that an exchange is under way. The RTS/CTS portion of the exchange is a required function of the MAC but may be disabled.

Medium Access Control

The 802.11 working group considered two types of proposals for a MAC algorithm: distributed access protocols, which, like Ethernet, distribute the decision to transmit over all the nodes using a carrier-sense mechanism; and centralized access protocols, which involve regulation of transmission by a centralized decision maker. A distributed access protocol makes sense for an ad hoc network of peer workstations (typically an IBSS) and may also be attractive in other wireless LAN configurations that consist primarily of bursty traffic. A centralized access protocol is natural for configurations in which a number of wireless stations are interconnected with each other and some sort of base station that attaches to a backbone wired LAN; it is especially useful if some of the data is time sensitive or high priority.

The end result for 802.11 is a MAC algorithm called DFWMAC (distributed foundation wireless MAC) that provides a distributed access control mechanism with an optional centralized control built on top of that. Figure 14.5 illustrates the architecture. The lower sublayer of the MAC layer is the distributed coordination function (DCF). DCF uses a contention algorithm to provide access to all traffic. Ordinary asynchronous traffic directly uses DCE The point coordination function (PCF) is a centralized MAC algorithm used to provide contention-free service. PCF is built on top of DCF and exploits features of DCF to assure access for its users. Let us consider these two sublayers in turn.

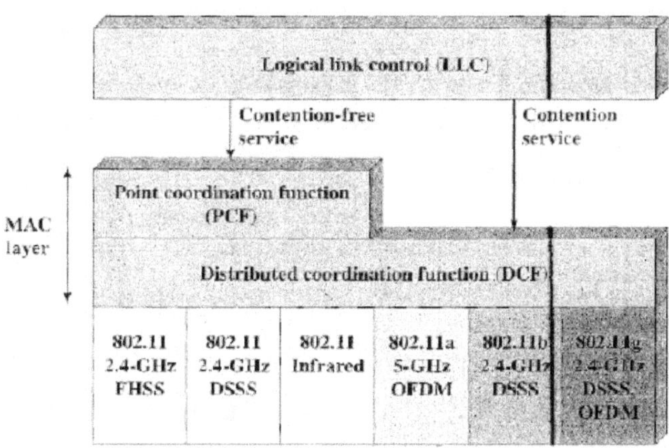

Figure 14.5 IEEE 802.11 Protocol Architecture

Distributed Coordination The DCF sublayer makes use of a simple CSMA (carrier sense multiple access) algorithm, which functions as follows. If a station has a MAC frame to transmit, it listens to the medium. If the medium is idle, the station may transmit; otherwise the station must wait until the current transmission is complete before transmitting. The DCF does not include a collision detection function (i.e., CSMA/CD) because collision detection is not practical on a wireless network. The dynamic range of the signals on the medium is very large, so that a transmitting station cannot effectively distinguish incoming weak signals from noise and the effects of its own transmission.

To ensure the smooth and fair functioning of this algorithm, DCF includes a set of delays that amounts to a priority scheme. Let us start by considering a single delay known as an interframe space (IFS). In fact, there are three different IFS values, but the algorithm is best explained by initially ignoring this detail. Using an IFS, the rules for CSMA access are as follows (Figure 14.6):

A station with a frame to transmit senses the medium. If the medium is idle, it waits to see if the medium remains idle for a time equal to IFS. If so, the station may transmit immediately. If the medium is busy (either because the station initially finds the medium busy or because the medium becomes busy during the IFS idle time), the station defers transmission and continues to monitor the medium until the current transmission is over. Once the current transmission is over, the station delays another IFS. If the medium remains idle for this period, then the station backs off a random amount of time and again senses the medium. If the medium is still idle, the station may transmit. During the back off time, if the medium becomes busy, the back off timer is halted and resumes when the medium becomes idle.

If the transmission is unsuccessful, which is determined by the absence of an acknowledgement, then it is assumed that a collision has occurred. To ensure that backoff maintains stability, a technique known as binary exponential backoffis used. A station will attempt to transmit repeatedly in the face of repeated collisions, but after each collision, the mean value of the random delay is doubled up to some maximum value. The binary exponential backoff provides a means of handling a heavy load. Repeated failed attempts to transmit result in longer and longer backoff times, which helps to smooth out the load. Without such a backoff, the following situation could occur. Two or more stations attempt to transmit at the same time, causing a collision. These stations then immediately attempt to retransmit, causing a new collision.

The preceding scheme is refined for DCF to provide priority-based access by the simple expedient of using three values for IFS:

- SIFS (short IFS): The shortest IFS, used for all immediate response actions, as explained in the following discussion PIFS (point coordination function IFS): A midlength IFS, used by the centralized controller in the PCF scheme when issuing polls DIFS (distributed coordination function IFS): The longest IFS, used as a minimum delay for asynchronous frames contending for access Figure 14.7a illustrates the use of these time values. Consider first the SIFS. Any station using SIFS to determine transmission opportunity has, in effect, the highest priority, because it will always gain access in preference to a station waiting an amount of time equal to PIFS or DIFS. The SIFS is used in the following circumstances:

- Acknowledgment (ACK): When a station receives a frame addressed only to itself (not multicast or broadcast) it responds with an ACK frame after waiting only for an SIFS gap. This has two desirable effects. First, because collision detection is not used, the likelihood of collisions is greater than with CSMA/CD, and the MAC-level ACK provides for efficient collision recovery. Second, the SIFS can be used to provide efficient delivery of an LLC protocol data unit (PDU) that requires multiple MAC frames. In this case, the following scenario occurs. A station with a multiframe LLC PDU to

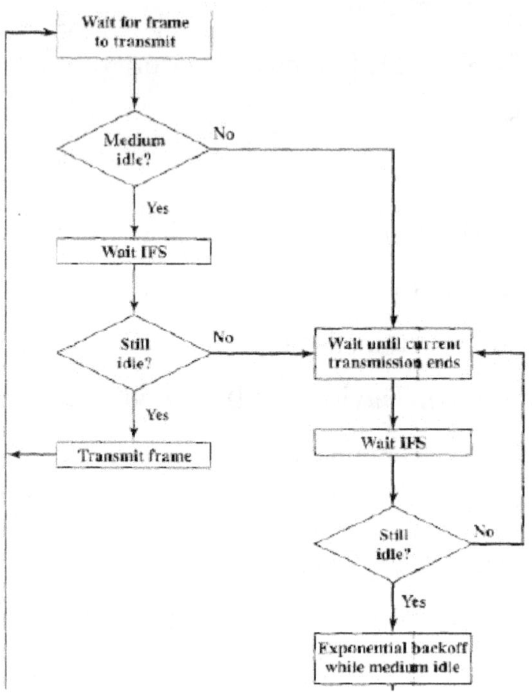

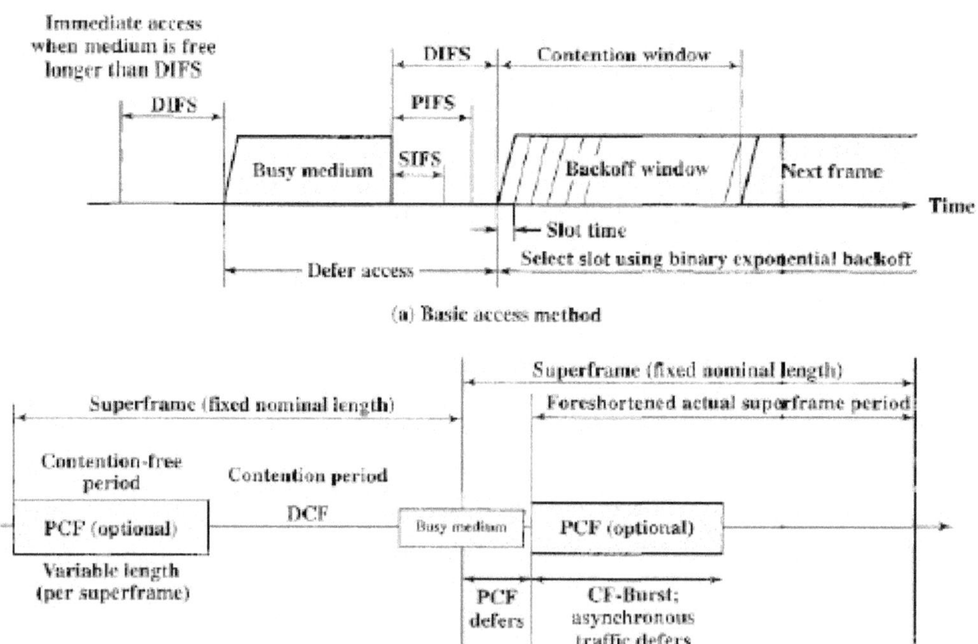

(a) Basic access method

(b) PCF superframe construction

Figure 14.7   IEEE 802.11 MAC Timing

transmit sends out the MAC frames one at a time. Each frame is acknowledged after SIFS by the recipient. When the source receives an ACK, it immediately (after SIFS) sends the next frame in the sequence. The result is that once a station has contended for the channel, it will maintain control of the channel until it has sent all of the fragments of an LLC PDU.

Clear to Send (CTS): A station can ensure that its data frame will get through by first issuing a small Request to Send (RT$) frame. The station to which this frame is addressed should immediately respond with aCTSframe if it is ready to receive. All other stations receive the RTS and defer using the medium.

Poll response: This is explained in the following discussion of PCP. The next longest IFS interval is the PIFS. This is used by the centralized controller in issuing polls and takes precedence over normal contention traffic. However, those frames transmitted using SIFS have precedence over a PCF poll. Finally, the DIFS interval is used for all ordinary asynchronous traffic. Point Coordination Function PCF is an alternative access method implemented on top of the Dep. The operation consists of polling by the centralized polling master (point coordinator). The point coordinator makes use of PIFS when issuing polls. Because PIFS is smaller than DIFS, the point coordinator can seize the medium and lock out all asynchronous traffic while it issues polls and receives responses. As an extreme, consider the following possible scenario. A wireless network is configured so that a number of stations with time-sensitive traffic are controlled by the point coordinator while remaining traffic contends for access using CSMA. The point coordinator could issue polls in a round-robin fashion to all stations configured for polling. When a poll is issued, the polled station may respond using SIFS. If the point coordinator receives a response, it issues another poll using PIFS. If no response is received during the expected turnaround time, the coordinator issues a poll. If the discipline of the preceding paragraph were implemented, the point coordinator would lock out all asynchronous traffic by repeatedly issuing polls.

To prevent this, an interval known as the super frame is defined. During the first part of this interval, the point coordinator issues polls in a round-robin fashion to all stations configured for polling. The point coordinator then idles for the remainder of the superframe, allowing a contention period for asynchronous access. Figure 14.7b illustrates the use of the superframe. At the beginning of a superframe, the point coordinator may optionally seize control and issues polls for a giveperiod of time. This interval varies because of the variable frame size issued by responding stations. The remainder of the superframe is available for contention based access. At the end of the superframe interval, the point coordinator contends for access to the medium using PIFS. If the medium is idle, the point coordinator gains immediate access and a full superframe period follows. However, the medium may be busy at the end of a superframe. In this case, the point coordinator must wait until the medium is idle to gain access; this results in a foreshortened superframe period for the next cycle.

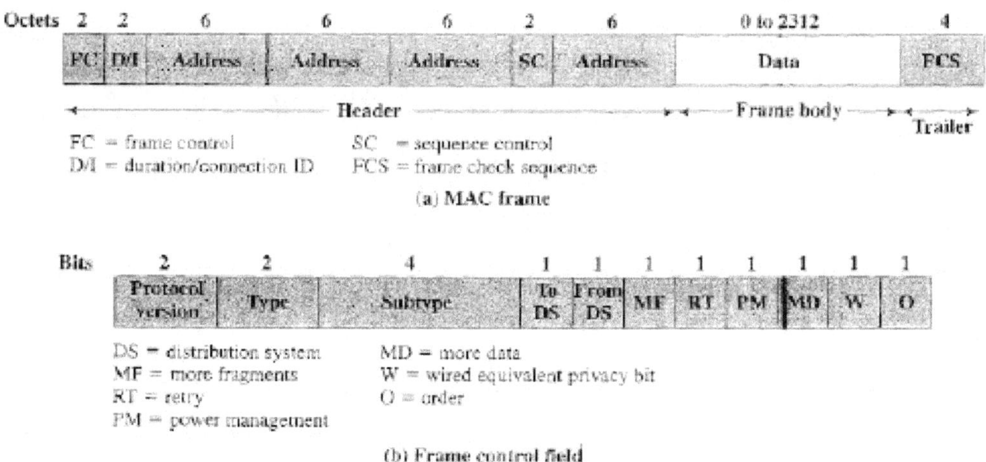

Figure 14.8   IEEE 802.11 MAC Frame Format

MAC Frame:

Figure 14.8a shows the 802.11 frame format when no security features are used. This general format is used for all data and control frames, but not all fields are used in all contexts. The fields are as follows:

- Frame Control: Indicates the type of frame and provides control information, as explained presently.
- Duration/Connection ID: If used as a duration field, indicates the time (in microseconds) the channel will be allocated for successful transmission of a MAC frame. In some control frames, this field contains an association, or connection, identifier.
- Addresses: The number and meaning of the 48-bit address fields depend on context. The transmitter address and receiver address are the MAC addresses of stations joined to the BSS that are transmitting and receiving frames over the wireless LAN.The service set ID (SSID) identifies the wireless LAN over which a frame is transmitted. For an IBSS, the

SSID is a random number generated at the time the network is formed. For a wireless LAN that is part of a larger configuration the SSID identifies the BSS over which the frame is transmitted; specifically, the SSID is the MAC-level address of the AP for this BSS (Figure 14.4). Finally the source address and destination address are the MAC addresses of stations, wireless or otherwise, that are the ultimate source and destination of this frame. The source address may be identical to the transmitter address and the destination address may be identical to the receiver address.

- Sequence Control: Contains a 4-bit fragment number subfield used for fragmentation and reassembly, and a 12-bit sequence number used to number frames sent between a given transmitter and receiver.

- Frame Body: Contains an MSDU or a fragment of an MSDUThe MSDU is a LLC protocol data unit or MAC control information.

- Frame Check Sequence: A 32-bit cyclic redundancy check. The frame control field, shown in Figure 14.8b, consists of the following fields: Protocol Version: 802.11 version, currently version O. Type: Identifies the frame as control, management, or data.

- Subtype: Further identifies the function of frame. Table 14.4 defines the valid combinations of type and subtype.

- To DS: The MAC coordination sets this bit to 1 in a frame destined to the distribution system. From DS: The MAC coordination sets this bit to 1 in a frame leaving the distribution system.

- More Fragments: Set to 1 if more fragments follow this one.

- Retry: Set to 1 if this is a retransmission of a previous frame.

Table 14.4 Valid Type and Subtype Combinations

Type Value	Type Description	Subtype Value	Subtype Description
00	Management	0000	Association request
00	Management	0001	Association response
00	Management	0010	Reassociation request
00	Management	0011	Reassociation response
00	Management	0100	Probe request
00	Management	0101	Probe response
00	Management	1000	Beacon
00	Management	1001	Announcement traffic indication message
00	Management	1010	Dissociation
00	Management	1011	Authentication
00	Management	1100	Deauthentication
01	Control	1010	Power save-poll
01	Control	1011	Request to send
01	Control	1100	Clear to send
01	Control	1101	Acknowledgment
01	Control	1110	Contention-Free (CF)-End
01	Control	1111	CF-End + CF-Ack
10	Data	0000	Data
10	Data	0001	Data + CF-Ack
10	Data	0010	Data + CF-Poll
10	Data	0011	Data + CF-Ack+CF-Poll
10	Data	0100	Null function (no data)

Power Management: Set to 1 if the transmitting station is in a sleep mode. More Data: Indicates that a station has additional data to send. Each block of data may be sent as one frame or a group of fragments in multiple frames. It WEP: Set to 1 if the optional wired equivalent protocol is implemented. WEP is used in the exchange of encryption keys for secure data exchange. This bit also is set if the newer WPA security mechanism is employed, as described in Section 14.6. Order: Set to 1 in any data frame sent using the Strictly Ordered service , which tells the receiving station that frames must be processed in order. We now look at the various MAC frame types. Control Frames Control frames assist in the reliable delivery of data frames.

There are six control frame subtypes:

- Power Save-Poll (PS-Poll): This frame is sent by any station to the station that includes the AP (access point). Its purpose is to request that the AP transmit a frame that has been buffered for this station while the station was in power saving mode.
- Request to Send (RTS): This is the first frame in the four-way frame exchange discussed under the subsection on reliable data delivery at the beginning of Section 14.3. The station

sending this message is alerting a potential destination, and all other stations within reception range, that it intends to send a data frame to that destination.

- Clear to Send (CTS): This is the second frame in the four-way exchange. It is sent by the destination station to the source station to grant permission to send a data frame.
- Acknowledgment: Provides an acknowledgment from the destination to the source that the immediately preceding data, management, or PS-Poll frame was received correctly.
- Contention-Free (CF)-End: Announces the end of a contention-free period that is part of the point coordination function.
- CF-End + CF-Ack: Acknowledges the CF-end.This frame ends the contention free period and releases stations from the restrictions associated with that period.

Data Frames There are eight data frame subtypes, organized into two groups. The first four subtypes define frames that carry upper-level data from the source station to the destination station. The four data-carrying frames are as follows:

- Data: This is the simplest data frame. It may be used in both a contention period and a contention-free period.
- Data + CF-Ack: May only be sent during a contention-free period. In addition to carrying data, this frame acknowledges previously received data.
- Data + CF-Poll: Used by a point coordinator to deliver data to a mobile station and also to request that the mobile station send a data frame that it may have buffered.
- Data + CF-Ack+ CF-Poll: Combines the functions of the Data + CF-Ack and Data + CF-Poll into a single frame.

The remaining four subtypes of data frames do not in fact carry any user data. The Null Function data frame carries no data, polls, or acknowledgments. It is used only to carry the power management bit in the frame control field to the AP, to indicate that the station is changing to a low-power operating state. The remaining three frames (CF-Ack, CF-Poll, CF-Ack+ CF-Poll) have the same functionality as the corresponding data frame subtypes in the preceding list (Data + CF-Ack, Data + CF-Poll, Data + CF-Ack+ CF-Poll) but without the data. Managetnent Frm:11.esManagement frames are used to manage communications between stations and APs. The following subtypes are included:

- Association Request: Sent by a station to an AP to request an association with this BSS. This frame includes capability information, such as whether encryption is to be used and whether this station is pollable.

- Association Response: Returned by the AP to the station to indicate whether it is accepting this association request.

- Reassociation Request: Sent by a station when it moves from one BSS to another and needs to make an association with the AP in the new BSS. The station uses reassociation rather than simply association so that the new AP knows to negotiate with the old AP for the forwarding of data frames.

- Reassociation Response: Returned by the AP to the station to indicate whether it is accepting this reassociation request.

- Probe Request: Used by a station to obtain information from another station or AP. This frame is used to locate an IEEE 802.11 BSS.

- Probe Response: Response to a probe request.

- Beacon: Transmitted periodically to allow mobile stations to locate and identify a BSS.

- Announcement Traffic Indication Message: Sent by a mobile station to alert other mobile stations that may have been in low power mode that this station has frames buffered and waiting to be delivered to the station addressed in this frame.

- II>Dissociation: Used by a station to terminate an association.

- ... Authentication: Multiple authentication frames are used in an exchange to authenticate one station to another.

- eDeauthentication: Sent by a station to another station or AP to indicate that it is terminating secure communications.

4.8 IEEE 802.11 PHYSICAL LAYER

The physical layer for IEEE 802.11 has been issued in four stages. The first part, simply called IEEE 802.11, includes the MAC layer and three physical layer specifications, two in the 2.4-GHz band (ISM) and one in the infrared, all operating at 1 and 2 Mbps. IEEE 802.11a operates in the 5-GHz band at data rates up to 54 Mbps.

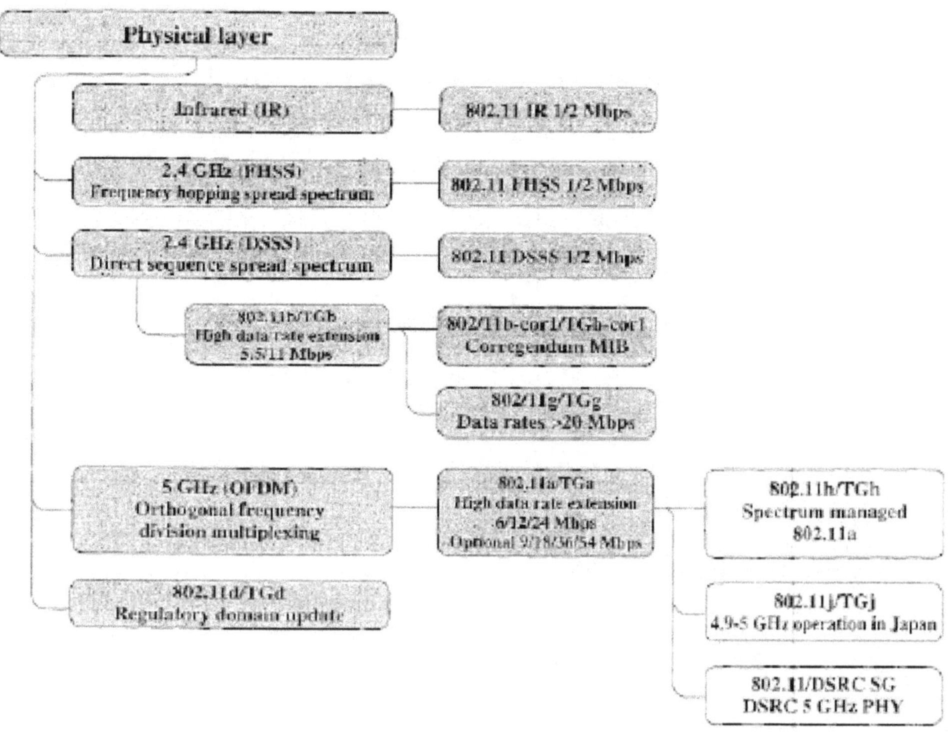

Figure 14.9   IEEE 802.11 Activities—Physical Layer

IEEE 802.lIb operates in the 2.4-GHz band at 5.5 and 11 Mbps. IEEE 802.11g also operates in the 2.4-GHz band, at data rates up to 54 Mbps. Figure 14.9 shows the relationship among the various standards developed for the physical layer, and Table 14.5 provides some details. We look at each of these in turn.Original IEEE 802.11 Physical LayerThree physical media are defined in the original 802.11 standard:

Direct sequence spread spectrum (DSSS) operating in the 2.4-GHz ISM band,at data rates of 1 Mbps and 2 Mbps. In the United States, the FCC (Federal Communications Commission) requires no licensing for the use of this band. The number of channels available depends on the bandwidth allocated by the various national regulatory agencies. This ranges from 13 in most European countries to just one available channel in Japan.

•Frequency-hopping spread spectrum (FHSS) operating in the 2.4-GHz Imbed, at data rates of 1 Mbps and 2 Mbps. The number of channels available ranges from 23 in Japan to 70 in the United States.

• Infrared at 1 Mbps and 2 Mbps operating at a wavelength between 850 and950nm.

Table 14.5   IEEE 802.11 Physical Layer Standards

	802.11	802.11a	802.11b	802.11g
Available bandwidth	83.5 MHz	300 MHz	83.5 MHz	83.5 MHz
Unlicensed frequency of operation	2.4–2.4835 GHz DSSS, FHSS	5.15–5.35 GHz OFDM 5.725–5.825 GHz OFDM	2.4–2.4835 GHz DSSS	2.4–2.4835 GHz DSSS, OFDM
Number of nonoverlapping channels	3 (indoor/outdoor)	4 indoor 4 (indoor/outdoor) 4 outdoor	3 (indoor/outdoor)	3 (indoor/outdoor)
Data rate per channel	1, 2 Mbps	6, 9, 12, 18, 24, 36, 48, 54 Mbps	1, 2, 5.5, 11 Mbps	1, 2, 5.5, 6, 9, 11, 12, 18, 24, 36, 48, 54 Mbps
Compatibility	802.11	Wi-Fi5	Wi-Fi	Wi-Fi at 11 Mbps and below

Table 14.6 summarizes key details.

Direct Sequence Spread Spectnlnl Up to three non overlapping channels, each with a data rate of 1 Mbps or 2 Mbps, can be used in the DSSS scheme. Each channel has a bandwidth of 5 MHz. The encoding scheme that is used is DBPSK (differential binary phase shift keying) for the 1 Mbps rate and DQPSK for the 2 Mbps rate. Recall from Chapter 7 that a DSSS system makes use of a chipping code, or pseudo noise sequence, to spread the data rate and hence the bandwidth of the signal. For IEEE 802.11, a Barker sequence is used. A Barker sequence is a binary {-I, +1} sequence {s(t)} of length n with the property that its autocorrelation values R(7") satisfy IR(7") I -< 1 for all iTl -<(n - 1). Further, the Barker property is preserved under the following transformations. s(t) ~ -s(t) and s(t) ~ -s(n - 1 - t) as well as under compositions of these transformations. Only the following Barker sequences are known:

$$
\begin{array}{ll}
n = 2 & + + \\
n = 3 & + + - \\
n = 4 & + + + - \\
n = 5 & + + + - + \\
n = 7 & + + + - - + - \\
n = 11 & + - + + - + + + - - - \\
n = 13 & + + + + + - - + + - + - +
\end{array}
$$

IEEE 802.11 DSSS uses the ll-chip Barker sequence. Each data binary 1 is mapped into the sequence {+- + +- +++- - - }, and each binary 0 is mapped into the sequence {-+--+---+++}.

Table 14.6   IEEE 802.11 Physical Layer Specifications

(a) Direct sequence spread spectrum (802.11, 802.11b)

Data Rate	Chipping Code Length	Modulation	Symbol Rate	Bits/Symbol
1 Mbps	11 (Barker sequence)	DBPSK	1 Msps	1
2 Mbps	11 (Barker sequence)	DQPSK	1 Msps	2
5.5 Mbps	8 (CCK)	DQPSK	1.375 Msps	4
11 Mbps	8 (CCK)	DQPSK	1.375 Msps	8

(b) Frequency hopping spread spectrum (802.11)

Data Rate	Modulation	Symbol Rate	Bits/Symbol
1 Mbps	Two-level GFSK	1 Msps	1
2 Mbps	Four-level GFSK	1 Msps	2

(c) Infrared (802.11)

Data Rate	Modulation	Symbol Rate	Bits/Symbol
1 Mbps	16-PPM	4 Msps	0.25
2 Mbps	4-PPM	4 Msps	0.5

(d) Orthogonal FDM (802.11a)

Data rate	Modulation	Coding Rate	Coded Bits per Subcarrier	Code Bits per OFDM Symbol	Data Bits per OFDM Symbol
6 Mbps	BPSK	1/2	1	48	24
9 Mbps	BPSK	3/4	1	48	36
12 Mbps	QPSK	1/2	2	96	48
18 Mbps	QPSK	3/4	2	96	72
24 Mbps	16-QAM	1/2	4	192	96
36 Mbps	16-QAM	3/4	4	192	144
48 Mbps	64-QAM	2/3	6	288	192
54 Mbps	64-QAM	3/4	6	288	216

Important characteristic of Barker sequences are their robustness againstinterference and their insensitivity to multipath propagation.Frequency-Hopping Spread Spectrulll Recall from Chapter 7 that a FHSSsystem makes use of a multiple channels, with the signal Hopping from one channelto another based on a pseudonoise sequence. In the case of the IEEE 802.11scheme, I-MHz channels are used.The details of the hopping scheme are adjustable. For example, the minimumhop rate for the United States is 2.5 hops per second. Tl::te minimum hopdistance in frequency is 6 MHz in North America and most of Europe and 5 MHzin Japan.

For modulation, the FHSS scheme uses two-level Gaussian FSK for the 1-Mbpssystem. The bits zero and one are encoded as deviations from the current carrier frequency.For 2 Mbps, a four-level GFSK scheme is used, in which four different deviationsfrom the center frequency define the four

2-bit combinations.Infrared The IEEE 802.11 infrared scheme is omnidirectional (Figure 13.6) ratherthan point to point. A range of up to 20 m is possible. The modulation scheme for the1-Mbps data rate is known as 16-PPM (pulse position modulation). In pulse positionmodulation (PPM), the input value determines the position ()f a narrow pulse relativeto the clocking time.The advantage ofPPM is that it reduces the output power requiredof the infrared source. For 16-PPM, each group of 4 data bits is mapped into one of the16-PPM symbols; each symbol is a string of 16 bits. Each 16-bit string consists of fifteenOs and one binary 1. For the 2-Mbps data rate, each group of 2 data bits is mapped intoone of four 4-bit sequences. Each sequence consists of three Os and one binary. The Actual transmission uses an intensity modulation scheme, in which the presence of a signalcorresponds to a binary 1 and the absence of a signal corresponds to binary O.

IEEE 802.11a

Channel Structure IEEE 802.11a makes use of the frequency band called theUniversal Networking Information Infrastructure (UNNI), which is divided intothree parts. The UNNI-1 band (5.15 to 5.25 GHz) is intended for indoor use; theUNNI-2 band (5.25 to 5.35 GHz) can be used either indoor or outdoor, and theUNNI-3 band (5.725 to 5.825 GHz) is for outdoor use.IEEE 80211.a has several advantages over IEEE 802.11b/g:

IEEE 802.lIa utilizes more available bandwidth than 802.11b/g. Each UNNI band provides four no overlapping channels for a total of 12 across the allocated spectrum. IEEE 802.lIa provides much higher data rates than 802.lIb and the same maximum data rate as 802.lIg.

IEEE 802.lIa uses a different, relatively uncluttered frequency spectrum(5 GHz).Figure 14.10 shows the channel structure used by 802.11a.The first part of the figure indicates a transmit spectrum mask, which is defined in 802.11b as follows:3 The transmitted spectrum mask shall have a 0 dBr (dB relative to the maximum spectral density of the signal) bandwidth not exceeding 18 MHz, - 20 dBr at 11 MHz frequency offset, - 28 dBr at 20 MHz frequency offset and -40 dBr at 30 MHz frequency offset and above. The transmitted spectral density of the transmitted signal shall fall within the spectral mask. The purpose of the spectrum mask is to constrain the spectral properties of the transmitted signal such that signals in adjacent channels do not interfere with one another. Figures 14.10b and 14.lOc show the 12 channels available for use in 802.lIb.3See Appendix B.2 for a discussion of power spectral density.

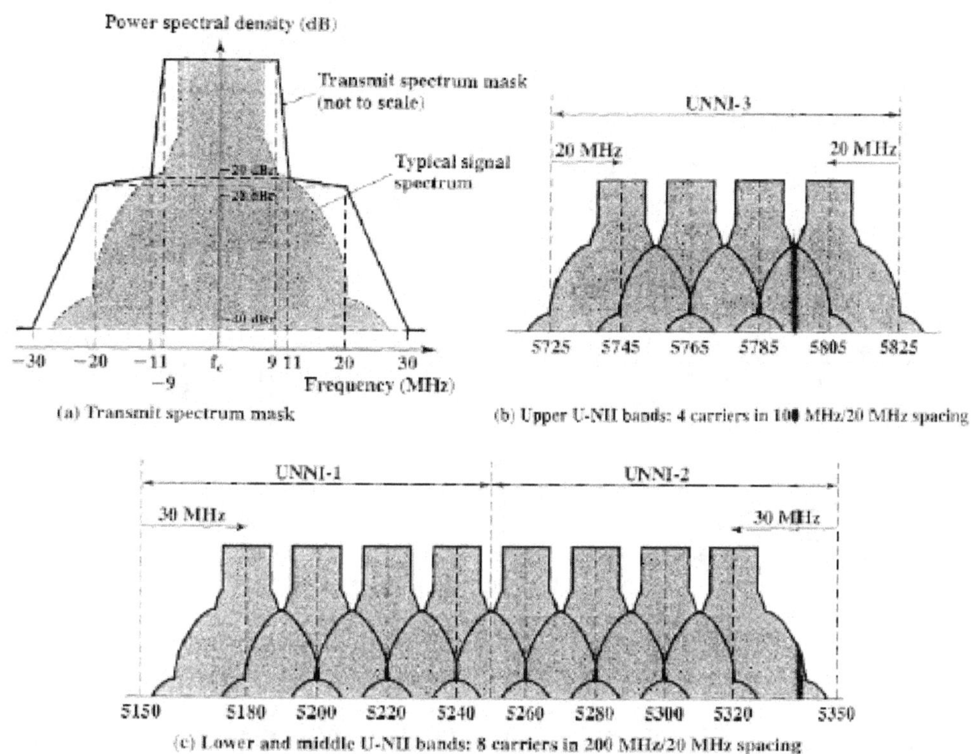

Coding and Modulation Unlike the 2.4-GHz specifications, IEEE 802.11 does not use a spread spectrum scheme but rather uses orthogonal frequency division multiplexing (OFDM). Recall from Section 11.2 that OFDM, also called multicarrier modulation, uses multiple carrier signals at different frequencies, sending some of the bits on each channel. This is similar to FDM. However, in the case of OFDM, all of the sub channels are dedicated to a single data source. To complement OFDM, the specification supports the use of a variety of modulation and coding alternatives. The system uses up to 48 subcarriers that are modulated using BPSK, QPSK, 16-QAM, or 64-QAM. Subcarrier frequency spacing is 0.3125 MHz. A convolutional code at a rate of 1/2,2/3, or 3/4 provides forward error correction. The combination of modulation technique and coding rate determines the data rate. Table 14.6d summarizes key parameters for 802.11a. Physical-Layer Frame Structure The primary purpose of the physical layer is to transmit medium access control (MAC) protocol data units.

(MPDUs) as directed by the 802.11 MAC layer. The PLCP sublayer provides the framing and signalling bits needed for the OFDM transmission and the PDM sublayer performs the actual encoding and transmission operation.

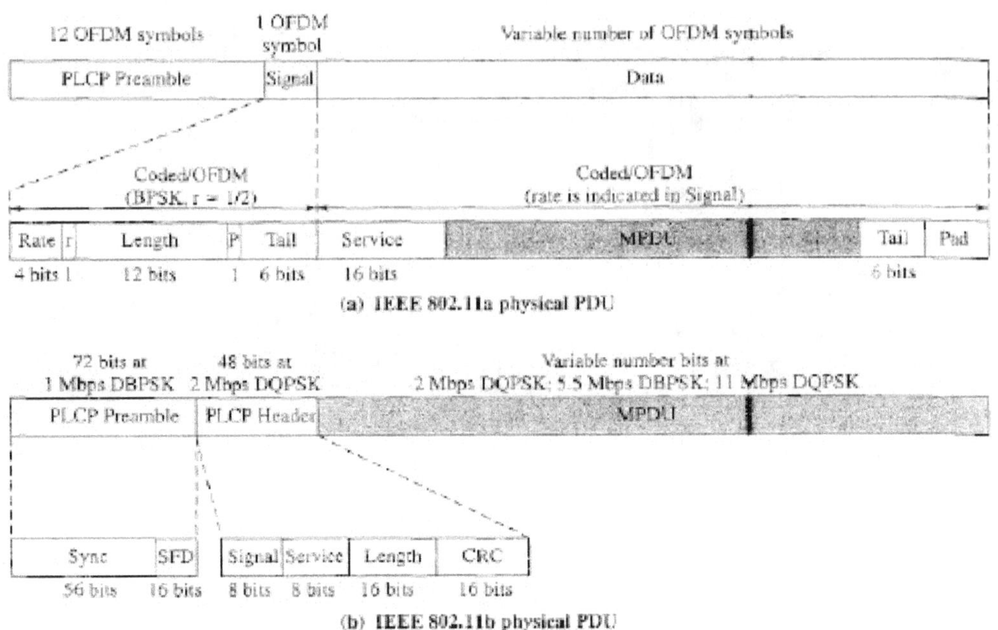

Figure 14.11   IEEE 802 Physical Level Protocol Data Units

Figure 14.11a illustrates the physical layer frame format. The PLCP Preamble field enables the receiver to acquire an incoming OFDM signal and synchronize the demodulator. Next is the Signal field, which consists of 24 bits encoded as a single OFDM symbol. The Preamble and Signal fields are transmitted at 6 Mbps using BPSK. The signal field consists of the following subfields:

- Rate: Specifies the data rate at which the data field portion of the frame is transmitted
- r: Reserved for future use
- Length: Number of octets in the MAC PDU
- P: An even parity bit for the 17 bits in the Rate, r, and Length subfields.
- Tail: Consist of 6 zero bits appended to the symbol to bring the convolutional encoder to zero state The Data field consists of a variable number of OFDM symbols transmitted at the data rate specified in the Rate subfield. Prior to transmission, all of the bits of the Data field are scrambled (see Appendix 14A for a discussion of scrambling).The Data field consists of four subfields:
- Service: Consists of 16 bits, with the first 6 bits set to zeros to synchronize the descrambler in the receiver, and the remaining 9 bits (all zeros) reserved for future use.
- MAC PDU: Handed down from the MAC layer. The format is shown in Figure 14.8.

- Tail: Produced by replacing the six scrambled bits following the MPDU end with 6 bits of all zeros; used to re-initialize the convolutional encoder.

- .. Pad: The number of bits required to make the Data field a multiple of the number of bits in an OFDM symbol (48,96,192, or 288).

IEEE S02.llb

IEEE 802.11b is an extension of the IEEE 802.11 DSSS scheme, providing data rates of 5.5 and 11 Mbps in the ISM band. The chipping rate is 11 MHz, which is the same as the original DSSS scheme, thus providing the same occupied bandwidth. To achieve a higher data rate in the same bandwidth at the same chipping rate, a modulation scheme known as complementary code keying (CCK) is used. The CCK modulation scheme is quite complex and is not examined in detail here. Figure 14.12 provides an overview of the scheme for the 11-Mbps rate. Input data are treated in blocks of 8 bits at a rate of 1.375 MHz (8 bits/symbol x 1.375 MHz = 11 Mbps). Six of these bits are mapped into one of 64 codes sequences based on the use of the 8 X 8 Walsh matrix (Figure 7.17). The output of the mapping, plus the two additional bits, forms the input to a QPSK modulator. An optional alternative to CCK is known as packet binary convolutional coding (PBCC). PBCC provides for potentially more efficient transmission at the cost of increased computation at the receiver. PBCC was incorporated into 802.llb in anticipation of its need for higher data rates for future enhancements to the standard.

Physical-Layer Frame Structure IEEE 802.11b defines two physical-layer frame formats, which differ only in the length of the preamble. The long preamble of 144 bits is the same as used in the original 802.11 DSSS scheme and allows interoperability with other legacy systems. The short preamble of 72 bits provides improved throughput efficiency. Figure 14.11b illustrates the physical layer frame format with the short preamble. The PLCP Preamble field enables the receiver to acquire an incoming signal and synchronize the demodulator. It consists of two sUbfields: a 56-bit Sync field for synchronization, and a 16-bit start-of-frame delimiter (SFD). The preamble is transmitted at 1 Mbps using differential BPSK and Barker code spreading.

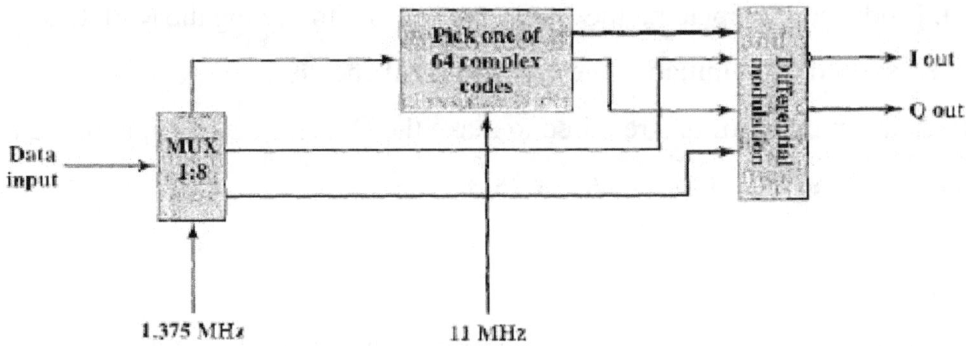

Figure 14.12   11-Mbps CCK Modulation Scheme

Following the preamble is the PLCP Header, which is transmitted at 2 Mbps using DQPSK. It consists of the following subfields:

- Signal: Specifies the data rate at which the MPDU portion of the frame is transmitted.
- Service: Only 3 bits of this 8-bit field are used in 802.11b. One bit indicates whether the transmit frequency and symbol clocks use the same local oscillator. Another bit indicates whether CCK or PBCC encoding is used. A third bit acts as an extension to the Length subfield.
- $ Length: Indicates the length of the MPDU field by specifying the number of microseconds necessary to transmit the MPDU. Given the data rate, the length of the MPDU in octets can be calculated. For any data rate over 8 Mbps, the length extension bit from the Service field is needed to resolve a rounding ambiguity. lilCRC: A 16-bit error-detection code used to protect t.lne Signal, Service, and Length fields.

The MPDU field consists of a variable number of bits transmitted at the data rate specified in the Signal subfield. Prior to transmission, all of the bits of the physicallayer PDU are scrambled (see Appendix 14A for a discussion of scrambling).

IEEE 802.11g

IEEE 802.11g extends 802.11b to data rates above 20 Mbps, up to 54 Mbps. Like 802.11b, 802.11g operates in the 2.4-GHz range and thus the two are compatible. The standard is designed so that 802.11b devices will work connecting to an 802.11g AP, and 802.11g devices will work connecting to and 802.11b AP, in both cases using the lower 802.11b data rate.

IEEE 802.11g offers a wider array of data rate and modulation scheme options, as shown in Table 14.7. IEEE 802.11g provides compatibility with 802.11 and 802.11b by specifying the same modulation and framing schemes as these standards for 1,2,5.5, and 11 Mbps. At data rates of 6,9,12,18,24,36,48, and 54 Mbps, 802.11g adopts the 802.11a OFDM scheme, adapted for the 2.4 GHz rate; this is referred to as ERP-OFDM, with ERP standing for extended rate physical layer. In addition, and ERP-PBCC scheme is used to provide data rates of 22 and 33 Mbps.

Table 14.7   IEEE 802.11g Physical Layer Options

Data Rate (Mbps)	Modulation Scheme	Data Rate (Mbps)	Modulation Scheme
1	DSSS	18	ERP-OFDM
2	DSSS	22	ERP-PBCC
5.5	CCK or PBCC	24	ERP-OFDM
6	ERP-OFDM	33	ERP-PBCC
9	ERP-OFDM	36	ERP-OFDM
11	CCK or PBCC	48	ERP-OFDM
12	ERP-OFDM	54	ERP-OFDM

Table 14.8   Estimated Distance (m) versus Data Rate

Data Rate (Mbps)	802.11b	802.11a	802.11g
1	90+	—	90+
2	75	—	75
5.5(b)/6(a/g)	60	60+	65
9	—	50	55
11(b)/12(a/g)	50	45	50
18	—	40	50
24	—	30	45
36	—	25	35
48	—	15	25
54	—	10	20

The IEEE 802.11 standards do not include a specification of speed versus distance objectives. Different vendors will give different values, depending on environment. Table 14.8, based on [LAYL04] gives estimated values for a typical office environment.

4.9 OTHER IEEE 802.11 STANDARDS

In addition to the standards so far discussed, which provide specific physical layer functionality, a number of other 802.11 standards have been issued Or are in the works.

IEEE 802.11c is concerned with bridge operation. A bridge is a device that links two LANs that have a similar or identical MAC protocol. It performs functions similar to those of an IP-Ievel router, but at the MAC layer. Typically, a bridge is simpler and more efficient than an IP router. The 802.11c task group completed its work on this standard in 2003, and it was folded into the IEEE 802.1D standard for LAN bridges. IEEE 802.11d is referred to as a regulatory domain update. It deals with issues related to regulatory differences in various countries.

IEEE 802.11e makes revisions to the MAClayer to improve quality of service and address some security issues. It accommodates time-scheduled and polled communication during null periods when no other data is being sent. In addition, it offers improvements to the efficiency of polling and enhancements to channel robustness. These enhancements should provide the quality required for such services as IP telephony and video streaming. Any station Implementing 802.11e is referred to as a QoS station, or QSTA. In a QSTA, the DCF and PCF (Figure 14.5) modules are replaced with a hybrid coordination function (HCF), which in tum consists of enhanced distributed channel access (EDCA) and HCF controlled channel access (HCCA). EDCA is an extension of the legacy DCF mechanism to include priorities. As with the PCF, HCCA centrally manages medium access, but does so in a more efficient and flexible manner.

IEEE 802.1lf addresses the issue of interoperability among access points(APs) from multiple vendors. In addition to providing communication among WLAN stations in its area, an AP can function as a bridge that connects two 802.11. LANs across another type of network, such as a wired LAN (e.g., Ethernet) or a wide area network. This standard facilitates the roaming of a device from one AP to another while insuring continuity of transmission. IEEE S02.11h deals with spectrum and power management issues. The objective is to make 802.11a products compliant with European regulatory requirements. In the EU, part of the 5-GHz band is used by the military for satellite communications. The standard includes a dynamic channel selection mechanism to ensure that the restricted portion of the frequency band is not selected. The standard also includes transmit power control features to adjust power to EU requirements.

IEEE S02.11i defines security and authentication mechanisms at the MAC layer. This standard is designed to address security deficiencies in the wire equivalent privacy (WEP) mechanism originally designed for the MAC layer of 802.1I. The 802.11i scheme uses stronger encryption and other enhancements to improve security and is discussed in Section 14.6.

IEEE S02.11k defines Radio Resource Measurement enhancements to provide mechanisms to higher layers for radio and network measurements. The standard defines what information should be made available to facilitate the management and maintenance of a wireless and mobile LANs. Among the data provided are the following:

To improve roaming decisions, an AP can provide a site report to a station when it determines that the station is moving away from it. The site report is an ordered list of APs, from best to worst service,that a station can use in changing over to another AP.

An AP can collect channel information from each station on the WLAN. Each station provides a noise histogram that displays all non-802.11 energy on that channel as perceived by the station. The AP also collects statistics on how long a channel is used during a given time. These data enable the AP to regulate access to a given channel. APs can query stations to collect statistics, such as retries, packets transmitted, and packets received. This gives the AP a more complete view of network performance.

802.11k extends the transmit power control procedures defined in 802.11h to other regulatory domains and frequency bands, to reduce interference and power consumption and to provide range control.

IEEE S02.11m is an ongoing task group activity to correct editorial and technical issues in the standard. The task group reviews documents generated by the other task groups to locate and correct inconsistencies and errors in the 802.11 standard and its approved amendments. IEEE S02.11n is studying a range of enhancements to both the physical and MAC layers to improve throughput. These include such items as multiple antennas, smart antennas, changes to signal encoding schemes, and changes to MAC access protocols. The current objective of the task group is a data rate of at least 100 Mbps,as measured at the interface between the 802.11 MAC layer and higher layers. In contrast, the 802.11 physical layer standards (Table 14.5) measure data rate atthe physical interface to the wireless medium. The motivation for measuring at theupper interface to the MAC layer is that the data rate experienced by the user may be significantly less than that at the physical layer. Overhead includes packet preambles, acknowledgments, contention windows, and various interface spacing parameters. The result is that the data rate coming out of the MAC layer may be on the order of one-half of the physical data rate. In addition to improving throughput, 802.11n addresses other performance-related requirements, including improved range at existing throughputs, increased resistance to interference, and more uniform coverage within an area.

4.10 WIFI PROTECTED ACCESS

The original 802.11 specification included a set of security features for privacy and authentication which, unfortunately, were quite weak. For privacy 802.11 defined the Wired Equivalent Privacy (WEP) algorithm. WEP makes use of the RC4 encryption algorithm using a 40-bit key.4 A later revision enables the use of a 104-bit key. For authentication, 802.11 requires that the two parties share. Secret key not shared by any other party and defines a protocol by which this key can be used for mutual authentication.

The privacy portion of the 802.11 standard contained major weaknesses. The 40-bit key is woefully inadequate. Even the 104-bit key proved to be vulnerable, due to a variety of weaknesses both internal and external to the protocol supporting WEP. These vulnerabilities include the heavy reuse of keys, the ease of data access in a wireless network, and the lack of any key management within the protocol. Similarly, there are a number of problems with the shared-key authentication scheme. The 802.11i task group has developed a set of capabilities to address the WLAN security issues. In order to accelerate the introduction of stwngsecurity into WLANs, the Wi-Fi Alliance promulgated WiFi Protected Access (\VPA) as a Wi-Fi standard. WPA is a set of security mechanisms that eliminates mos1 802.11 security issues and was based on the current state of the 802.11i standard. As 802.11i evolves, WPA will evolve to maintain compatibility.

IEEE 802.11i addresses three main security areas: authentication, key management, and data transfer privacy. To improve authentication, 802.11i~equires the use of an authentication server (AS) and defines a more robust authentication protocol. The AS also plays a role in key distribution. For privacy, 802.1li provides three different encryption schemes. The scheme that provides a long-term solution makes use of the Advanced Encryption Standard (AES) with 128-bit keys. However, because the use of AES would require expensive upgrades to existing equipment, alternative schemes based on 104-bit RC4 are also defined. Figure 14.13 gives a general overview of 802.11i operation. First, an exchange between a station and an AP enables the two to agree on a set of security capabilities to be used. Then an exchange involving the AS and the station pro vides for secure authentication. The AS is responsible for key distribution to the A P, which in turn manages and distributes keys to stations. Finally, strong encryption isused to protect data transfer between the station and the AP.

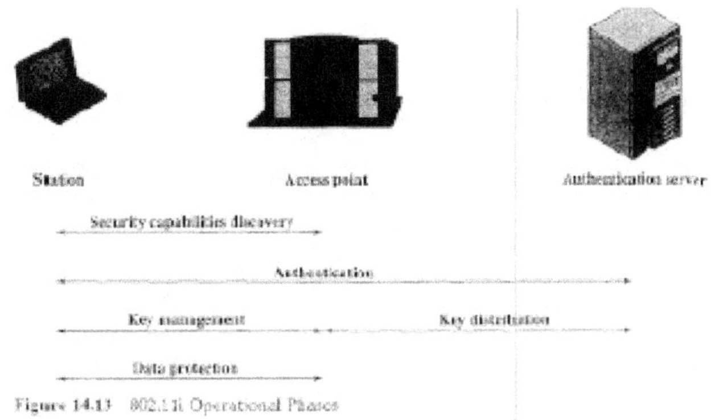

Figure 14.13   802.11i Operational Phases

The 802.11i architecture consists of three main ingredients:

• Authentication: A protocol is used to define an exchange between a user and an AS that provides mutual authentication and generates temporary keys to be used between the client and the AP over the wireless link.
• Access control: This function enforces the use of the authentication function, routes the messages properly, and facilitates key exchange. It can work with a variety of authentication protocols.

Privacy with message integrity: MAC-level data (E .g., an LLC PDU) are encrypted, along with a message integrity code that ensures that the data have not been altered. Authentication operates at a level above the LLC an MAC protocols and is considered beyond the scope of 802.11. There are a number of popular authentication protocols in use, including the Extensible Authenticate on Protocol (EAP) and the Remote Authentication Dial-In User Service (RADIU~). These are not covered in this book. The remainder of this section examines access control and privacy with message integrity.

Access Controls IEEE 802.11i makes use of another standard that was designed to provide access control functions for LANs. The standard is IEEE 802.11,Port-Based Network Access Control. IEEE 802.1X uses the terms supplicant, authenticator, and authentication server (AS). In the context of an 802.11 WLAN, the first two terms correspond to the wireless station and the AP. The AS is typically a separate device on the wired side of the network (i.e., accessible over the DS) but could also reside directly on the authenticator.

Before a supplicant is authenticated by the AS, using an authentication protocol, the authenticator only passes control or authentication messages between the supplicant and the AS; the 802.1X control channel is unblocked but the 802.11 data channel is blocked. Once a supplicant is authenticated and keys a: e provided, the authenticator can forward data from the supplicant, subject to pI defined access control limitations for the supplicant to the network. Under these Circumstances, the data channel is unblocked.

As indicated in Figure 14.14, 802.1X uses the concepts of controlled and uncontrolled ports. Ports are logical entities defined within the authenticator and refer to physical network connections. For a WLAN, the authenticator (the AP) may have only two physical ports, one connecting to the DS and I ne for wireless communication within its BSS. Each logical port is mapped to 0: e of these two physical ports. An uncontrolled port allows the exchange of PDUs between the supplicant and other the AS regardless of the authentication stat of the supplicant.A controlled port allows the exchange of PDUs between a supplicant and other systems on the LAN only if the current state of the supplicant authorizes such an exchange.

The 802.1X framework, with an upper-layer authentication protocol, fits nicely with a BSS architecture that includes a number of wireless stations

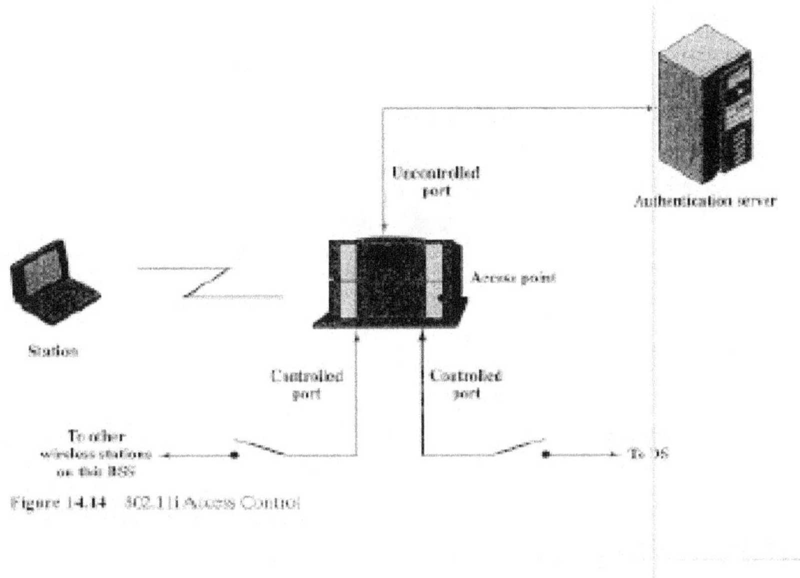

Figure 14.14   802.11i Access Control

an AP. However, for an IBSS, there is no AP. For an IBS , 802.11i provides a more complex solution that, in essence, involves pairwise authentication between stations on the IBSS.

Privacy with Message Integrity IEEE 802.11i defines two schemes for protecting data transmitted in 802.11 MAC PDUs. The first scheme is known as the Temporal Key Integrity Protocol (TKIP) or WPA-l. TKIP is designed to require only software change to devices that are implemented with WEP and uses the same RC4 encryption algorithm as WEP. The Second scheme is known as Counter Mode-CBC MAC Proto 01 (CCMP) or WPA2. CCMP makes use of the Advanced Encryption Standard (ES) encryption protocol.We begin with an overview of TKIP.

TKIP To understand TK1p, it is useful to start by examining the MAC frame,shown in Figure 14.15a. TKIP begins with an unsecured MA frame (Figure 14.8)and adds four fields: an initialization vector (IV), an extended IV (EIV), a messageintegrity check (MIC), and an integrity check value (ICV). The initialization vector is a value that was introduced for use with WEPRC4 encryption algorithm. RC4 is known as a stream encryption algorithm andworks in the following manner. The initial 104-bit RC4 k~ Yacts as the startingpoint for an algorithm that generates a key stream, which is simply an unlimitednumber of bits whose value is determined by the starting key. Encryption isachieved by a bit-by-bit XOR of the key stream with the stream of bits to be encrypted. If the same key stream starting point is used on each MAC frame, it is

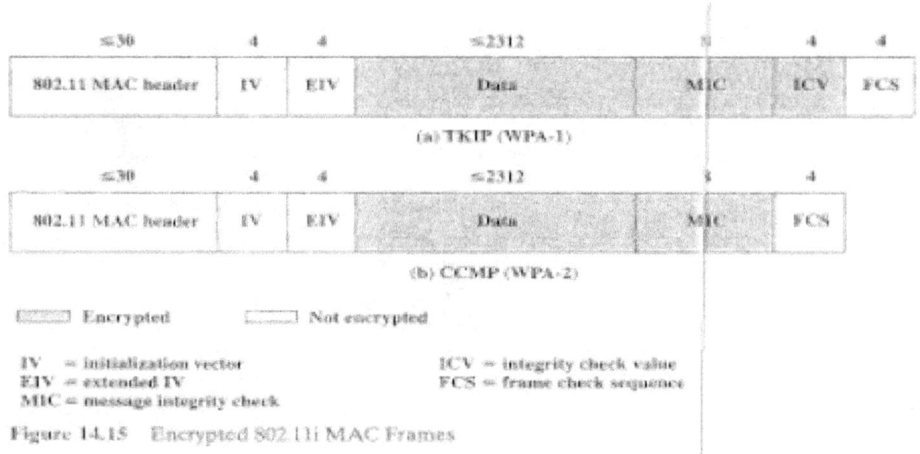

Figure 14.15   Encrypted 802.11i MAC Frames

easier to attack the system. To counter this threat, a 24-bit IV i: concatenated with the RC4 key before the key stream is generated. In effect, e 128-bit key issued. If a different IV is used for each frame, then the key stream will be different for each frame. The IV is transmitted in the clear (unencrypted) so that the receiver can combine the IV with the shared secret RC4 key for decryption. In the frame format, 4 bytes are reserved for the IV, but only the first bytes contain the 24-bit value.

The 24-bit IV is too short to provide adequate security. To deal with this problem, TKIP incorporates an extended IV. The EIV serves two purposes. First, a48-bit IV is extracted from the combination of the IV and EIV fields. This IV is combined with the 104-bit RC4 key to produce the encryption key. However, rather than just appending the IV to the RC4 key, the 48-bit IV, the RC4 key , and the transmitter MAC address serve as inputs to a mixing function that pro uses a 128-bitRC4 encryption key. This produces a stronger key. In addition, bytes from the IV and EIV also function as a sequence counter, which is incremented by one for each new frame transmitted. The sequence counter is designed to counter a replay attack, in which a third party captures a MAC frame and later retransmits i to produce an unintended effect. Because the receiving entity discards any frame that is out of sequence, the replay attack is thwarted.

The integrity check value was also introduced for use with \\ EP. The ICV isa cyclic redundancy check (CRC) calculated on all the fields of the frame. This field is then encrypted, along with the data field, using the same RC4 key. Although both the ICV and FCS fields use a CRC calculation, they serve different purposes. The FCS field is used to detect bit errors in transmission, as was explained in Section 8.1. The ICV field is used for message authentication, aconcept that is described in Appendix 12B. When a WEP MAC frame arrives and is decrypted, the receiver recalculates the ICV and compares the calculated value to the received value. If the two differ, it is assumed that the Date field has been altered in transit. The theory behind the ICV is that if an attacker alters an encrypted data message, the ICV will show this. Because the ICV is also encrypted, it is difficult for an attacker to modify the ICV so as to] match the modifications to the encrypted data field.

It can be shown that the ICV is easily defeated [EDNEOLJ]. To deal with this problem, TKIP adds a new message integrity code. For backward compatibility, the ICV field is retained. The MIC is a new algorithm, called Michael, that computes a 64-bit value calculated using the source and destination MAC address values and the Data field. This value is then encrypted using a separateRC4 key from that used for encrypting the Data and ICV fields. The use of a more complex algorithm, a separate encryption key, and a 6< -bit length all make the MIC and substantially stronger message authentication feature than the ICV. CCMP Figure 14.15b shows the format of a MAC frame using (CMP. The only format difference is that CCMP does not include the legacy ICV field. The most significant difference is that AES is used as the encryption algorithm.

4.11 BLUETOOTH

The concept behind Bluetooth is to provide a universal sho t-range wireless capability. Using the 2.4-GHz band, available globally for unlicersed low-power uses, two Bluetooth devices within 10 m of each other can share Our to 720 kbps of capacity. Bluetooth is intended to support an open-ended list of applications, including data (e.g., schedules and telephone numbers), audio, graphics, and even video. For example, audio devices can include headsets, cordless and standard phones, home stereos, and digital MP3 players. The following are examples of some 0: the capability Bluetooth can provide consumers:

- Make calls from a wireless headset connected remotely to a cell phone.
- Eliminate cables linking computers to printers, keyboards, and the mouse.
- Hook up MP3 players wirelessly to other machines t download music.

- Set up home networks so that a couch potato can remotely monitor air conditioning,the oven, and children's Internet surfing.
- Call home from a remote location to turn appliances on and off, set the alarm,and monitor activity.

Bluetooth Applications

Bluetooth is designed to operate in an environment of many users. Up to eightdevices can communicate in a small network called a piconet. Ten of thesepiconets can coexist in the same coverage range of the Bluetooth radio. To providesecurity, each link is encoded and protected against eavesdropping andinterference Bluetooth provides support for three general applications areusing short range wireless connectivity:

- Data and voice access points: Bluetooth facilitates real-time voice and data transmissions by providing effortless wireless connection of portable and stationary communications devices.
- Cable replacement: Bluetooth eliminates the need for numerous, often proprietary, cable attachments for connection of practically any kind of communication device. Connections are instant and are maintained even when devices are not within line of sight. The range of each radio is approximately 1Dm but can be extended to 100 m with an optional amplifier.
- Ad hoc networking: A device equipped with a Bluetooth radio canestablish instant connection to another Bluetooth radio as soonas it comesinto range.

Table 15.1 gives some examples of Bluetooth uses.

Table 15.1   Bluetooth User Scenarios [HAAR98]

Three-in-one phone When you are in the office, your phone functions as an intercom (no telephony charge). At home, it functions as a cordless phone (fixed-line charge). When you are on the move, it functions as a mobile phone (cellular charge).	**Briefcase e-mail** Access e-mail while your portable PC is still in the briefcase. When your PC receives an e-mail message, you are notified by your mobile phone. You can also use the phone to browse incoming e-mail and read messages.
Internet bridge Use your portable PC to surf the Internet anywhere, whether you are connected wirelessly through a mobile phone (cellular) or through a wired connection (PSTN, ISDN, LAN, xDSL).	**Delayed messages** Compose e-mail on your PC while you are on an airplane. When you land and are allowed to switch on your mobile phone, the messages are sent immediately.
Interactive conference In meetings and at conferences, you can share information instantly with other participants. You can also operate a projector remotely without wire connections.	**Automatic synchronization** Automatically synchronize your desktop computer, portable PC, notebook, and mobile phone. As soon as you enter the office, the address list and calendar in your notebook automatically updates the files on your desktop computer or vice versa.
The ultimate headset Connect a headset to your mobile PC or to any wired connection and free your hands for more important tasks at the office or in your car.	**Instant digital postcard** Connect a camera cordlessly to your mobile phone or to any wire-bound connection. Add comments from you mobile phone, a notebook, or portable PC and send them instantly.
Portable PC speakerphone Connect cordless headsets to your portable PC, and use it as a speaker phone regardless of whether you are in the office, your car, or at home.	**Cordless desktop** Connect your desktop/laptop computer cordlessly to printers, scanner, keyboard, mouse, and the LAN.

Bluetooth Standards

The Bluetooth standards present a formidable bulk-well over 1500 pages, divided into two groups: core and profile. The core specifications describe the details of the various layers of the Bluetooth protocol architecture, from the radio interface to link control. Related topics are covered, such as interoperability with related technologies, testing requirements, and a definition of various Bluetooth timers and their associated values.

The profile specifications are concerned with the use 0 Bluetooth technology to support various applications. Each profile specification discusses the use of the technology defined in the core specifications to implement a particular usage model. The profile specification includes a description of which aspects of the core specifications are mandatory, optional, and not applicable. The purpose of a profile specification is to define a standard of interoperability so that products from different vendors that claim to support a given usage morel will work together. In general terms, profile specifications fall into one of two categories: cable replacement or wireless audio. The cable replacement profiles provide a convenient means for logically connecting devices in proximity to one another and for exchanging data. For example, when two devices first come within ran e of one another, they can automatically query each other for a common profile. TJ is might then cause the end users of the device to be alerted, or cause some automat c data exchange to take place. The wireless audio profiles are concerned with establishing short-range voice connections.

Protocol Architecture

Bluetooth is defined as a layered protocol architecture (Figure 15.1) consisting of core Protocols, cable replacement and telephony control protocol, and adopted protocols.

The core protocols form a five-layer stack consisting 0 the following elements:
- Radio: Specifies details of the air interface, including. Frequency, the use of frequencyhopping, modulation scheme, and transmit power.
- Baseband: Concerned with connection establishment' within a piconet, addressing,packet format, timing, and power control.
- Link manager protocol (LMP): Responsible for Ii k setup between Bluetoothdevices and ongoing link management. This includes security aspectssuch as authentication and encryption, plus the control and negotiation of baseband packet sizes.
- Logical link control and adaptation protocol (L2Ci P): Adapts upper-layerprotocols to the baseband layer. L2CAP provides both connectionless andconnection-oriented services.
- Service discovery protocol (SDP): Device information, services, and the characteristicsof the services can be queried to enable the establishment of aconnection between two or more Bluetooth devices.RFCOMM is the cable replacement protocol include in the Bluetooth specification.RFCOMM presents a virtual serial port that is designed to make replacement

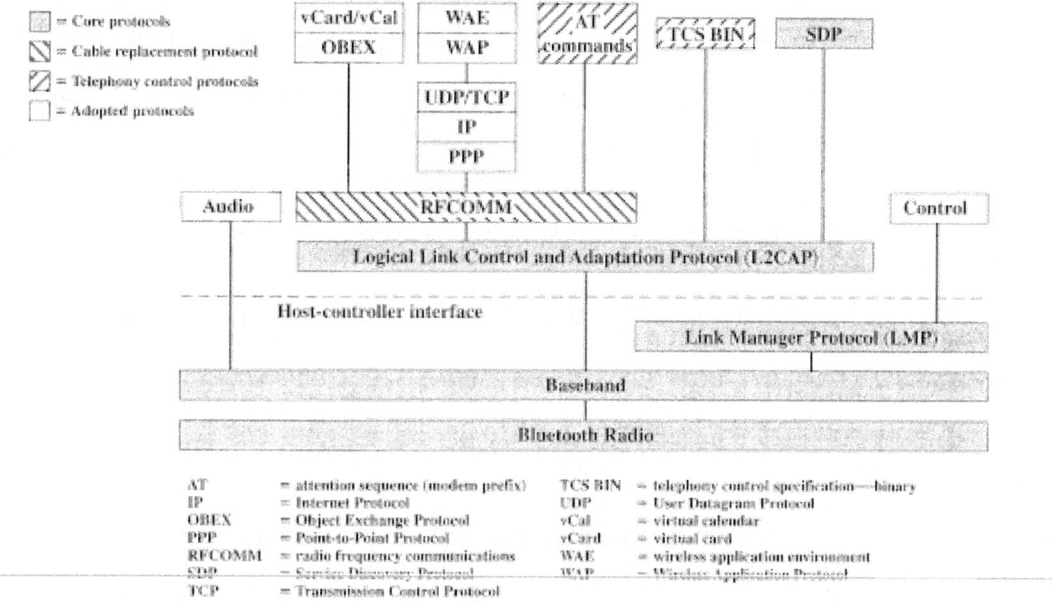

Figure 15.1   Bluetooth Protocol Stack

of cable technologies as transparent as possible. Serial port are one of the most common types of communications interfaces used with computing and communications devices. Hence, RFCOMM enables the replacement of serial port cables with the minimum of modification of existing devices. RFCO~ M provides for binary data transport and emulates EIA-232 control signals over the Bluetooth baseband layer. EIA-232 (formerly known as RS-232) is a widely used serial port interface standard.

Bluetooth specifies a telephony control protocol. TCS I IN (telephony control specification-binary) is a bit-oriented protocol that defines the call control signalling for the establishment of speech and data calls between Bluetooth devices. In addition, it defines mobility management procedures for handling groups of Bluetooth TCS devices.

- The adopted protocols are defined in specifications issued by other standards making organizations and incorporated into the overall Bluetooth architecture. The Bluetooth strategy is to invent only necessary protocols and use existing standards whenever possible. The adopted protocols include the following The point-to-point protocol is an Internet standard protocol for transporting TCP/UDP/IP: These are the foundation protocols of the TCP/IP protocol suite (described in Chapter 4).

- OBEX: The object exchange protocol is a session level protocol developed by the Infrared Data Association (IrDA) for the exchange of objects. OBEX provides functionality similar to that of HTTP, but in a simpler fashion. It also provides a model for representing objects and opera ions. Examples of content formats transferred by OBEX are vCard and v calendar, which provide the format of an electronic business card and personal calendar entries and scheduling information, respectively.
- WAEIWAP: Bluetooth incorporates the wireless al plication environment and the wireless application protocol into its architecture (described in Chapter 12).

Usage Models

A number of usage models are defined in Bluetooth profile documents. In essence, a usage model is set of protocols that implement a particular Bluetooth-based application. Each profile defines the protocols and protocol feat res supporting a particular usage model. Figure 15.2, taken from [METT99], illustrates the highest-priority usage models:

File transfer: The file transfer usage model supports t] e transfer of directories, files, documents, images, and streaming media forma s. This usage model also includes the capability to browse folders on a remote device.

- •Internet bridge: With this usage model, a PC is wirelessly connected to mobile phone or cordless modern to provide dial-up networking and fax capabilities. For dial-up networking, AT commands are wed to control the mobile phone or modem, and another protocol stack (e.g., PPP over RFCOMM) is used for data transfer. For fax transfer, the fax software op rates directly over RFCOMM.
- LAN access: This usage model enables devices on a picante to access a LAN. Once connected, a device functions as if it were directly connected (wired) to the LAN.

Synchronization: This model provides a device-to-device synchronization of PIM (personal information management) information, such a phone book, calendar, message, and note information. IrMC (Ir mobile communications) is an IrDA protocol that provides a client/server capability for transferring updated PIM information from one device to another.

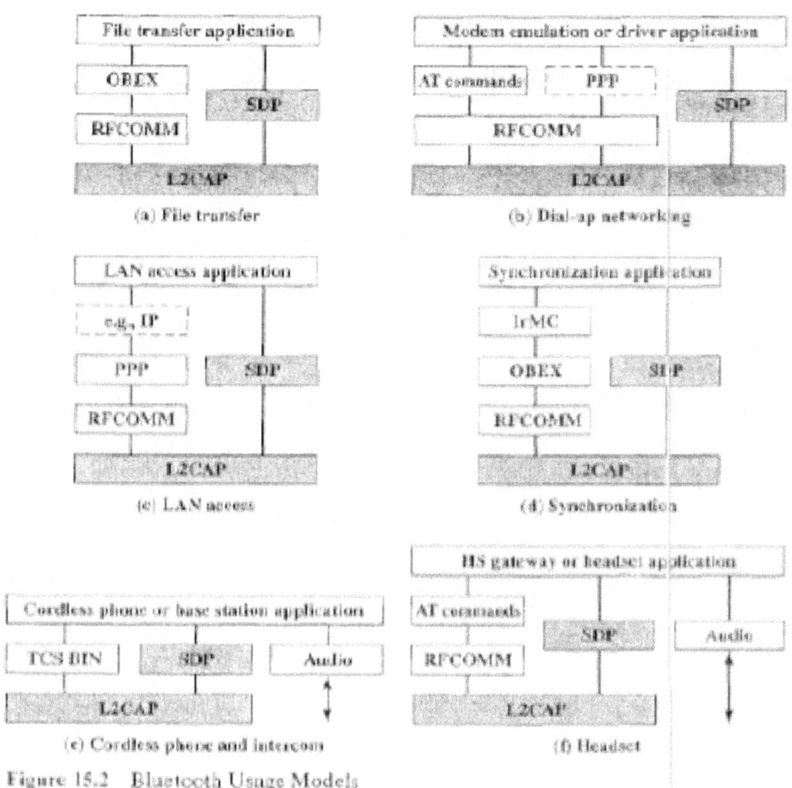

Figure 15.2   Bluetooth Usage Models

Three-in-one phone: Telephone handsets that implement this usage model may act as a cordless phone connecting to a voice base station, s an intercom device for connecting to other telephones, and as a cellular phone.

Headset: The headset can act as a remote device's audio input and output interface Pico nets and Scatter nets

As was mentioned, the basic unit of networking in Bluetooth 's a piconet, consisting of a master and from one to seven active slave devices. The radio designated as the master makes the determination of the channel (frequency-hopping sequence) and phase (timing offset, i.e., when to transmit) that shall be used by all devices on this piconet. The radio designated as master makes this determination using its Own device address as a parameter, while the slave devices must tune to the same channel and phase. A slave may only communicate with the master and may only communicate when granted permission by the master. A device in one piconet may also exist as part of another piconet and may function as either a slave or master in each piconet (Figure 15.3).

This form of overlapping is called a scatternet. Figure 15.4, based on one in [HAAROOa], contrasts the piconet/scatternet architecture with other forms of wireless networks.

The advantage of the piconet/scatternet scheme i~ that it allows many devices to share the same physical area and make efficient use of the bandwidth. A Bluetooth system uses a frequency-hopping scheme wi:h a carrier spacing of 1 MHz. Typically, up to 80 different frequencies are used fClr a total bandwidth of 80 MHz. If frequency hopping were not used, then a single channel would correspond to a single I-MHz band. With frequency hoppinga logical channel is defined by the frequency-hopping sequence. At any give 1 time, the bandwidth available is 1 MHz, with a maximum of eight devices sharing the bandwidth. Different logical channels (different hopping sequences) car. simultaneously share the same 80-MHz bandwidth. Collisions will occur when devices in different

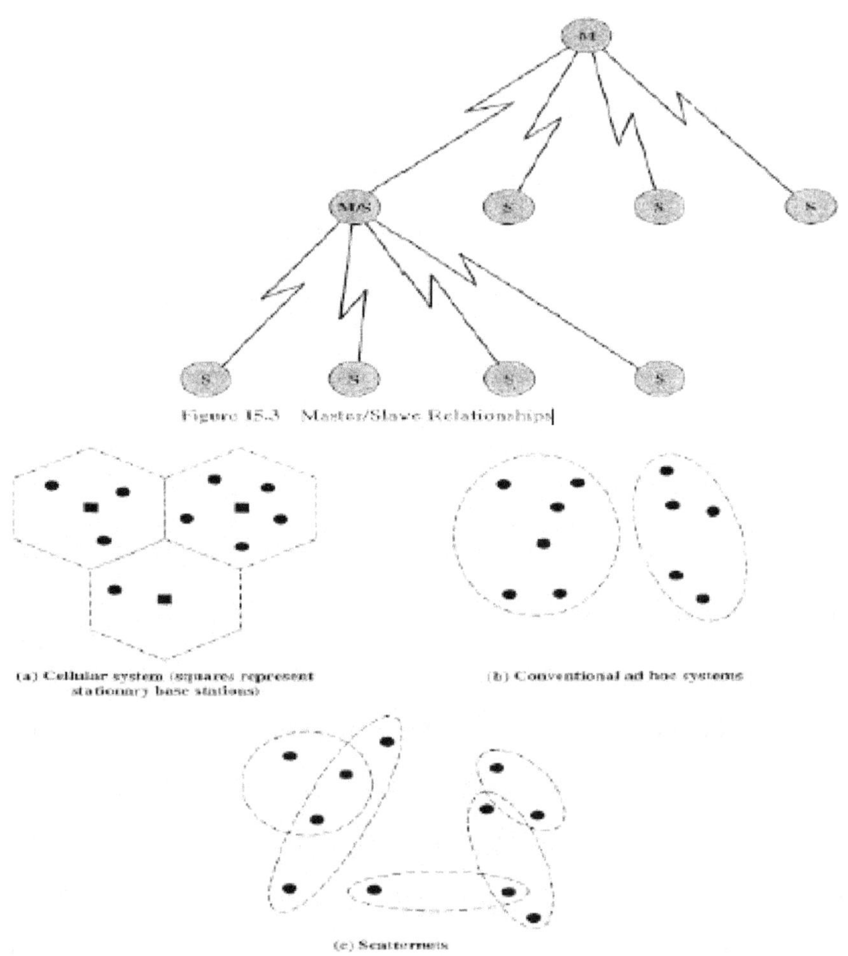

Figure 15.3   Master/Slave Relationships

Figure 15.4   Wireless Network Configurations

piconets, on different logical channels, happen to use the same hop frequency at the same time. As the number of piconets in an area increases, the number of collisions increases, and performance degrades. In summary, the physical area and total bandwidth are shared by the scatternet. The logical channel and data transfer are shared by a piconet.

4.12 RADIO SPECIFICATION:

The Bluetooth radio specification is a short document that gives the basic details of radio transmission for Bluetooth devices. Some of the key parameters are summarized in Table 15.2.

One aspect of the radio specification is a definition of three classes of transmitters based on output power:

• Class 1: Outputs 100 mW (+20 dBm) for maximum range, with a minimum of 1 mW (0 dBm). In this class, power control is mandatory, ranging from 4 to 20 dBm. This mode provides the greatest distance.

Class 2: Outputs 2.4 roW (+4 dBm) at maximum, with a minimum of 0.25 mW(-6 dBm). power control is optional.

Class 3: Lowest power. Nominal output is 1 mW.

Table 15.2　Bluetooth Radio and Baseband Parameters

Topology	Up to 7 simultaneous links in a logical star
Modulation	GFSK
Peak data rate	1 Mbps
RF bandwidth	220 kHz (−3dB), 1 MHz (−20dB)
RF band	2.4 GHz, ISM band
RF carriers	23/79
Carrier spacing	1 MHz
Transmit power	0.1 W
Piconet access	FH-TDD-TDMA
Frequency hop rate	1600 hops/s
Scatternet access	FH-CDMA

Bluetooth makes use of the 2.4-GHz band within the ISM (industrial, scientific, and medical) band. In most countries, the bandwid1h is sufficient to define79 I-MHz physical channels (Table 15.3). Power control is used to keep the devices from emitting any more RF power than necessary. The power control algorithm is implemented using the link management protocol between a master and the slaves in a piconet. Modulation for Bluetooth is Gaussian FSK, with a binary one represented by a positive frequency deviation and a binary zero represented by a negative frequency deviation from the center frequency. The minimum deviation is 115 kHz.

4.13 BASEBAND SPECIFICATIONS:

One of the most complex of the Bluetooth documents is thebaseband specification.

In this section we provide an overview of the key elements

Table 15.3   International Bluetooth Frequency Allocations

Area	Regulatory Range	RF Channels
U.S., most of Europe, and most other countries	2.4 to 2.4835 GHz	$f = 2402 + n$ MHz, $n = 0, \ldots, 78$
Japan	2.471 to 2.497 GHz	$f = 2473 + n$ MHz, $n = 0, \ldots, 22$
Spain	2.445 to 2.475 GHz	$f = 2449 + n$ MHz, $n = 0, \ldots, 22$
France	2.4465 to 2.4835 GHz	$f = 2454 + n$ MHz, $n = 0, \ldots, 22$

Frequency Hopping

Frequency hopping (FH) in Bluetooth serves two purposes:

1. It provides resistance to interference and multipath effects.
2. It provides a form of multiple access among co-located devices in different piconets.

The FH scheme works as follows. The total bandwidth is d: vided into 79 (in almost all countries) physical channels, each of bandwidth 1 MIIz. FH occurs by jumping from one physical channel to another in a pseudorandom sequence. The same hopping sequence is shared by all of the devices on a singlepiconet; we will refer to this as an FH channel2 The hop rate is 1600 hops per second, so that each physical channel is occupied for a duration of 0.625 ms. Each 0.625- ms time period is referred to as a slot, and these are numbered sequentially. Bluetooth radios communicate using a time division duplex (TDD) discipline. Recall from Chapter 11 that TDD is a link transmission technique in which data are transmitted in one direction at a time, with transmission alternating between the two directions. Because more than two devices share the piconet medium the access technique is TDMA. Thus piconet access can be characterized as FH-TDD-TDMA. Figure 15.5 illustrates the technique.3 In the figure, k denotes the slot number, and f(k) is the physical channel selected during slot period k.

Transmission of a packet starts at the beginning of a slot. Pack;;t lengths requiring 1,3, or 5 slots are allowed. For multisport packets, the radio remains at the same frequency until the entire packet has been sent (Figure 15.6). In the next slot after the multisport packet, the radio returns to the frequency required for its hopping sequence, so that during transmission, two or four hop frequencies have been skipped. Using TDD prevents crosstalk between transmit and receive operations in the radio transceiver, which is essential if a one-chip implementation is desired. Note that because transmission and reception take place at different tin Le slots, different frequencies are used.

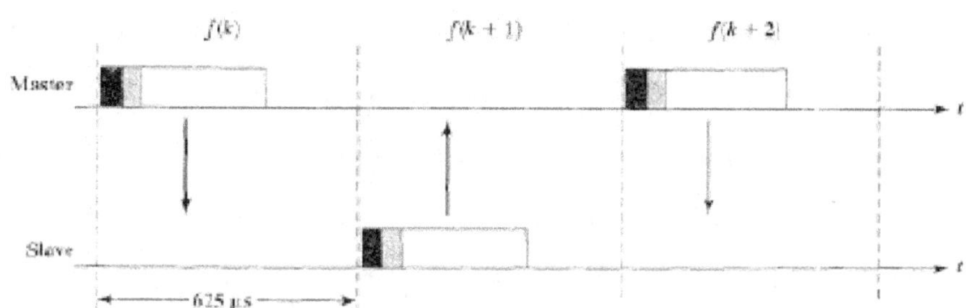

Figure 15.5   Frequency-Hop Time Division Duplex

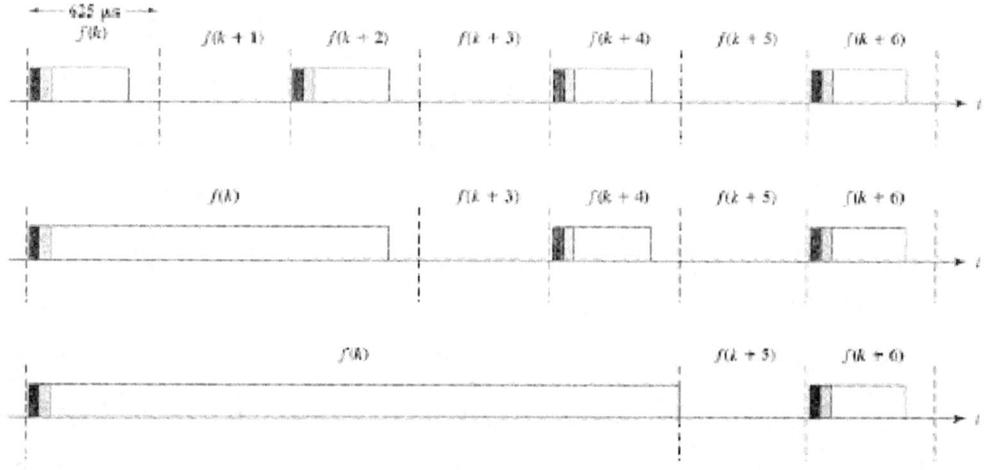

Figure 15.6   Examples of Multislot Packets

The FH sequence is determined by the master in a piconet called is a function of the master's Bluetooth address. A rather complex mathematical 0 Iteration involving permutations and exclusive-OR (XOR) operations is used to generate a pseudorandom hop sequence.

Because different piconets in the same area will have different masters, they will use different hop sequences. Thus, most of the time, transmission on two devices on different piconets in the same area will be on different physical channels. Occasionally, two piconets will use the same physical channel during the same time slot, causing a collision and lost data. However, because this will happen infrequently, it is readily accommodated with forward error correction and error detection ARQ techniques. Thus, a form of code division multiple access (CDMA) isachieved between devices on different piconets in the same scatternet,this isreferred to as FH-CDMA. II

Physical Links I,

Two types of links can be established between a master and a slave

- Synchronous connection oriented (SCQ): Allocates afixed bandwidthbetween a point-to-point connection involving the master and a single slave.The master maintains the SCO link by using reserved slots at regularintervals. The basic unit of reservation is two consecutive slots (one in eachtransmission direction). The master can support up to th lee simultaneousSCO links while a slave can support two or three SCO links.SCO packets are never retransmitted.

- Asynchronous connectionless (ACL): A point-to-multipoint link between themaster and all the slaves in the piconet. In slots not reserved by SCO links, themaster can exchange packets with any slave on a per-slot basis, including aslave already engaged in an SCO link. Only a single ACL link can exist. Formost ACL packets, packet retransmission is applied. I ISCO links are used primarily to exchange time-bounded data requiring guaranteeddata rate but without guaranteed delivery. One example, us !:d in a number ofBluetooth profiles, is digitally encoded audio data with built-in tolerance to lostdata. The guaranteed data rate is achieved through the reservation of a particularnumber of slots. IACL links provide a packet-switched style of connection. No bandwidth reservationis possible and delivery may be guaranteed through error detection andretransmission.

A slave is permitted to return an ACL packet in theslave-to-masterslot if and only if it has been addressed in the preceding master-Io-slave slot. ForACL links, I-slot, 3-slot, and 5-slot packets have been defined. I)ata can be senteither unprotected (although ARQ can be used at a higher layer) ir protected with a 2/3 forward error correction code. The maximum data rate that c 1m be achieved iswith a 5-slot unprotected packet with asymmetric capacity allocation, resulting in721 kbps in the forward direction and 57.6 kbps in the reverse direction. Table 15.4summarizes all of the possibilities.

Table 15.4   Achievable Data Rates on the ACL Link

Type	Symmetric (kbps)	Asymmetric (kbps)	
DM1	108.8	108.8	108.8
DH1	172.8	172.8	172.8
DM3	256.0	384.0	54.4
DH3	384.0	576.0	86.4
DM5	286.7	477.8	36.3
DH5	432.6	721.0	57.6

DMx = x-slot FEC-encoded
DHx = x-slot unprotected

Packets

The packet format for all Bluetooth packets is shown in Figure 15.7. It consists of three fields:

Access code: Used for timing synchronization, offset compensation, paging, and inquiry

1. Header: Used to identify packet type and to carry protocol control information
2. Payload: If present, contains user voice or data and, in most cases, a payload header

Access Code There are three types of access codes:

1. Channel access code (CAC): Identifies a piconet(unique for a piconet)
2. Device access code (DAC): Used for paging and its subsequentresponses

Inquiry access code (lAC): Used for inquiry purpose:

An access code consists of a preamble, a sync word, called a trailer. The preambleis used for DC compensation. It consists of the pattern 0101 if the least significant(leftmost) bit in the sync word is 0 and the pattern 1010 if the least significant bit in the sync word is 1.similarly, the trailer is 0101 if the most significant bit (rightmost)of the sync word is 1 and 1010 if the most significant bit is O.The 64-bit sync word consists of three components (Figure 15.8) and is worthexamining in some detail. Each Bluetooth device is assigned a globally unique 48-bitaddress. The 24 least significant bits are referred to as the 10Wier address part (LAP) andare used in forming the sync word. For a CAC, the LAP olE the master is used; for aDAC, the LAP of the paged unit. There are two different lACs. The general lAC(GIAC) is a general inquiry message used to discover which

Bluetooth devices are inrange, and for this a special reserved value of LAP is available. A dedicated lAC(DIAC) is common for a dedicated group of Bluetooth units that share a common characteristic, and a previously defined LAP corresponding to that characteristic is used.

Using the appropriate LAP, the sync word is formed as follows:
To the 24-bit LAP, append the 6 bits 001101 if the most significant bit (MSB)of the LAP is 0, and append 110010 if the MSB is 1.This forms a 7-bit Barker sequence. The purpose of including a Barker sequence is to further improve the autocorrelation properties of the sync word.

Generate a 64-bit pseudo noise (PN) sequence, Po, Pl' ,P63' The sequence is defined by the equation $P(X) = 1 + X2 + X3 + X5 + r$ and can be implemented with a 6-bit linear feedback shift register. 11: e seed value for the PN sequence is 100000. Take the bitwise XOR of P34> P35, ,P63and the 30--bit sequence produced in step 1. This "scrambles" the information, removing unwanted regularities.

Generate a 34-bit error-correcting code for the scrambled information block and place this at the beginning to form a 64-bit code word. Thus, we have a (64,30) code. To generate this code, start with a (63,30) BCH opde.6 Then define the generator polynomial $g(X) = (1 + X)g'(X)$, where $g'(X)$ is the generator polynomial for the (63,30) BCH code. This produces the d sired 34-bit code.

Take the bitwise XOR of Po, Pa',P63and the 64-ipit sequence produced in step 4. This step descrambles the information part of1 the code word so that the original LAP and Barker sequence are transmitted. The step also scrambles the block code. The scrambling of the information part of the codeword in step 3 is designed to strengthen the error-correcting properties of the block code. The subsequent descrambling enables the receiver to recover the LAP easily. In the words of the specification, the scrambling of the 34-bit error code removes tb e cyclic properties of the underlying code. This might give better transmission spectral qualities and also improve autocorrelation properties.

Packet Header The header format for all Bluetooth packets is shown in Figure 15.7c. It consists of six fields:

AM_ADDR: Recall that a piconet includes at most seven active slaves. The 3-bit AM Address contains the "active mode" address (temporary address assigned to this slave in this piconet) of one of the slaves. A transmission from the master to a slave contains that slave's address; a transmission from a slave contains its address. The 0 value is reserved for a broadcast ::rom the master to all slaves in the piconet.

Type: Identifies the type of packet (Table 15.5). Four type codes are reserved for control packets common to both SCQ and ACL lines. The remaining packet types are used to convey user information. For SeQ links, the HVl,HV2, HV3 packets each carry 64-kbps voice. The difference is the amount of error protection provided, which dictates how frequently a packet must be sent to maintain the 64-kbps data rate. The DV packet carries both voice and data. For ACL links, 6 different packets are defined. These, together with the DMI packet, carry user data with different amounts of error protection and different data rates (Table 15.4). There is another packet type common to both physical links; it consists of only the access code, with a fixed length of 68 bits(does not include trailer). This is referred to as the ID packet and is used in the inquiry and access procedures.

Flow: Provides a I-bit flow control mechanism for ACL tr 3.ffic only. When apacket with Flow = 0 is received, the station receiving the packet must temporarily halt the transmission ofACL packets on this link. V\'hen a packet with Flow = 1 is received, transmission may resume.

ARQN: Provides a I-bit acknowledgment mechanism for ACL traffic protected by a CRC (Table 15.5). If the reception was successful, an ACK(ARQN = 1) is returned; otherwise a NAK (ARQN = 0) is returned. When no return message regarding acknowledge is received, a NAK is assumed implicitly. If a NAK is received, the relevant packet is retransmitted.

SEQN: Provides a I-bit sequential numbering schemes. Transmitted packets are alternately labelled with a 1 or O. This is required to filter out retransmission sat the destination; if a retransmission occurs due to Cl failing ACK, the destination receives the same packet twice.

Header error control (HEC): An 8-bit error detection code used to protect the packet header. Payload Format For some packet types, the baseband specification defines a format for the payload field. For voice payloads, no header is defined. For all of the

4.14 LINK MANAGER SPECIFICATION:

LMP manages various aspects of the radio link between a master and a slave. The protocol involves the exchange of messages in the form of LMP PDUs (protocol data units) between the LMP entities in the master and slave. Messages are always sent as single slot packets with a 1-byte payload header that identifies the message type and a payload body that contains additional information pertinent to this message.

The procedures defined for LMP are grouped into 24 functional areas, each of which involves the exchange of one or more messages. Table 15.7 lists these areas, together with the PDUs involved in each area. We briefly look at each area in turn. The two general response messages are used to reply to other PDUs in a number of different procedures. The accepted PDU includes the opcode of the message that is accepted. The not accepted PDU includes the opcode of the message that is not accepted and the reason why it is not accepted. LMP supports various security services with mechanisms for managing authentication, encryption, and key distribution. These services include

Authentication: Authentication is defined in the baseband specification but involves the exchange of two LMP PDUs, one containing the random number and one containing the signed response (Figure 15.14).

Pairing: This service allows mutually authenticated users to automatically establish a link encryption key. As a first step, an initialization key is generated by both sides and used in the authentication procedure to authenticate that the two sides have the same key. The initialization key is generated from a common personal identification number (PIN) entered in both devices. The two sides then exchange messages to determine if the link key to be used for future encryptions will be a secret key already configured or a combination key that is calculated based on the master's link key.

Change link key: If two devices are paired and use a combination key, then that key can be changed. One side generates a new key and sends it to the other side XOR with the old link key. The other side accepts or rejects the key.

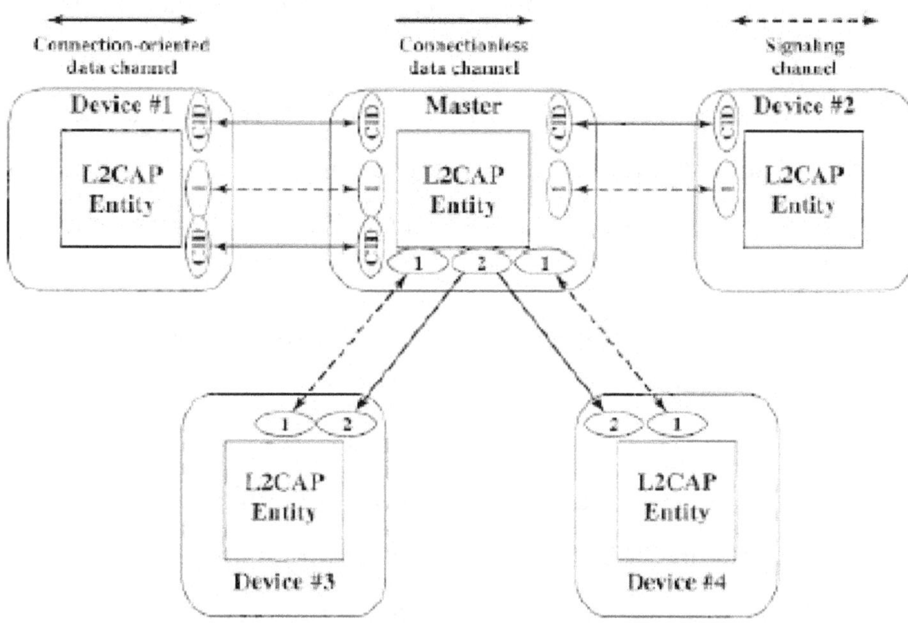

Figure 15.14   L2CAP Channels

4& Change current link key: The current link key can be changed temporarily. The exchange involves the use of random numbers and XOR calculations to generate the temporary key, which is used for a single session. 4& Encryption: LMP is not directly involved in link encryption but provides services to manage the encryption process. A number of parameters may be negotiated, including the operating encryption mode (no encryption, point-to point only, point-to-point and broadcast), the size of the key, and the random seed key use to start a new encryption session.

LMP is also used to begin and end the use of encryption. LMP provides mechanisms for synchronizing the clocks in the various piconet participants:

Clock offset request: When a slave receives the FRS packet, the difference is computed between its own clock and the master's clock value included in the payload of the FRS packet. The clock offset is also updated each time a packet is received from the master. The master can request this clock offset anytime during the connection. By saving this clock offset the master knows on what

RF channel the slave wakes up to PAGE SCAN after it has left the piconet. This can be used to speed up the paging time the next time the same device is paged.

• Slot offset information: An initiating device can transmit a message that describes timing differences (time difference between slot boundaries) between two adjacent piconets.

Timing accuracy information request: Used by a device to retrieve the accuracyparameters of another device's timing subsystem. Parameters include long-term clock drift and clock jitter.LMP includes two PDUs that are used to exchange information about the communicating devices:

LMP version: Allows each LMP entity to determine the LMP version implemented in the other. So far, there is only one version.

Supported features: The Bluetooth radio and link controller may support only a subset of the packet types and features described in Baseband Specification and Radio Specification. The PDU LMP features req and LMP features res are used to exchange this information. Table 15.8 lists the features that may be exchanged.

A Bluetooth device has a number of states and modes that it can occupy. LMP provides the following PDUs to manage these modes.

Switch master/slave role: Allows a slave to become the master of the piconet. For example, this is needed when a paging device must be the master. If a new device needs to issue a page, it can use this service.

Name request: Enables a device to request the text name of another device.

Detach: Enables a device to remove itself from a connection. This can be issued by either master or slave.

Table 15.8 LMP Supported Feature List

Feature
3-slot packets
5-slot packets
Encryption
Slot offset
Timing accuracy
Switch
Hold mode
Sniff mode
Park mode
RSSI
Channel quality-driven data rate
SCO link
HV2 packets
HV3 packets
μ-law log
A-law log
CVSD
Paging scheme
Power control

$ Hold mode: Places the link between a master and slave in hold mode for a specified time.

Sniff mode: To enter sniff mode, master and slave negotiate a sniff interval sniff and a sniff offset, D sniff, which specifies the timing of the sniff slots. The offset determines the time of the first sniff slot; after that the sniff slots follows periodically with the sniff interval T sniff.

Park mode: Places a slave in park mode.

Power control: Used by a device to direct another device to increase or decrease the second device's transmit power.

sChannel quality-driven change between DM and DH: A device is configured to use DM packets always or to use DR packets always or to adjust its packet type automatically according to the quality of the channel. This service allows an explicit change among these three alternatives. The difference between Demand DR is that the payload in a DM packet is protected with a 2/3 FEC code, whereas the payload of a DR is not protected with any FEC

Quality of service: Two parameters define Bluetooth GoS. The poll interval, which is the maximum time between transmissions from a master to a particular slave, is used for capacity allocation and latency control. The number of repetitions for broadcast packets (NBC). Broadcast packets are not acknowledged and so the automatic retransmission of all broadcast packets improves reliability.

SCQ links: Used to establish an SCQ link.

sControl of multisport packets: Arbitrates the maximum number of time slots apacket can cover. The default value is one. This mechanism can be used to select 3 or 5.

8 Paging scheme: Controls the type of paging scheme to be used between devices on the piconet. There is a default scheme that is mandatory for implementation. Additional optional schemes may be defined.

Link supervision: Controls the maximum time a device should wait before declaring the failure of a link.

4.15 LOGICAL LINK CONTROL AND ADAPTION PROTOCOL:

Like Logical Link Control (LLC) in the IEEE 802 specification, L2CAP provides alink-layer protocol between entities across a shared-medium network. As with LLC,L2CAP provides a number of services and relies on a lower layer (in this case, the baseband layer) for flow and error control.L2CAP makes use of ACL links; it does not provide support for SCQ links.

- Using ACL links, L2CAP provides two alternative services to upper-layer protocols:
- Connectionless service: This is a reliable datagram style of service.
- Connection-mode service: This service is similar to that offered by RDLC

A logical connection is set up between two users exchanging data, and flowcontrol and error control are provided.

L2CAP provides three types of logical channels:

- Connectionless: Supports the connectionless service. Each channel is unidirectional. This channel type is typically used for broadcast from the master to multiple slaves.
- Connection oriented: Supports the connection-oriented service. Each channels bidirectional (full duplex). A quality of service (QoS) flow specification is assigned in each direction.
- Signalling: Provides for the exchange of signalling messages between L2CAPentities.

Figure 15.14 provides an example of the use of L2CAP logical channels. Associated with each logical channel is a channel identifier (CID). For connection-oriented channels, a unique CID is assigned at each end of the channel to identify this connection and associate it with an L2CAP user on each end. Connectionless channels are identified by a CID value of 2, and signalling channels are identified by a CD value of 1. Thus, between the master and any slave, there is only one connectionless channel and one signalling channel, but there may be multiple connection-oriented channels.L2CAP Packets Figure 15.15 shows the format of L2CAP packets. For the connectionless service, the packet format consists of the following fields:

Length: Length of the information payload plus PSM fields, in bytes.

Channel ID: A value of 2, indicating the connectionless channel.
protocol/service multiplexer (PSM): Identifies the higher-layer recipient for the payload in this packet.

Information payload: Higher-layer user data. This field may be up to 65533(216- 3) bytes in length. connection-oriented packets have the same format as connectionless packets, but without the PSM field. The PSM field is not needed because the CID identifies the upper-layer recipient of the data. The information payload field may be up to65535 (216- 1) bytes in length. Signalling command packets have the same header format as the connection oriented packets. In this case, the CID value is 1, indicating the signaling channel.The payload of a signaling packet consists of one or more L2CAP commands, each of which consists of four fields:

code: Identifies the type of command.

identifier: Used to match a request with its reply. The requesting device sets this field and the responding device uses the same value in its response. A different identifier must be used for each original command. length: Length of the data field for this command, in bytes.

Data: Additional data, if necessary, relating to this command.

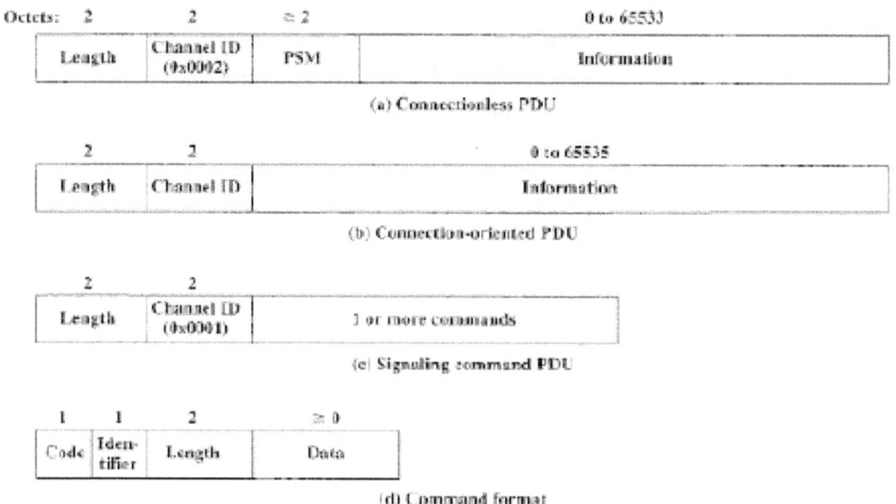

Figure 15.15   L2CAP Formats

Table 15.9   L2CAP Signaling Command Codes

Code	Description	Parameters
0x01	Command reject	Reason
0x02	Connection request	PSM, Source CID
0x03	Connection response	Destination CID, Source CID, Result, Status
0x04	Configure request	Destination CID, Flags, Options
0x05	Configure response	Source CID, Flags, Result, Options
0x06	Disconnection request	Destination CID, Source CID
0x07	Disconnection response	Destination CID, Source CID
0x08	Echo request	Data (optional)
0x09	Echo response	Data (optional)
0x0A	Information request	InfoType
0x0B	Information response	InfoType, Result, Data (optional)

Signaling commands

There are eleven commands in five categories (Table 15.9). The command reject command can be sent in response to any command to reject it. Reasons for rejection include invalid CID or length exceeded. Connection commands are used to establish a new logical connection. There quest command includes a PSM value indicating the L2CAP user for this connection. Three values are so far defined, for the service discovery protocol, RFCOMM, and the telephony control protocol. Other PSM values are assigned dynamically and are implementation dependent. The request command also includes the CID value that will be assigned to this connection by the source. The response command includes the source CID and the destination CID, the latter assigned to this channel by the respondent. The result parameter indicates the outcome (successful, pending, rejected) and, if the result is pending, the status field indicates the current status that makes this a pending connection (e.g., authentication pending, authorization pending).

Configure commands are sent to establish an initial logical link transmission contract between two L2CAP entities and to renegotiate this contract whenever appropriate. Each configuration parameter in a configuration request is related exclusively to either the outgoing or the incoming data traffic. The request command includes a flags field; currently the only flag is an indicator of whether additional configuration commands will be sent. The options field contains a list of parameters and their values to be negotiated. Each parameter is defined by three fields:

Type (1 byte): The 7 least significant bits of this byte identify the option. If the most significant bit is set to 0, the option is mandatory and, if not recognized, the recipient must refuse the configuration request. If the most significant bitis set to 1, the option is optional and may be ignored by the recipient.

Length (1 byte): The length of the option payload. A length of 0 indicates no payload.

Option payload: Further information about this option. The following parameters may be negotiated:

Maximum transmission unit (MTU): The largest L2CAP packet payload, in bytes, that the originator of the request can accept for that channel. The MTU is asymmetric and the sender of the request shall specify the MTU it can receive on this channel if it differs from the default value. L2CAP implementations must support a minimum MTU size of 48 bytes. The default value is 672 bytes. This is not a negotiated value but simply informs the recipient of the size of MTU that the sender of this request can accept.

Flush timeout option: Recall in our discussion of the baseband specification that as part of the ARQ mechanism, a payload will be flushed after failure on repeated attempts to retransmit. The flush timeout is the amount of time the originator will attempt to transmit an L2CAP packet successfully before giving up and flushing the packet.

Quality of service (QoS): Identifies the traffic flow specification for the local device's traffic (outgoing traffic) over this channel. This parameter is described in the following subsection. In the latter two cases, a negotiation takes place, in which the recipient can accept the flush timeout and QoS parameters or request an adjustment. The initial sender can then accept or reject the adjustment.

The configure response command also includes a Flags field with the same meanings in the configuration request command. The Result field in the response command Indicates whether the preceding request is accepted or rejected. The Options field contains the same list of parameters as from the corresponding request command. For a successful result, these parameters contain the return values for any wild card parameters (see discussion of QoS, subsequently). For an unsuccessful result, rejected parameters should be sent in the response with the values that would have been accepted if sent in the original request.

- The disconnection commands are used to terminate a logical channel.
- The echo commands are used to solicit a response from a remote L2CAP entity.
- These commands are typically used for testing the link or passing vendor-specificinformation using the optional data field.

- The information commands are used to solicit implementation-specific information from a remote L2CAP entity.

Quality of Service

The QoS parameter in L2CAP defines a traffic flow specification based on RFC1363.10 In essence, a flow specification is a set of parameters that indicate a performance level that the transmitter will attempt to achieve. When included in a Configuration Request, this option describes the outgoing traffic flow from the device sending the request to the device receiving it. When included in a positive Configuration Response, this option describes the incoming

traffic flow agreement as seen from the device sending the response. When included in a negative Configuration Response, this option describes the preferred incoming traffic flow from the perspective of the device sending the response. The flow specification consists of the following parameters: GI Service type

- Token rate (bytes/second)
- Token bucket size (bytes)
- Peak bandwidth (bytes/second)
- Latency (microseconds)
- (II Delay variation (microseconds)

The service type parameter indicates the level of service for this flow. A value of 0 indicates that no traffic will be transmitted on this channel. A value of 1 indicates best effort service; the device will transmit data as quickly as possible but with no guarantees about performance. A value of 2 indicates a guaranteed service; the sender will transmit data that conform to the remaining QoS parameters. The token rate and token bucket size parameters define a token bucket scheme that is often used in QoS specifications. The advantage of this scheme is that it provides concise description of the peak and average traffic load the recipient can expect and it also provides a convenient mechanism by which the sender can implement the traffic flow policy.

A token bucket traffic specification consists of two parameters: a token replenishment rate R and a bucket size B. The token rate R specifies the continually sustainable data rate; that is, over a relatively long period of time, the averagedata rate to be supported for this flow is R. The bucket size B specifies theamount by which the data rate can exceed R for short periods of time. The exactcondition is as follows: During any time period T, the amount of data sent cannotexceed RT + B.

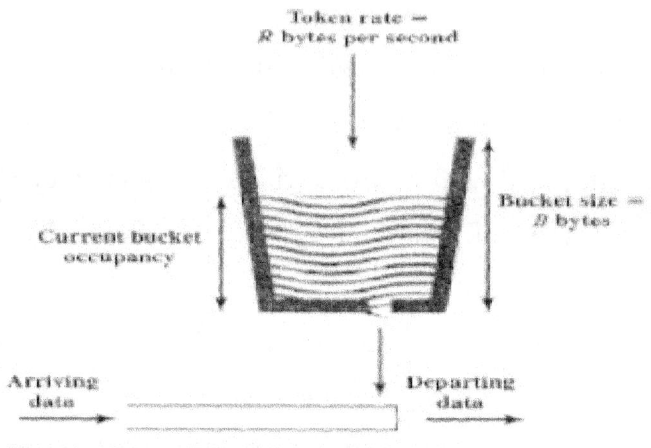

Figure 15.16   Token Bucket Scheme

figure 15.16 illustrates this scheme and explains the use of the term bucket. Thebucket represents a counter that indicates the allowable number of bytes of data thatcan be sent at any time. The bucket fills with byte tokens at the rate of R (i.e., thecounter is incremented R times per second), up to the bucket capacity (up to themaximum counter value). Data arrive from the L2CAP user and are assembled intopackets, which are queued for transmission. A packet may be transmitted if there aresufficient byte tokens to match the packet size. If so, the packet is transmitted and thebucket is drained of the corresponding number of tokens. If there are insufficienttokens available, then the packet exceeds the specification for this flow. The treatmentfor such packets is not specified in the document; typically, the packet will simply be queued for transmission until sufficient tokens are available.Over the long run, the rate of data allowed by the token bucket is R. However,if there is an idle or relatively slow period, the bucket capacity builds up, so that atmost an additional B bytes above the stated rate can be accepted. Thus, B is a measureof the degree of burstiness of the data flow that is allowed.For L2CAP, a value of zero for the two parameters implies that the tokenscheme is not needed for this application and will not be used. A value of all 1s is thewild card value. For best effort service, the wild card indicates that the requestor wantsas large a token or as large a token bucket size, respectively, as the responder willgrant. For guaranteed service, the wild card indicates that the maximum data rate orbucket size, respectively, is available at the time of the request. The peak bandwidth, expressed in bytes per second, limits how fast packetsmay be sent back-to-back from applications. Some intermediate systems can takeadvantage of this information, resulting in more efficient resource allocation. Considerthat if the token bucket is full, it is possible for the flow to send a series ofback-to-back packets equal to the size of the token bucket. If the token bucket sizeis large, this back-to-back run may be long enough to exceed the recipient's capacity.To limit this effect, the maximum transmission rate bounds how fast successivepackets may be placed on the network.

The latency is the maximum acceptable delay between transmission of a bit bythe sender and its initial transmission over the air, expressed in microseconds.

The delay variation is the difference, in microseconds, between the maximumand minimum possible delay that a packet will experience. This value is used byapplications to determine the amount of buffer space needed at the receiving sidein order to restore the original data transmission pattern. If a receiving applicationrequires data to be delivered in the same pattern that the data were transmitted, itmay be necessary for the receiving host briefly to buffer data as they are receivedso that the receiver can restore the old transmission pattern. An example of this isa case where an application wishes to send and transmit data such as voice samples,which are generated and played at regular intervals. The amount of bufferspace that the receiving host is willing to provide determines the amount of variationin delay permitted for individual packets within a given flow

4.16 IEEE 802.15.

The IEEE 802.15 Working Group for Wireless Personal Area Networks (PANs) wasformed to develop standards for short range wireless PANs (WPANs).A PAN is communicationsnetwork within a small area in which all of the devices on the networkare typically owned by one person or perhaps a family. Devices on a PAN may includeportable and mobile devices, such as PCs, Personal Digital Assistants (PDAs), peripherals,cell phones, pagers, and consumer electronic devices. The first effort by theworking group was to develop 802.15.1, with the goal of creating a formal standard ofthe Bluetooth specification; this standard was approved in 2002.Because most or all of the planned 802.15 standards would operate in the samefrequency bands as used by 802.11

devices, both the 802.11 and 802.15 workinggroups were concerned about the ability of these various devices to successfullycoexist. The 802.15.2 Task Group was formed to develop recommended practices forcoexistence. This work resulted in a recommended practices document in 2003.Following the 802.15.1 standard, the 802.15 work went in two directions. The802.15.3 task group is interested in developing standards for devices that are lowcost and low power compared to 802.11 devices, but with significantly higher datarates than 802.15.1. An initial standard for 802.15.3 was issued in 2003 and, as of thiswriting, work continues on 802.15.3a, which will provide higher data rates than802.15.3, using the same MAC layer. Meanwhile, the 802.15.4 task group developeda standard for very low cost, very low power devices at data rates lower than802.15.1, with a standard issued in 2003.Figure 15.17 shows the current status of the 802.15 work. Each of the threewireless PAN standards has not only different physical layer specifications but differentrequirements for the MAC layer. Accordingly, each has a unique MAC specification.Figure 15.18, based on one in [ZHEN04], gives an indication of the relativescope of application of the wireless LAN and PAN standards. As can be seen,

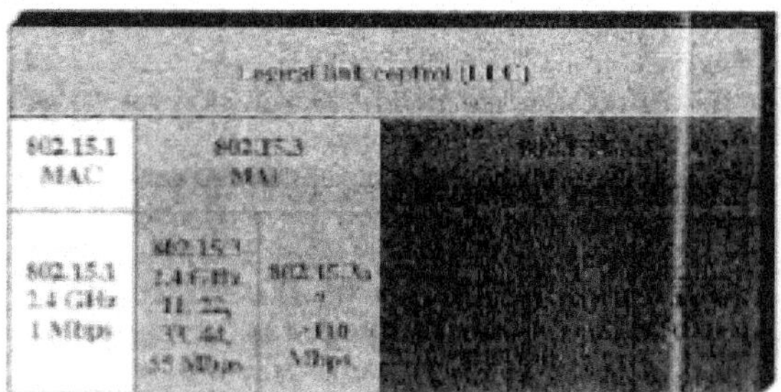

Figure 15.17   IEEE 802.15 Protocol Architecture

the 802.15 wireless PAN standards are intended for very short range, up to about10 m, which enables the use of low power, low cost devices. This section provides an overview of 802.15.3 and 802.15.4.

4.17 IEEE 802.15.3

The 802.15.3 task group is concerned with the development of high data rateWPANs. Examples of applications that would fit a WPAN profile but would alsorequire a relatively high data rate include [GILB04]

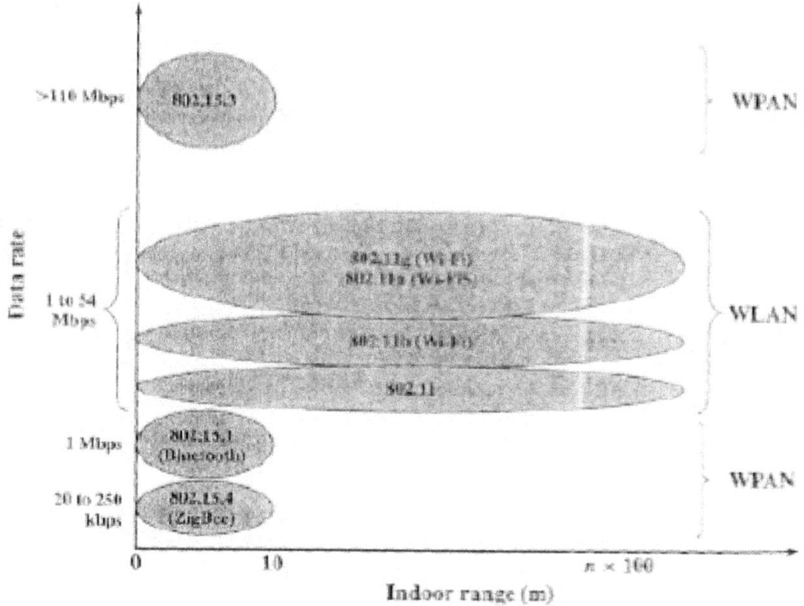

Figure 15.18 Wireless Local Networks

- Connecting digital still cameras to printers or kiosks

- Laptop to projector connection

- Connecting a personal digital assistant (PDA) to a camera or PDA to a printer

- Speakers in a 5:1 surround-sound system connecting to the receiver

- Video distribution from a set-top box or cable modem

- Sending music from a CD or MP3 player to headphones or speakers

- Video camera display on television

- Remote view finders for video or digital still cameras

These applications are mainly in the consumer electronics area and generatethe following requirements:

- Short range: On the order of 10m.

- High throughput: Greater than 20 Mbps to support video and/or multichannel audio.

- Low power usage: To be useful in battery-powered portable devices.

- Low cost: To be reasonable for inexpensive consumer electronic devices.

- QoS (quality of service) capable: To provide guaranteed data rate and otherOoS features for applications sensitive to throughput or latency.

- Dynamic environment: Refers to a piconet architecture in which mobile,portable, and stationary devices

- enter and leave the piconet often. For mobiledevice, a speed of less than 7 kilometers per hour is addressed.

- Simple connectivity: To make networking easy and eliminate the need for a technically sophisticated user.

- Privacy: To assure the user that only the intended recipients can understandwhat is being transmitted. These requirements are not readily met with an IEEE 802.11 network, whichwas not designed with this set of applications and requirements in mind.

Table 15.10 IEEE 802.15.3 Physical Layer Characteristics

Modulation	Coding	Data Rate
QPSK	8-state TCM	11 Mbps
DQPSK	None	22 Mbps
16-QAM	8-state TCM	33 Mbps
32-QAM	8-state TCM	44 Mbps
64-QAM	8-state TCM	55 Mbps

QPSK = quadrature phase-shift keying
DQPSK = differential QPSK
QAM = quadrature amplitude modulation
TCM = trellis-coded modulation

Mediuul Access Control An 802.15.3 network consists of a collection of devices(DEVs). One of the DEVs also acts as a piconet coordinator (PNC). The PNCassigns time for connections between devices; all commands are between the PNCand DEVs. Note the contrast between a PNC and an 802.11 access point (AP). TheAP provides a link to other networks and acts as a relay point for all MAC frames.The PNC is used to control access to the time resources of the piconet and is notinvolved in the exchange of data frames between DEVs.The OoS feature of the 802.15.3 MAC layer is based on the use of a TDMA (time division multiple access) architecture with the provision of guaranteed timeslots (GTSs).Physical Layer The 802.15.3 physical layer operates in the 2.4-GHz band, using five modulation formats with an 11 Mbaud symbol rate to achieve data rates from11 to 55 Mbps. Table 15.10 summarizes the key parameters. The most significantaspect of the scheme is the use of trellis -coded modulation (TCM). TCM is an oldtechnique, used in voice-grade telephone network modems. In the remainder of thissubsection, we provide an overview ofTCM.

Before proceeding, we briefly review some definitions from Chapter 6(Table 6.1).A bit I s the fundamental unit that takes on the values 0 or 1. A signal element,or symbol, is that part of a signal that occupies the shortest interval of a signalingcode; typically, it is a pulse of constant frequency, phase, and amplitude andmay represent one or more bits.

The signaling rate is measured in signaling elementsper second, or baud.In all of the approaches to transmission that we have seen so far in this book,signal encoding, or modulation, is performed separately from encoding for forwarderror correction. Furthermore, error control is achieved by adding additional bits tothe data bits, which has the effect of lower the data transmission rate per channelbandwidth. When faced with a combination of a channel of limited bandwidth and ahigh data rate requirement, an effective approach is to combine modulation andcoding and treat them as a single entity. This approach is referred to asTCM and hasthree basic features:

The number of different signal elements used is larger than what is requiredfor the given modulation scheme and data rate. The additional signal elementsallow redundancy for forward error correction without sacrificingdata rate. Convolutional coding is used to introduce dependency between successive signalelements, such that only certain sequences of signal elements are allowed. Decoding is done by modeling the coder as a trellis and using a Viterbi-typedecoding algorithm to perform error correction.The concepts mentioned in points (2) and (3) are discussed in Section 8.3.

Recall that the convolutional code gives rise to a state transition diagram that canbe laid out in a trellis pattern. Also, decoding involves use of a Viterbi algorithm, typically with a metric based on Hamming distance. In the case of TCM, the metric used is Euclidean distance. We next explain these concepts using a simple examplebased on a QPSK modulation scheme. Keep in mind that TCM can be used withmore complex modulation schemes, such s QAM. Any analog modulation scheme based on phase and/or amplitude, such asPSK or QAM, can be defined by a two-dimensional layout that indicates thephase and amplitude of each signal element. Recall from Chapter 6 that QPSK,uses phase shifts separated by multiples of 7T/2 (90°) to define signal elements

$$
\text{QPSK} \quad s(t) = \begin{cases}
A\cos\left(2\pi f_c t + \dfrac{\pi}{4}\right) & 11 \\[1em]
A\cos\left(2\pi f_c t + \dfrac{3\pi}{4}\right) & 01 \\[1em]
A\cos\left(2\pi f_c t - \dfrac{3\pi}{4}\right) & 00 \\[1em]
A\cos\left(2\pi f_c t - \dfrac{\pi}{4}\right) & 10
\end{cases}
$$

Each signal element represents two bits rather than one. Figure 15.19a shows thisscheme on a graph, where each signal element is represent by a point at unit distancefrom the origin, representing amplitude, and at an angle from the horizontal,representing phase. The minimum Euclidean distance between signal elements onthe graph is a measure of the difficulty of decoding the signal. Of course, in the caseof a pure PSK scheme, such as QPSK, the minimum phase angle between signal elementsis an equivalent measure. However, in more complex schemes, such as QAM,signal elements will differ both by phase and amplitude, and so the more generalmeasure of Euclidean distance is used.

ForTCM, we expand the number of signal points to eight (Figure 15.19b), separatedby a minimum of 45°. This would seem to make the decoding problem worse,because now the decoder must be able to distinguish a phase shift of 45° rather thana phase shift of 90°. However, the TCM code can be defined in such a way as to prohibitphase shifts of less than 90°. Thus we have not lost any discrimination power.Furthermore, the use of an additional bit adds redundancy which, if coded properly,allows for forward error correction so as to reduce errors.Figure 15.19c shows the way in which convolutional encoding is used. Input is taken two bits At a time to produce a signal element. One of the bits, designated al (n) for the nth pair of input bits, bypasses the convolutional encoder. The other bit of thepair, ao(n), passes through a (2,1,3) encoder (compare Figure 8.9a).

The two encoderoutput bits are combined with the passed-through bit to produce a 3-bit output that designatesone of the eight signal elements. Figure 15.19d shows the allowable state transitionsusing a trellis diagram (compare Figure 8.10). The four possible states are definedby the two preceding input bits. Thus, state 10 corresponds to ao(n - 1) = 1 andao(n - 2) = O. The transition from a state is determined by the two input bits and eachtransition produces three output bits and a move to a new state. For example, one of thetransitions from state 00 to state 10 is labeled 011010 (90°). The first part of the labelrefers to the two input bits: al (n) = 0 and ao(n) = 1. The second part of the label refersto the three output bits: b2(n) = 0, b1(n) = 1, bo(n) = O. The final part of the labelindicates the phase shift corresponding to the three output bits. For states 01 and 11, thefirst part of the label is not included but left as an exercise for the reader. Note that successivestate transitions are constrained to produce a minimum phase shift of 90°.

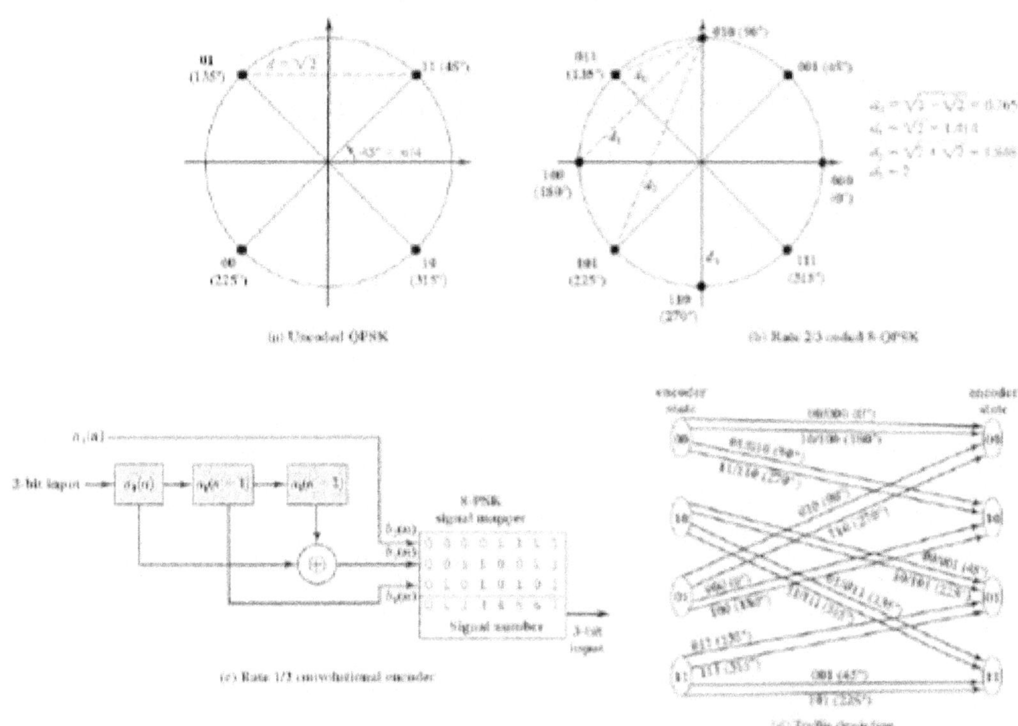

Figure 15.19   Example of Trellis-Coded Modulation

Table 15.11   Sequence and Error Determination for Example 15.1

States	Signals	Symbol Errors (°)	Total Error (°)
10-01-10-01	1-4-1	2.5, 62.5, 12.5	77.5
10-01-10-11	1-4-3	2.5, 62.5, 102.5	167.5
10-01-00-00	1-6-0	2.5, 27.5, 32.5	62.5
10-01-00-10	1-6-2	2.5, 27.5, 57.5	87.5
10-11-11-11	3-5-1	92.5, 17.5, 12.5	122.5
10-11-11-01	3-5-3	92.5, 17.5, 102.5	212.5
10-11-01-10	3-7-0	92.5, 72.5, 32.5	197.5
10-11-01-00	3-7-2	92.5, 72.5, 57.5	222.5

IEEE 802.15.3a

The WPAN Higher Rate Alternate PHY Task Group (TG3a) is chartered to draftand publish a new standard that will provide a higher speed (110 Mbps or greater)PHY amendment to the draft P802.15.3 standard. This will address streaming videoand other multimedia Applications. The new

PHY will use the P802.15.3 MAC withlimited modification. As of the time of writing, this work is still in progress.

IEEE 802.15.4

The WPAN Low Rate Task Group (TG4) is chartered to investigate a low data ratesolution with multimonth to multiyear battery life and very low complexity. Thisstandard specifies two physical layers: an 868-MHz/915-MHz direct sequencespread spectrum PHY and a 2.4-GHz direct sequence spread spectrum PHY. The2.4-GHz PHY supports an over air data rate of 250 kb/s and the 868-MHz/915-MHz

Chapter -5

MOBILE DATA NETWORKS

Mobile data networks we refer to those services, technologies, and standards that are related to data services over wide area coverage areas spanning more than the local area or campus. Examples include metropolitan area wireless data ser- vices such as Metricom's Ricochet service and those that operate over the same coverage areas as cellular networks such as CDPD or GPRS

5.1 INTRODUCTION

SMS services can also be considered a part of these systems. Short messaging services are embedded in digital cellular systems such as GSM. These services use the 10-digit keypad of the mobile terminal to type and display a message and use the digital cellular network facilities to deliver the message. In traditional mobile data services, the subscriber uses computer keyboards to enter the message. Considering this larger picture for mobile data services or wireless WANs, as shown in Figure 9.1 we can classify mobile data networks into three categories: independent, shared, and overlay networks based on the way they relate to the cellular infrastructure.

5.1.1 Independent Mobile Data

Independent networks have their own spectrum that is not coordinated with any other service and their own infrastructure that is not shared with any other service. These networks are divided into two groups according to the status of their operating frequency band. The first group uses independent spectrum in licensed bands. Examples of such networks are ARDIS and Mobitex, and historically they were the first mobile data services that were introduced. Such networks were not economically successful because the revenues generated, mostly from the vertical applications, could not justify the cost of the implementation of the infrastructure. For these networks to survive, either a sizable vertical market is needed, or the cost of implementation of the infrastructure should be reduced, or a horizontal killer application is needed. The TETRA network (see Table 1.7) is designed for public safety application that is a prosperous vertical market. It was defined by the ETS1

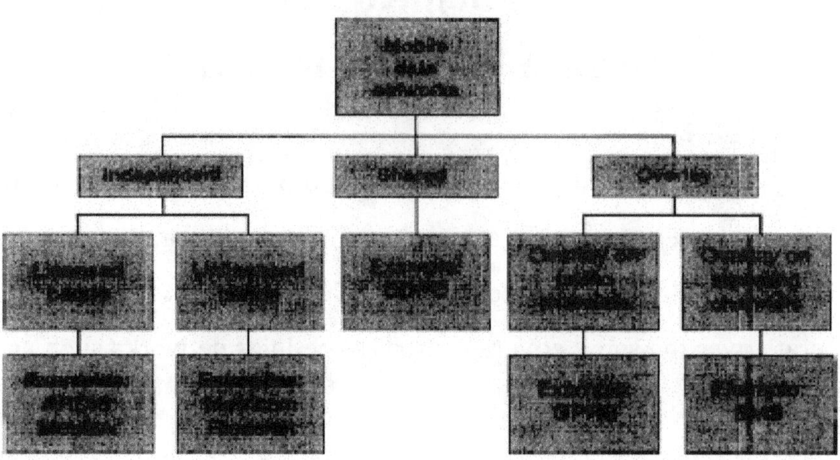

Figure 5.1 Classification of mobile data networks.

to meet the needs of professional mobile radio users. As a result, in spite of the fates of the previously mentioned mobile data projects, at the time of this writing, a number of companies in EU are engaged in manufacturing TETRA equipment. These companies have already reached agreements with the public safety organiza- tions in Europe to use manufactured equipment in their future public land mobile data networks. Reduction of the cost of the infrastructure and killer applications are envisioned in the shared and overlay systems that are discussed in the following two sections.

The second group of independent mobile data networks makes use of unli- censed spectrum that is shared among a variety of applications and users. Metri- com's Ricochet service, which used the 915 MHz unlicensed ISM band spectrum, was an example of this service. This service was deployed in airports and some met- ropolitan areas for wireless Internet access.

5.1.2 Shared Mobile Data

These networks share the spectrum and part of the infrastructure with an already existing voice-oriented analog service. The services operate in the same radio chan - nels used for analog voice, but they have their own air-interface and MAC proto - cols. In addition to dedicated channels for data, these mobile data services can also use the available unused voice channels. These systems share an existing system in- frastructure, therefore the initial investment is not huge, and it could be made as gradually as possible. Initial deployment could be made in areas where there is subscriber demand and subsequent penetration into other areas is considered as the customer base enlarges. The CDPD service (see Table 1.7 for overview), which shares spectrum and part of the infrastructure with AMPS, is an example of such networks. It does have an independent air-interface and MAC layer, along with ad- ditional infrastructure required for operation of data services. The CDPD standard was completed in the early 1990s, and the expectation was that by the year 2000, nearly 13 million subscribers would be using it. However, this expectation was never met, and generating income remained as the main obstacle for this service. Recently CDPD services have picked up with the availability of modems for palm computing devices. In the next section, we provide the details of implementation of CDPD to familiarize the reader with the implementation aspects of a data-oriented service.

5.1.3 Overlay Mobile Data

The last group of mobile data networks is an overla y on existing networks and ser- vices. This means that the data service will not only make use of the spectrum allo- cated for another service but also the MAC frames and air-interface of an existing voice-oriented digital cellular system. GPRS and GSM's SMS are examples of such overlays. They make use of free time slots available within the traffic channels and signaling channels in GSM. This way, the amount of new infrastructure required is reduced to a bare minimum. Most of the extra components required are imple- mented in software, making it inexpensive and easy to deploy. GPRS type of ser- vices uses computer keyboards to communicate longer messages, and SMS use the cellular phone dialing keypad to communicate short messages. Sections 9.3 and 9.4 of this chapter provide further details on GPRS and SMS.

5.2 CDPD [TAY97], [CDPD95], (SAL99a,b]

has been one of the longest surviving wide area mobile data technologies worldwide. It is a shared mobile dat‹t network that shares part of the infrastructure and the entire spectrum with AMPS in the United States. It is, however, an open standard, making its implementation easier and more widespread. CDPD initially had mixed success because the coverage was not universal, the data rates low, and prices prohibitive. CDPD has been more popular with vertical applications such as inventory for vending machines, fleet management, and so on. With the emergence of new handheld computers and palm-based devices, CDPD is making resurgence as a service for low data rate text- based Web, email, and short messaging horizontal applications. For example, modems are available for popular PalmOS and Windows CE devices that provide unlimited CDPD

In 1991, McCaw and IBM came up with the idea of developing a packet data overlay on AMPS. By the end of 1991, a telephone network—oriented prototype ar-chitecture was in place. This preliminary version was discussed in 1992 at a CDPD technical conference in Santa Clara by which point of time, CDPD als‹n had the support of several regional telephone companies such as Ameritech, Bell Atlantic, GTE, McCaw, Nynex, PacTel, Southwest Bell, and US West. The first field trials were held in the San Francisco Bay area in 1992. At the same time, there was a recognition of the complexity of the telephony oriented architecture, and so open standards based on data networking standards and the OSI model were investi- gated around this time. Ultimately the latter approach based on data networking standards was selected, and the first official specifications were released in July 1993. The specifications were based on an open architecture, and the mobility man- agement technique closely follows and is a precursor of the Mobile-IP standard. This specification was accepted by several of the major cellular telephony service providers. The CDPD forum was created in 1994, which attracted about 100 mem- bers. In 1995, release 1.1 of the CDPD standard came out. CDPD has been de- ployed by many of the former regional Bell operating companies as well as AT&T wireless.

5.2.1 What Is CDPD?

The design of CDPD was based on several design objectives that are often repeated in designing overlay networks or new networks. Some of these design goals are dis- cussed. A lot of emphasis was laid on open architectures and reusing as much of the existing RF infrastructure as possible. The design goals of CDPD included location independence and independence from service provider, so that coverage could be maximized; application transparency and multiprotocol support, interoperability be- tween products from multiple vendors, minimal invention, and use of COTS tech- nology as far as possible; and optimal usage of RF where air-interface efficiency is given priority over other resources. CDPD used primitive RF technology for cost reasons, and for this purpose the well-known GMSK modulation scheme was cho- sen. The raw signaling rate is

19.2 kbps, and with Reed-Solomon (RS) coding the ef- fective data rate is 14.4 kbps full duplex before control overhead. The design was intended to be evolutionary and based on the OS I model with support for native IP, so that if new transport layer or application layer protocols were implemented there was no need for changes. The prominent features of CDPD have been its openness and freedom from all proprietary technology, support for multivendor interoper- ability, and simplicity in design. There is, however, constraint on the design of CDPD because it is a shared mobile data network and AMPS has priority over the usage of the spectrum. CDPD employs a technique called RF sniffing to detect whether an AMPS call is trying to access a frequency channel, and hopping to move from such a band to another to give the voice call priority. About 20 percent of AMPS frequency channels that can be used for CDPD are idle at a given time.

When the telephone system selects a new channel for a voice call, if CDPD is using that channel it should exit within 40 ms. The MDBS should find an alternative channel and allocate it to the mobile end-system. The MDBS informs the mobile that the downlink is being changed to another channel and hops to this channel. A timed hop is a mandatory channel hop that is planned to happen after a fixed time. A forced hop is due to a voice call request. If no channels are avail- able, CDPD enters "blackout."

5.2.2 CDPD Services

In a manner similar to our discussion of GSM, we start with the services that CDPD offers. Network services are the basic form of services offered by CDPD. This is simply support for transfer of data from one location to another via popular or standard network layer protocols. In particular, CDPD supports connectionless layer 3 protocols (IP or connectionless network protocol—CLNP) and in that sense acts simply as a wireless extension to the Internet.

Network support services are ser- vices necessary to maintain the operation of the mobile data network such as man- agement, accounting, security, and so on. These services include mobility and radio resource management and are usually transparent to the user. Such services add "intelligence" to the network. The last category of services includes network appli- cation services. These are value added services such as limited size messaging on top of the network services and need explicit subscription.

5.2.3 Reference Architecture in CDPD

Figure 5.2 shows the reference architecture for CDPD. There are three key CDPD interfaces that form logical boundaries for a CDPD service provider's network. They are essential for the proper operation of CDPD. There are some interfaces internal to the "cloud." Such interfaces are only recommended, and a service provider can implement them differently. Each interface specifies a protocol stack corresponding to the OSI model and primitives are defined at each "layer" that can request and obtain services from the layer below.

5.2.4 Interface Details

The A-Interface is the air link interface, and parts 400—409 of the CDPD spec-ifications specify it. The E-InterfaCe is the external interface, and it is the means by which CDPD operates with the rest of data network. Over this interface IP and CLNP are supported, and IPv6 will be supported as it becomes deploye d. Other protocols are supported by encapsulation because they are outside the CDPD specs. Mobility is transparent to the network beyond the E-interface. The I- Interface is the interservice provider interface. The North American market is partitioned into a multiplicity of service providers and the I-interface enables seam- less nationwide service. It supports all of the E-interface protocols plus two CDPD specific protocols—the mobile network locatian protocol (MNLP) whic-h is the

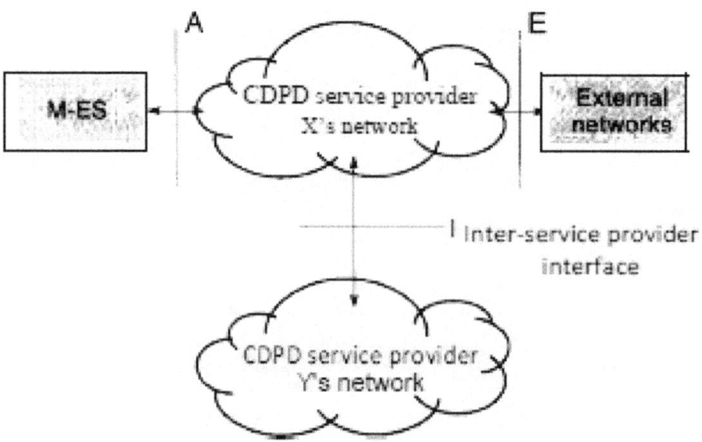

Figure 5.2 Reference architecture for CDPD

protocol by which mobile users from one system are supported by another system and is a key piece of CDPD mobility management scheme.

Network management and accounting protocols are also defined at the 1-interface. All the protocols are based on CLNP (except reverse channel lP packets).

5.2.5 Physical Architecture

The physical elements of the CDPD architecture and their relationship with the three interfaces are shown in Figure 9.3. These elements are the mobile end system, the mobile data BS, and the mobile data intermediate system, along with some servers for accounting and network management and databases called the mobile home and mobile serving functions.

The mobile-end system (M-ES) is the ultimate source and destination of pro- tocol data units (PDUs). It is equipped with a CDPD radio and software, and ex- ample M-ESs are telemetry devices, laptops, vending machines, and so on. In the M-ES, protocols are specified up to layer 3. An M-ES can be full duplex or half du- plex and supports all standard APIs. Communication is implemented via conven- tional means like sockets, NDIS, and so on. An M-ES has three functional units: subscriber unit (SU), subscriber identity module (SIM), and mobile application subsystem (MAS). The subscriber unit establishes and maintains data communica- tion, executes CDPD air-interface protocols, and includes administrative and man- agement layers. The SIM is a repository of identity and authentication credentials, and the SIM card is very similar to GSM. In fact it is based on GSM standards. The MAS deals with the higher layer protocols and can perform remote database ac- cess, email, vending machine inventory, and so on. The MASs span a wide range of

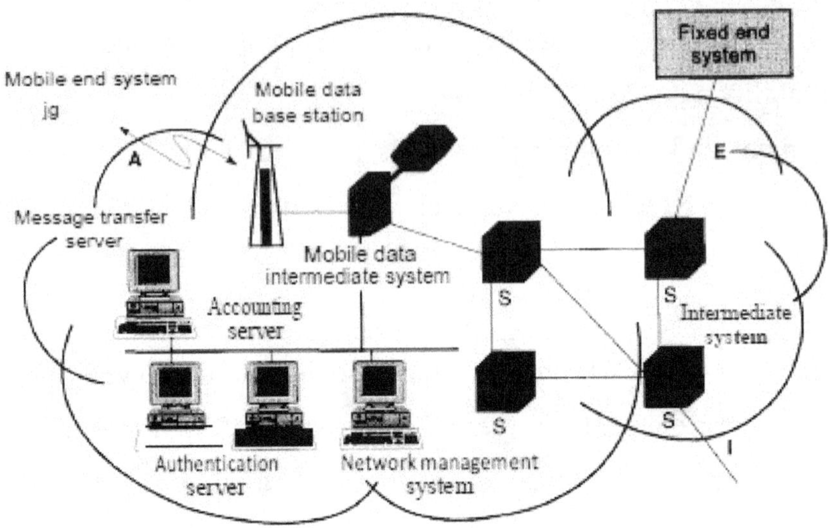

Figure 5.3 Physical elements in the CDPD architecture.

features. Some support both CDPD and an AMPS modem. Others can support voice communications as well. The M-ES employs a variety of power sources such as internal batteries, vehicular power source, or a laptop-based PC card.

The MDBS is the system end (network side) of the MAC sublayer over the air interface. It is equivalent to the BSS in GSM and is pretty much the BS electronics for CDPD. It is also like an Ethernet hub and acts as a link layer relay or bridge. It communicates with the M-ES through the A-interface and performs modulation of data bits and demodulation of the RF signal. It actively participates in the medium access scheme called digital sense multiple access (DSMA) (see Chapter 4). It is Layer 3 addressable for network management.

The MD-IS is the focal point of CDPD mobility management and packet for-warding. It has a mobile serving function (MSF) that serves as the foundation for registration of a mobile and a mobile home function (MHF) that serves as an anchor point for locating a mobile. It tracks the local point of access of the mobile de- vices and is responsible for presenting the external interface on behalf of the M-ES and for routing all traffic to and from the M-ES. It also performs accounting ser- vices. The MDBS to MD-IS interface is not specified though there are recommendations. Because it is internal to the CDPD cloud, proprietary implementations are possible although most service providers follow the recommendations. The inter- mediate system (IS) is a fancy name for

137

a router, and it handles packet f‹irwarding. Border ISs are further required to provide security filtering and access control functions that are not part of the CDPD specifications.

The fixed-end system (FES) is a conventional network node th‹tt includes most PCs, workstations, and so on that are transport layer peers of the M-ES. An Internal F-ES operates within the boundaries of the CDPD network and is under the control of the service provider. It usually operates functionally in the role of administrative servers and value-added servers. This is an example of the flexibility of CDPD.

Internal FESs include an accounting server (AS), an authentication server, a directory server, a network management system, and a message transfer system. For example, the AS is in charge of collection and distribution of accounting data such as packet count, packet size, source and destination address, geographic in- formation, time of transmission, and so on. CDPD employs pay by the byte (air- link usage) charging rather than time of connection. The network management system is based on general network management schemes of the OSI model using the common management interface protocol (CMIP), or optionally, simple net- work management protocol (SNMPv2).

5.2.6 Mobility Support in CDPD

As in the case of most mobile networks, mechanisms are in place in CDPD to sup-port the mobile environment. We consider radio resources, mobility m‹inagement, and security in this section. Mobility Management Handoff in CDPD occurs when an M-ES moves from one cell to another or if the CDPD channel quality deteriorates, the current CDPD channel is requested by an AMPS voice call (forced hop), or the load on CDPD channels in the current cell is much more than the load on the channels in an overlapping cell.

The physical layer of CDPD provides the ability to tune to a specific RF channel, the ability to measure the received signal strength indication (RSS I) of the received signal, the ability to set the power of the M-ES transmitted signal to a specified level, and the ability to suspend and resume monitoring of RF channels in the M-ES. Both uplink and downlink channels are slotted. There is no con- tention on the downlink, and the MDBS will transmit link layer frames sequen- tially. On the uplink, a DSMA/CD (digital sense multiple-access with collision detection) protocol is employed. Collision detection is at the BS and informed to the MHs on the downlink.

On the downlink, multiple cell configuration messages are broadcast, including for the given cell and its neighbors, the cell identifier, a reference channel for the cell, a value that provides the difference in power be- tween the reference channel, and the actual CDPD data channel, a RSS bias to compare the RSS of the reference channels of the given cell and adjacent cells, and a list of channels allocated to CDPD within the given cell. RSS measurements are always done on the reference channel because the CDPD channel list may keep changing [CDPD95].

Upon powering on, the MH scans the air and locks on to the strongest "ac- ceptable" CDPD channel stream it can find and registers with the mobile-data in- termediate system (MD-IS) that serves the base station. This is done via the mobile network registration protocol (MNRP) whereby the MH announces its presence and also authenticates itself. Registration protects against fraud and enables CDPD network to know the mobile location and update its mobility databases. The MH continues to listen to the CDPD channel unless it (or the CDPD network) initiates a handoff.

CDPD mobility management is based on principles similar to mobile-IP. The details are shown in Figure 9.4. The MD-IS is the central element in the process. An MD-IS is logically separated into a home MD-IS and a serving MD-IS. A home MD-IS contains a subscription database for its geographic area.

Each subscriber is registered in his home MD-IS associated with his home area. The IP address of a subscriber points to his home MD-IS. At the home MD-IS, an MHF maintains in- formation about the current location of MHs associated with (homed at) that home MD-IS.

The MHF also encapsulates any packet that is addressed to an M-ES homed with it directing it to an MSF associated with the serving MD-IS, whose serving area the M-ES is currently visiting.

A serving MD-lS manages one serving area. Mobile data BSs that provide coverage in this area are connected to the serv- ing MD- IS, whose MSF contains information about all subscribers currently visit- ing the area and registered with it.

The MSF employs the mobile network location protocol (MNLP) to notify the MHF about the presence of the M-ES in its service area. The channel stream in which a subscriber is active is also indicated.

The MSF decapsulates forwarded packets and routes them to the correct channel stream in the cell.

MSF: Mobile Serving Function

MHF: Mobile Home Function

MD-IS: Mobile Data Intermediate System MNLP:

Mobile Network Location Protocol MNRP:

Mobile Network Registration Protocol

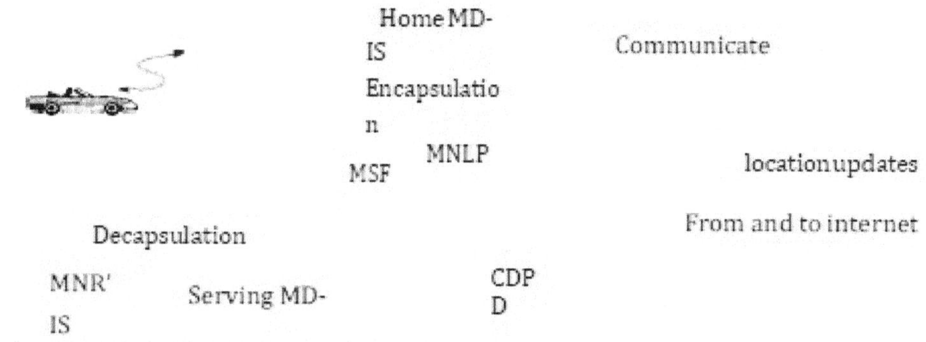

Figure 5.4 Mobility management in CDPD.

The handoff procedure in CDPD is shown in Figure 9.5. The handoff' initiation and decision in CDPD are as follows. The handoff is mobile controlled. "Fhe M-ES always measures the signal strength of the reference channel [SAL99b]. An M-ES scans for alternative channels when its signal deteriorates. Because certain cells may have large shadowing effects within them, the operator can set a RSSI scan value to determine when a M-ES should start scanning for alternative channels. An M-ES will ignore a drop in signal level if the RSSI scan value is large enough or start scanning

Figure 9.5 Handoff procedure in CDPD.

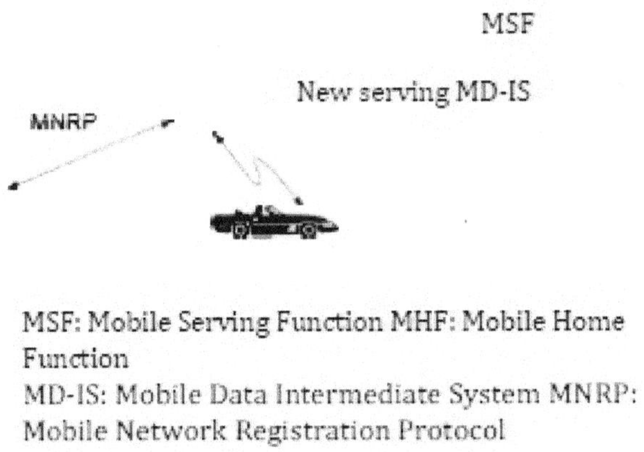

MSF: Mobile Serving Function MHF: Mobile Home Function

MD-IS: Mobile Data Intermediate System MNRP:

Mobile Network Registration Protocol for alternative channels if it is small. This value is also useful (and should be made small) when the signal strength does not drop even when the M-ES has moved well into a neighboring cell. When additional thresholds for RSSI hysteresis, block error rate (BLER) and/or symbol error rate (SER) are reached, the M-ES will go through a list of channels of adjacent cells that the current BS is broadcastinp• and tune in to the one with the best signal strength. The M-ES informs the new BS that it has en- tered its cell. The mobile serving function of the new MD -IS uses a redirect -request and redirect-confirm procedure with the mobile home function of M-ES. The mo- bile home function also informs the old serving MD-IS about the handoff and di- rects it through its MSF to redirect packets it may have received for the M-ES to the new serving MD-IS or flush them. Depending on the nature of handoff (interoperator or intraoperator), the delay of registration and traffic redirection will vary.

5.2.7   Security

The security functions in CDPD are limited to data link confidentiality and M-ES authentication. There are some mechanisms for key management, the ability to upgrade, access control based on location, a network entity identifier (NE I), and screening lists.

CDPD authentication is performed by the mobile network registration proto- col management entit y (MME) that exists in both the MD-IS and M-ES. It uses the NEI along with an authentication sequence number (ASN) and an authentication random number (ARN) for authentication. The M-ES and network both maintain two sets of ARN/ASN-tuples (in case a fresh ARN is lost due to poor radio cover- age) . The shared historical record is the basis for authentication. It is updated every 24 hours. Authentication may be initiated at any time by the network.

CDPD confidentiality is based on encrypting all data using a secret key that is different in each session. The usual concept of using public key for exchanging keys and secret keys for block data encryption is employed. The session key generation is based on "Diffie-Hellman" key exchange with 256 bit values. It is, however, sus- ceptible to the man-in-the-middle attack. RC-4 is used for block data encryption, and it is not a very secure secret key algorithm. Consequently, security limitations exist in CDPD. The CDPD network is not authenticated to the mobile as mas- querading as a CDPD network is assumed to be impossible. Data confidentiality is not end-to-end, and it is assumed to be a higher layer issue. There are no mecha- nisms for data integrity, nonrepudiation, or traffic flow confidentiality.

5.2.8 Radio Resource Management

RRM is handled by a management layer in CDPD [SAL99b] and contains the procedures to handle the dynamically changing RF environment. In particular it takes care of (1) acquiring and releasing channels due to competition between CDPD and AMPS, and handoff from one cell to another or from one channel to another. Its function is to continuously provide the best possible RF channel between the M-ES and the fixed network. The procedures are distributed between the M-ES and the net- work. The element algorithms, and procedures reside in the MDBS on the network side. The RRM also ensures that transmission power levels are set dynamically to minimize cochannel interference and optimize communication quality on the reverse channel. In the MDBS, the RRM handles distribution of network configur‹ttion data, and power control data help the M-ES to track channel hops, perform handoffs, and satisfy power control requirements. On the M-ES side, the RRM has the algorithms and procedures to acquire and track CDPD forward channel transmissions, maintain the best possible CDPD channel in the area where the M-ES is located, and keep transmission power at the required level. All these may be assisted by data transmit- ted by the network. Unlike voice networks, the M-ES is supposed to handle RRM be- cause the nature of transmission is extremely bursty. As such, the RRM functionality can be provided with or without the assistance of data provided by the netwc›rk.

Example 5.4: Messaging for Power Control in CDPD

The channel stream identification (CSI) message (see Figure 9.6) on the downlink provides information about the current channel and also contains the following parameters: a cell identifier, a channel stream identifier, the service provider identity (SPI), a wide area service identifier (WASI), and finally a power product and maximum power level. The transmission power of the M-ES is calculated via the formula [SALOO]:

Transmission power (dBW) = Power product (dB) — 143 dBW — RSSI (clBW) RSSI is the received signal strength indication that is calculated from I he re-ceived signal.

5.2.9 Protocol Layers in CDPD

The CDPD standard specifies a protocol stack for CDPD as shown in I'igure 5.7. There are four layers: the physical layer, the MAC layer, the data link layer, and the subnetwork dependent convergence protocol (SNDCP) layer.

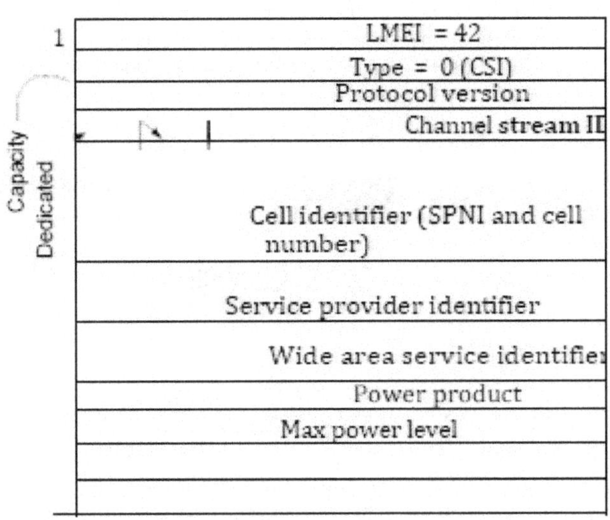

Figure 5.6 The channel stream identification message format.

The physical layer specifies two distinct one-way RF channels. The [forward Channel is from the MDBS to the M-ES and the reverse channel is tromp the M-ES to the MDBS.

They are shown in Figures 5.8 and 5.9, respectively. Each channel is 30 kHz wide and corresponds to the same frequencies as AMPS. The transmission is digital GMSK at 19.2 kbps.

Example 5.5: Error Control Coding in CDPD

The physical layer is robust by employing a (63,47) RS coding. On the forward channel, one RS-block is transmitted every 21.575 ms, so that the raw bit rate is 420 bits/21.875 ms = 19.2 kbps. Up to eight symbol errors can be corrected with this code, but the CDPD specifications suggest correcting only up to seven sym- t)o1 errors. The undetected symbol error rate is 2.75 1 bits

Data segment

bits = 6 bits / 47 symbols Add 8 bits to identify MDBS & MD-IS

378 bits = 6 bits / 63 symbols

(83,47) RS-coding with a 64-ary alphabet

420 bits = 7 x 6 + 378 bits

Figure 9.8 The forward channel in CDPD.

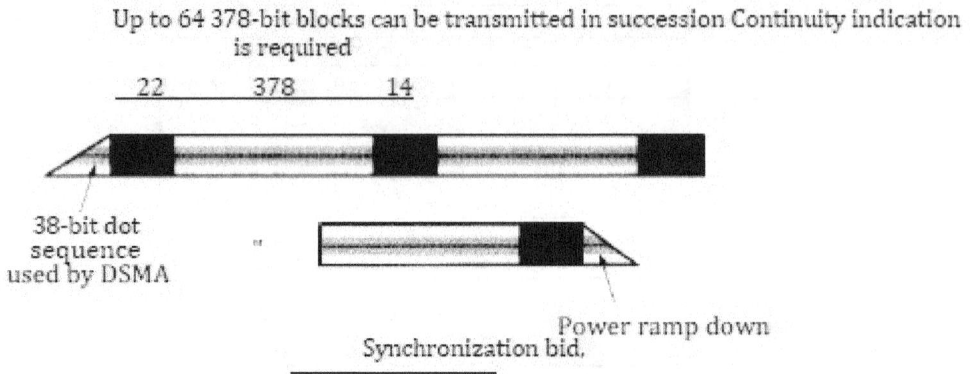

Figure 9.9 The reverse channel in CDPD.

The MAC layer follows the familiar CSMA/CD scheme typified by Ethernet. The forward channel has only one transmitter, the MDBS, and there is no con- tention for this channel. The reverse channel has multiple M-ESs competing for ac- cess. An M-ES may transmit on a channel whenever it has data to send and the channel is not already occupied by another transmission. The following steps are followed: (1) An M-ES must assess the state of the channel to see if it is available;

If the channel is occupied, there is a random back-off period (nonpersistent);

The M-ES transmits if the channel is free; and (4) If two MESs find the chan- nel free and transmit simultaneously, there is a collision that must be detected to ensure retransmission. On a wireless link, there are problems with collision detec- tion (see Chapter 4). Carrier sensing is easier at baseband than at RF frc'quencies. The receive and transmit frequencies are different. Also, transmissions from ground level can be detected at a tower but not at the ground level. Circuitry cost and power consumption become prohibitive for collision detection by a MES, so the channel-busy status and collision detection is enabled by the MDBS. A digital indicator is provided on the forward channel in order to indicate reverse channel status. This indicator is called the BUSY/IDLE indicator and it is set to BUSY whenever the MDBS senses reverse channel transmissions. The channels are slot- ted so that transmissions occur only in time slots. Another flag on the forward channel called decode status indicates whether the transmission was successfully de- coded. Five bits are used to indicate busy/idle status and M-ESs use a simple major- ity to decide whether the channel is busy or idle.

Example 5.6: Flexibility in the MAC Protocol

The MAC protocol specifies a Mindle Time that is the minimum amount tit time a mobile must wait after one burst to transmit again to ensure fairness. Two counts Mincount and Max count specify limits of back-off delay periods in the case where there are too many or too few users. For example, if Mincount = 4, on the first observation that the channel is busy or the first collision, the mobile backs off for a random number uniformly distributed between zero and 2' = 16 slots. On a consecutive observation of busy channel, the distribution changes to twice the number of slots, for instance, random in (0,52) slots. The value Maxcount — 8 im-plies, the maximum distribution interval is 2' = 256 slots. Max_blocks is the maxi-mum number of RS-blocks that can be transmitted in a burst. It's default value is 64, which implies that at most a 2 kbyte packet can be sent.

The data link layer uses the mobile data link protocol (MDLP) to connect the MD-IS and the M-ES. This is at the LLC (logical link control) layer equivalent of the b02.3 protocol. The "logical link" is identified by a "temporary equipment identifier" (TEI). The TEI reduces load on the air-interface and ensures privacy of the user. MDLP is similar to the LAPD of ISDN, and it uses a sliding window protocol. A selective reject mechanism is used. The sender has to retransmit only that frame that is acknowledged by an SREJ message. There is, however, no CRC check as in LAPD and the error control is shifted to the MAC layer.

Exarriple 9.7: Other Data Link Features
Zap frames are used by the MD-IS to disable transmissions from a mobile for a given period of time. This is in case a M-ES does not follow the CDPD protocol in

backing off or is not correctly working. A sleep mode is also available to power down if not transmitting to save battery life. The link layer is maintained in sus-pended mode, and all timers are saved. If a mobile does not transmit for a time period called T203 it is assumed to have gone to sleep. T203 is used to determine the "wake-up" time. Every T204 seconds the network broadcasts a list of TEIs that have outstanding data packets to receive. Before sleeping the mobile tracks the last T204 broadcast and wakes up at the next T204 to listen to the broatcast. After N203 TEI broadcasts, if a mobile is not up, the network discards the Pack-ets. Packet forwarding is also possiP›1c by storing it in the network for future transmissions.

The SNDCP maps MDLP services to those expected by IP or CLNP. It man- ages the difference between maximum data link frame size of 130 bytes, network packet size of up to 2048 bytes, and multiple network connections using the same MDLP. The functions of SNDCP include segmentation and reassembly, multiplex- ing, header compression, TCP/IP header compression using the Van Jacobson method, and the CLNP header compression using similar process and data encryp- tion. Details of CDPD protocols, message formats, and so on can be found in [TA Y97].

5.3 GPRS AND HIGHER DATA RAT£S

GPRS is an overlay on top of the GSM physical layer and network entities. It ex- tends data capabilities of GSM and provides connection to external packet data networks through the GSM infrastructure with short access time to the network.

5.3.1 What Is GPRS?

GPRS [KALOO], [CAI97], [BRA97] is an enhancement of the GSM. It uses exactly the same physical radio channels as GSM, and only new logical GPRS radio› channels are defined. Allocation of these channels is flexible: from one to eight radio interface timeslots can be allocated per TDMA frame. The active users share t'imeslots, and uplink and downlink are allocated separately. Physical channels are taken from the common pool of available channels in the cell. Allocation to circuit switched services and GPRS is done dynamically according to a "capacity on demand" principle. This means that the capacity allocation for GPRS is based on the actual need tor packet transfers. GPRS does not require permanently allocated physical channels. GPRS of- hers permanent connections to the Internet with volume based charging that enables a user to obtain a less expensive connection to the Internet. The GPRS MSs (termi- nals) are of three types. Class A terminals operate GPRS and other GSM services si- multaneously. Class B terminals can monitor all services, but operate either GPRS or another service, such as GSM, one at a time. Class C terminals operate only GPRS service. This way there are options to have high-end or low-end terminals.

GPRS has some limitations in that there is only a limited cell capacity for all users and speeds much lower in reality. There is no store and forward service in case the MS is not available. The more popular short messaging service provides this feature, as we shall see in the next section.

The adaptation of GPRS to the IS -136 TDMA cellular standard is called GPRS- 136. It is very similar to GPRS except that it uses 30 kHz physical channels instead of 200 kHz physical channels. Also there is no separate BSC. It can use co- herent 8-PSK in addition to u/4-DQPSK to increase throughput over a limited area. This concept is similar to the 2.5G data service called enhanced datii rates for glohal evolution (EDGE). Hooks in the standard allow the possibility of 16-QAM, IG-PSK, or 1G-DQ PSK in the future [SAROO].

5.3.1.1 GPRS Network Services

GPRS provides the following network services—point-to-multipoint (PTM-M) that is a multicast service to all subscribers in a given area, point-to-multipoint (PTM-G) that is a multicast service to predetermined group that may be dispersed over a geographic area, and point-to-point (PTP) service which is packet data transfer. This is of two types: connectionless based on IP and CLNP called PTP- CLNS and connection-oriented based on X.25 (PTP-CONS). GPRS also provides a bearer service for GSM's SMS discussed later in this chapter. There is also an anonymous access for MS at no charge. This is for example similar to an 500 num- ber service where an agency that charges toll could allow an MS to access its credit card verification service for free.

GPRS has parameters that specify a QoS based on service precedence, a pri- ority of a service in relation to another service (high, normal, and low), reliability, and transmission characteristics required. Three reliability cases are defined and four delay classes. Here delay is defined as the end-to-end delay between two MSs or between an MS and the interface to the network external to GPRS. The relia- bility and delay classes are outlined in Tables 9.1 and 9.2. Transmission character- istics are specified by the maximum and mean bit rates. The maximum bit rate value can be between 8 kbps and 11 Mbps. The mean bit rate value is 0.22 bps to 111 kbps.

5.3.2   Reference Architecture in GPRS

As already mentioned, GPRS reuses the GSM architecture to a very large extent. There are a few new network entities called GPRS support nodes (GSN) that are responsible for delivery and routing of data packets between the mobile station and external packet network. There are two types of GSNs, the serving GPRS sup- port node (SGSN) and the Gateway GPRS support node (GGSN).

These are com- parable to the MD-IS in CDPD. There is also a new database called the GPRS register (GR) that is colocated with the HLR. It stores routing information and maps the IMSI to a PDN address (lP address for example). Figure 9.10 shows this reference architecture.

The U,, interface is the air-interface and connects the MS to the BSS. The in- terface between the BSS and the SGSN is called the Gb interface and that between the SGSN and the GGSN is called the G,, interface. The SGSN is a router that is similar to the foreign agent in Mobile-IP. It controls access to MSs that may be at- tached to a group of BSCs. This is called a routing area (RA) or service area of the SGSN. The SGSN is responsible for delivery of packets to the MS in its service area and from the MS to the Internet. It also performs the logical link manage- ment, authentication, and charging functions. The GGSN acts as a logical interface to the Internet. It maintains routing information related to a MS, so that it can route packets to the SGSN servicing the MS. It analyses the PDN address of the MS and converts it to the corresponding IMSI and is equivalent to the HA in Mobile-IP.

5.3.3 Mobility Support in GPRS
 In a manner similar to GSM and CDPD, there are mechanisms in GPRS t‹i support mobility. We will discuss these issues in the following sections.

Class	Lost Packet	Dupifcated Packet	Out-of-Sequence Packet	Corrupted Packet
2	10*'	10*'	1(1*'	10''
3	10 '	10°''	10°'	10°'

Table 9.2 Delay Classes

Class	128 Byte Packet		1,024 Byte Packet	
	Mean Delay	95% Delay	Mean Delay	95 % Delhiy
1	< 0.5s fis	< 1.5s 25s	< 2s < 15s	7s 75s
2		250s	75s	e 375s
3	< 50s	Best	Best Effort	Best
4	Best Effort	Effort		Effort

5.3.3.1 Attachment Procedure

Before accessing GPRS services, the MS must register with the GPRS net-work and become "known" to the PDN. The MS performs an attachment procedure with an SGSN that includes authentication (by checking with the GR).

The MS is al- located a temporary logical link identity (TLLI) by the SGSN and a PDP (packet data protocol) context is created for the MS. The PDP context is a set of parameters

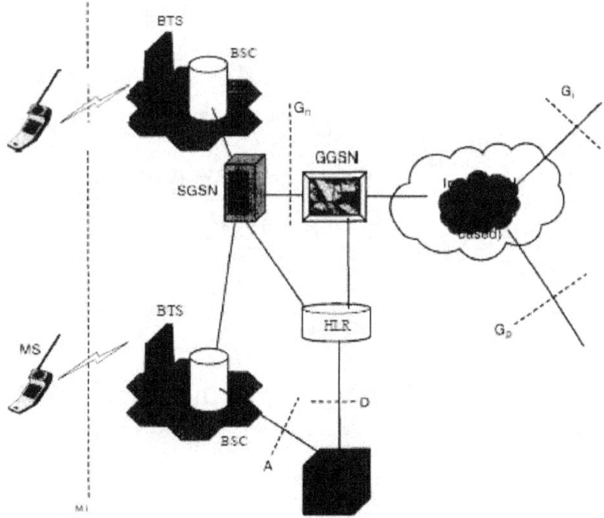

Figure 5.10 GPRS system architecture

created for each session and contains the PDP type, such as IPv4, the PDP address assigned to the MS, the requested QoS parameters, and the GGSN address that serves the point ot access to the PDN. The PDP context is stored in the MS, the SGSN, and the GGSN. A user may have several PDP contexts enabled at a time. The PDP address may be statically or dynamically assigned (static address is the common situation). The PDP context is used to route packets accordingly.

5.3.3.2 Location and Handoff Management

The location and mobility management procedures in GPRS are based on keeping track of the MSs location and having the ability to route packets to it ac- cordingly. The SGSN and the GGSN play the role of foreign and HAs (visiting and home databases) in GPRS. Location management depends on three states in which the MS can be (Fig- ure 9.11). In the IDLE state the MS is not reachable, and all PDP contexts are deleted. In the STANDBY state, movement across routing areas is updated to the SGSN but not across cells. In the READY state, every movement of the MS is indicated to the SGSN. The reason for the three states is based on discussions similar to those in Chapter 6. If the MS updates its location too often, it consumes battery power and wastes the air-interface resources.

If it updates too infrequently, a system wide paging is needed; this is also a waste of resources. A standby state focuses the area to the service area of the SGSN. In the standby state, there is a medium chance of packets addressed to the MS. The ready state pinpoints the area when the chances of packets reaching are high.

Routing area updates that are part of the standby state are of two types. In the intra-SGSN RA update, the SGSN already has the user profile and PDP context. A new temporary mobile subscriber identity is issued as part of routing area update "accept." The HLR need not be updated.

In an inter-SGSN RA update, the new RA is serviced by a new SGSN. The new SGSN requests the old SGSN to send the PDP contexts of the MS. The new SGSN informs the home GGSN, the GR, and other GGSNs about the user's new routing context.

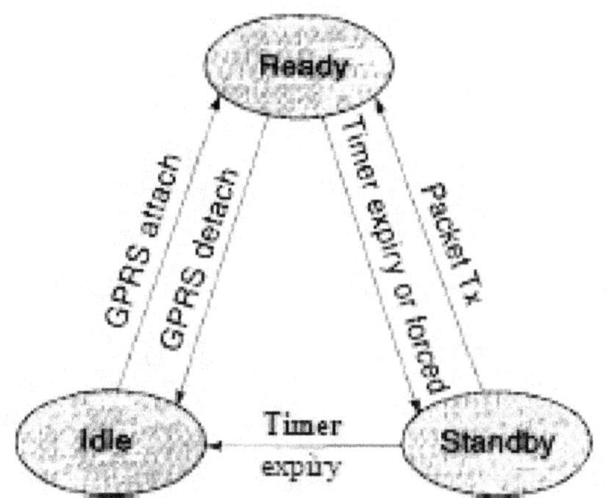

Figure 9.11 Location management in

GPRS

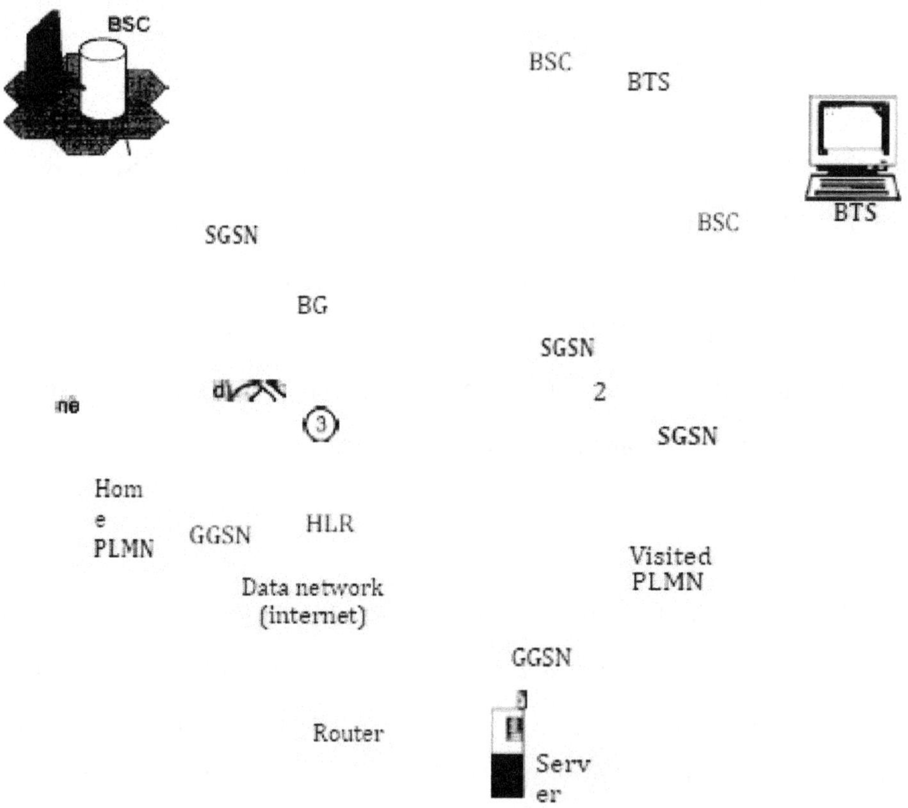

Figure 5.12 Handoff management in GPRS.

mobility management in GPRS starts at handoff initiation. The MS listens to the BCCH and decides which cell it has to select. Proprietary algorithms are em- ployed that use RSS, cell ranking, path loss, power budget, and so on. The MS is re- sponsible for cell reselection independently, and this is done in the same way as GSM. The MS measures the RSS of the current BCCH and compares it with the RSS of the BCCH of adjacent cells and decides on which cell to attach it to. There is, however, an option available to operators to make the BSS ask reports from the MH (as in GSM), and then the handoff is done as in GSM (MAHO). Pla in GPRS specific information can be sent in a packet BCCH (PBCCH), but the RSS is al- ways measured from the BCCH. There are also other principles, which may be considered in handoff decision such as path loss, cell-ranking, and so on. The hand- off procedure is very similar to mobile IP.

The location is updated with a routing update procedure, as shown in Fig 5.12. When a MS changes a routing area (RA), it sends an RA update request con-taining the cell identity and the identity of previous routing area, to the new SGSN (1). Note that an intra-SGSN routing area update (as discussed above) is also possible.

when the same SGSN serves the new RA. The new SGSN asks the old SGSN to provide the routing context (GGSN address and tunneling information) of the MS (2). The new SGSN then updates the GGSN of the home network with the new SGSN address and new tunneling information (3). The new SGSN also updates the HLR. The HLR cancels the MS information context in the old SGSN and loads the subscriber data to the new SGSN. The new SGSN acknowledges the MS. The pre- vious SGSN is requested to transmit undelivered data to the new SGSN.

5.3.3.3 Power Control and Security

Power control and security mechanisms are very similar to the way in which they are implemented in GSM (see Chapter 7). The ciphering algorithm is used to provide confidentiality and integrity protection of GPRS user data used for PTP mobile-originated and mobile-terminated data transmission and point- to- multipoint group (PTM-G) mobile terminated data transmission. The algorithm is restricted to the MS-SGSN encryption.

5.3.4 Protocol Layers in GPRS

In ‹order to transport different network layer packets, GPRS specifies a protocol stack like CDPD and GSM (see Figure 9.13). This is the transport plane (where user data is transferred over the GPRS/GSM infrastructure). There is also a GPRS signaling plane to enable signaling between various elements in the archi- tecture (like messaging between the SGSN and BSS etc.). GPRS employs out-of- band signaling in support of actual data transmission. Signaling between SGSN, HLR, VLR, and EIR is similar to GSM and extends only the GPRS related func- tionality. So it is based on SS-7. Between the MS and SGSN, a GPRS mobility management and session management (GMM/SM) protocol is used for signaling purposes.

The GPRS transport plane has different layers in different elements. The physical layers between the MS-BSS, BSS-SGSN, and SGSN-GGSN are indicated

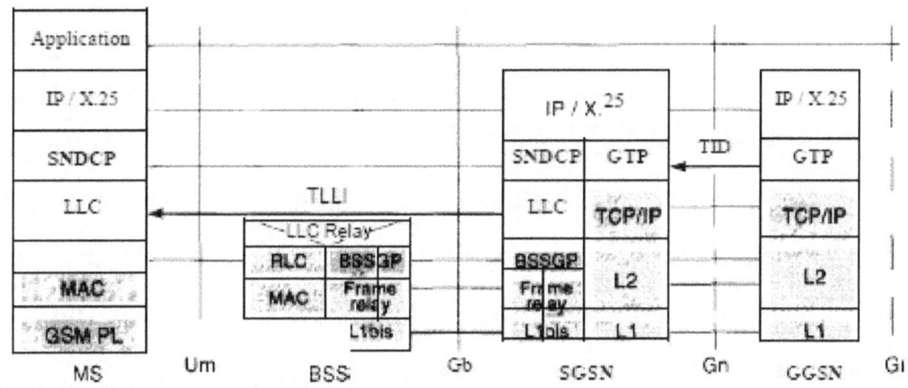

Figure 5.13 GPRS transport plane.

Figure 5.13 GPRS transport plane.

in Figure 5.13. Over the air, the physical layer is the same as GSM (i.e., it uses GMSK). Its functionalities include forward error correction and indication of un- correctable code words, interleaving of radio "blocks," synchronization, monitor- ing of radio link signal quality, and so on. All other functions are similar to GSM. GPRS allows a MS to transmit on multiple time slots of the same TDMA frame un- like GSM. A very flexible channel allocation is possible since 1— 8 time sl‹›ts can be allocated per TDMA frame to a single MS. Uplink and downlink slots can be

154

allo - cated differently to support asymmetric data traffic. Some channels may be allo- cated solely for GPRS. These are called packet data channels (PDCH).

Allocation of radio resources is also slightly different compared with GSM. A cell may or may not support GPRS and if it does support GPRS, radio resources are dynamically allocated between GSM and GPRS services. Any GPRS information is broadcast on the CCHs. PDCHs may be dynamically allocated ‹ deal located by the network (usually the BSC). If an MS is unaware that the PDCH has been deal located, it may cause interference to a voice call. In such a case, fast release of PDCHs is achieved by a broadcast of a deal location message on a PACCH. The uplink and downlink transmissions are independent. The medium access protocol is called "Master-Slave Dynamic Rate Access" or MSDRA. Here, the organization of time-slot assignment is done centrally by the BSS. A "master" PDCH includes common control channels that carry the signaling information required to initiate packet transfer.

The "slave" PDCH includes user data and dedicated signaling information for an MS. Several logical traffic and control GPRS channels are defined analogous to GSM. For example, PDTCH is the packet data traffic channel and PBCCH is the packet broadcast control channel. For random access to obtain a traffic channel, the packet random access, access grant, and paging channels are called PRACH, PAGCH, and PPCH, respectively. Additionally there is a packet notification channel (PNCH) that notifies arrival of a packet for the MS and a packet associated control channel (PACCH) used to send ACKs for received packets. A packet timing-advance control channel (PTCCH) is used for adaptive frame synchronization.

The packet transfer on the uplink and downlink are shown in Figures 5.14 and 5.15, respectively. They are quite similar to the process in GSM. Some of the differences are as follows. If a MS does not get an ACK, it will back off for a random time and try again. On the uplink, the Master-Slave mechanism utilizes a 3-bit uplink status flag (USF) on the downlink to indicate what PDCHs are available. A list of PDCHs and their USFs are specified in this USF. The packet resource or im - mediate assignment message indicates what USF state is reserved for the mobile on a PDCH. Channel assignment can also be done so that a MS can send packets uninterrupted for a predetermined amount of time.

On the downlink, data transmission to a mobile can be interrupted if a high-priority message needs to be sent. Instead of paging, a resource assignment message may be sent to the MS if it is already in a "ready" state. GPRS supports IP and X.25 packets at the network layer to be used lay end-to-end applications. The SNDCP supports a variety of network protocols (IP, X.25, CLNP, etc.). All network layer packets share the same SNDCP. It multiplexes and demultiplexes the network layer payload and forms the interface between the link layer (LLC) and the network layer. Also the SNDCP handles packets based on QoS.

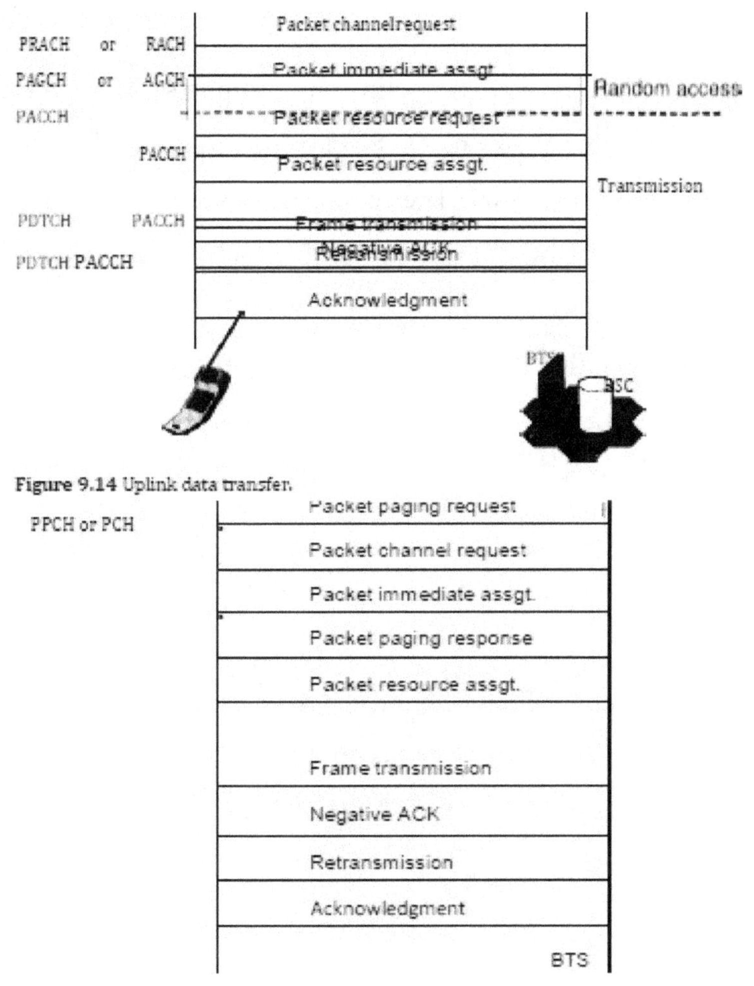

Figure 9.14 Uplink data transfer.

Figure 5.15 Downlink data transfer.   BSC

5.3.4.1 Paging Transmission

The LLC layer forms a logical link between the MS and the SGSN (similar to CDPD's MDLP). Each MS has a temporary logical link identity (TLLI) tc› identify itself in the LLC header. The LLC performs sequence control, error recovery, flow control, and encryption. It has an acknowledged mode (with retransmission for network layer payloads) and an unacknowledged mode (for signaling and SMS). The LLC also supports various OoS classes. Figure 9.16 shows how packets flow from higher layers, applications, and signaling levels to the SNDCP and the LLC. The packet transformation data flow is shown in Figure 9.17. The end result is blocks of 114 bits that are transmitted in bursts similar to GSM.

There are two levels of connections (tunneling mechanisms) implemented in the GPRS infrastructure as shown in Figures 9.13 and 9.18, one between the MS and the SGSN and the second between the SGSN and the GGSN. The two-level tunneling mechanism corresponds to a two-level mobility management: LLC "tun- nels" (or virtual circuits) correspond to small area mobility, while GPRS tunneling protocol (GTP) tunnels correspond to wide area mobility. A new logical link is cre- ated each time the MS makes a handoff in the ready state between itself and the SGSN. If the SGSN does not change, the tunneling of the packet beyond the SGSN remains the same with the same GTP.

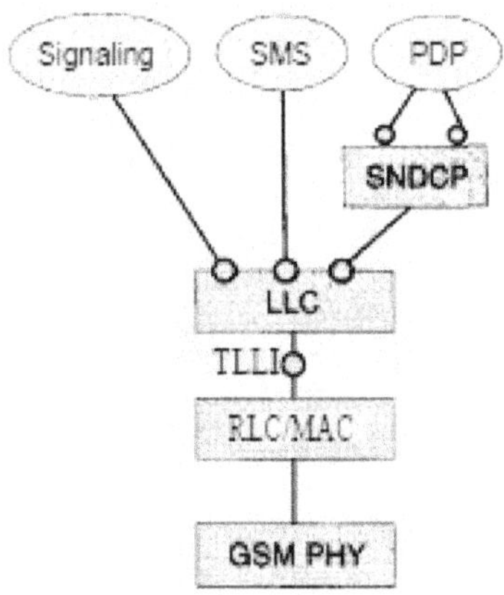

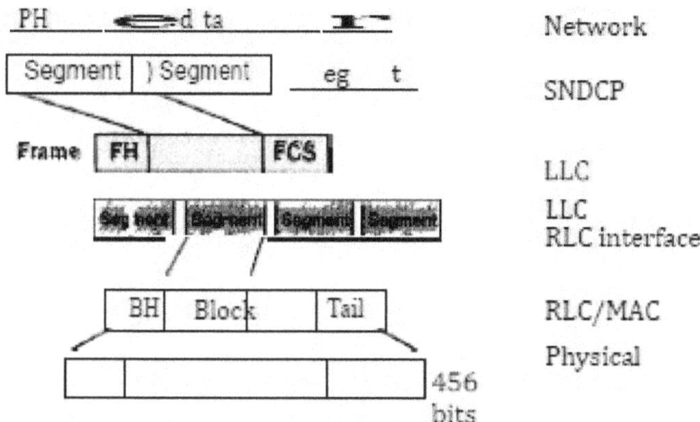

The BSS Gateway protocol (BSSGP) operates between the BSS and the SGSN relaying the LLC packets from the MS to the SGSN. Many MS LL(?s can be multiplexed over one BSSGP. Its primary function is to relay radio related, QoS, and routing information between the BSS and SGSN and paging requests from SGSN to the BSS. It supports flushing of old messages from BSS. The data transfer is unconfirmed between BSS and SGSN. The GTP allows multiprotocol packets to be tunneled through the GPRS backbone. A tunnel lD (TID) is created using the signaling plane that tracks the PDP context of each MS session. GTP can multiplex various payloads. The GTP

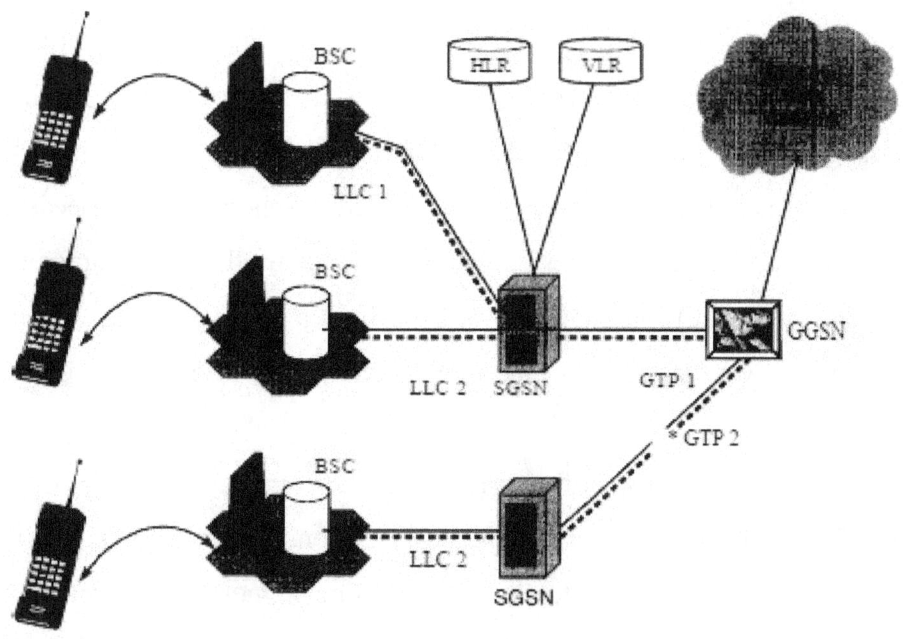

Figure 5.18 Two-level tunneling in GPRS

packet is carried by either UDP/IP or TCP/IP, depending on whether the payload is IP or X.25, respectively.

5.4 SMS

The proliferation of GSM enabled the introduction of the .short messaging service (SMS), which has become extremely popular in Europe. It is similar to the peer-to- peer instant messaging services on the Internet. Users of SMS [PEEOOa], [PEE00b] can exchange alphanumeric messages of up to 160 characters (mapped into 140 bytes) within seconds of submission of the message. The service is available wher- ever GSM exists and makes it a very attractive wide area data service.

5.4.1 What Is SMS?

SMS was developed as part of GSM Phase 2 specifications (see Chapter 7 i. It oper - ates over all GSM networks making use of the GSM infrastructure completely. It uses the same network entities (with the addition of a SMS center—ShlSC), the same physical layer, and intelligently reuses the logical channels of the (GSM sys- tem to transmit the very short alphanumeric messages.

5.4.1.1 Service Description

SMS has both an almost instant delivery service if the destination MS is active or a store and forward service if the MS is inactive. Two types of services are speci- fied: In the cell broadcast service, the message is transmitted to all MSs that are ac- tive in a cell and that are subscribed to the service. This is an unconfirmed, one-way service used to send weather forecasts, stock quotes, and so on. In the PTP service, an MS may send a message to another MS using a handset keypad, a PDA, or a laptop connected to the handset, or by calling a paging center. Recently, SMS mes- sages can be transmitted via dial-up to the service center and the Internet as well [PE E00a].

A short message (SM) can have a specified priority level, future delivery time, expiration time, or it might be one of several short predefined messages. A sender may request acknowledgment of message receipt. A recipient can manually acknowledge a message or may have predefined messages for acknowledgement An SM will be delivered and acknowledged whether a call is in progress be-cause of the way logical channels in GSM are used for SMS. We discus.s this in a later section.

5.4.1.2 Overview of SMS Operation

The SMS makes use of the GSM infrastructure, protocols, and the physical layer to manage the delivery of messages. Note that the service has a store-and-forward na-ture. As a result, each message is treated individually. Each message is maintained and transmitted by the SMSC. The SMSC sorts and routes the messages appropri- ately. The short messages are transmitted through the GSM infrastructure using SS-7. Details of the packet formats and messaging can be found in [PEE0()a].

Figure 5 .19 shows the reference architecture and the layered protocol archi- tecture for SMS. There are two cases of short messages: a mobile originated SM and a mobile terminated short message. A SM originating from an MS has to be first delivered to a service center. Before that, it reaches an MSC for processing. A dedicated function in the MSC called the SMS-interworking MSC (SMS-IWMSC) allows the forwarding of the SM to the SMSC using a global SMSC ID. An SM that terminates at the MS is forwarded by the SMSC to the SMS-gatewa y MS C (SMS-GMSC) function in an MSC. As in the case of GSM, it either queries the HLR or sends it to the SMS-GMSC function at the home MSC of the recipient. Subse - quently, the SM is forwarded to the appropriate MSC that has the responsibility of finally delivering the message to the MS. This delivery is performed by querying the VLR for details about the location of the MS, the BSC controlling the BTS pro-viding coverage to the MS, and so on.

There are four layers in SMS—the application layer (AL), the transfer layer (TL), the relay layer (RL), and the link layer (LL). The AL can generatc and dis- play the alphanumeric message. The SMS -TL services the SMS -AL to exchange SMs and receive confirmation of receipt of SMs. It can obtain a delivery report or status of the SM sent in either direction. The RL relays the SMS PDUs through the LL. There are six PDUs types in SMS that convey the short message—from the SMSC to the MS and vice versa, convey a failure cause, and convey status reports and commands.

Over the air, the SMs are transmitted in time slots that are freed up in the control channels. If the MS is in an idle state (see Chapter 10), the short messages are sent over the SDCCH at 184 bits within approximately 240 ms. If the MS is in the active state (i.e., it is handling a call), the SDCCH is used for call sc t-up and maintenance. In that case, the SACCH has to be used for delivering the SM. This occurs at around 168 bits every 480 ms and is much slower. Failures can occur if there is a state change when the SM is in transit. The short message will have ter be transmitted later.

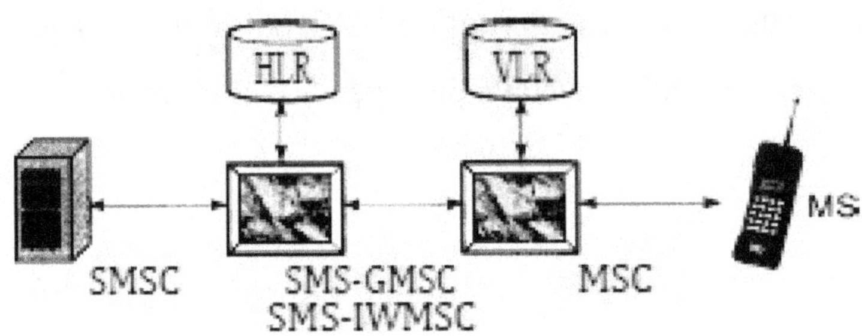

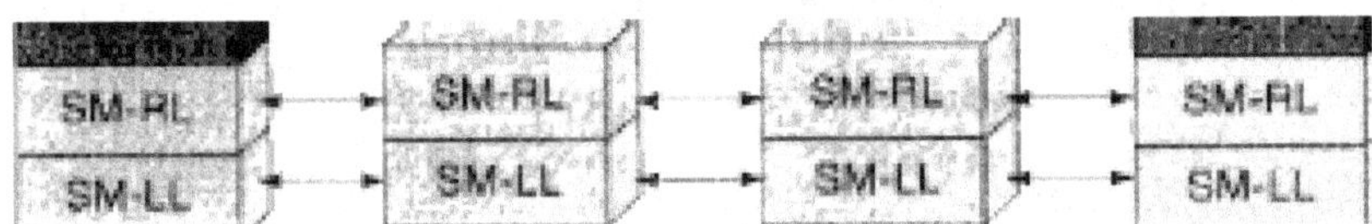

Figure 9.19   Reference and layered protocol architecture for SMS

In the case of cell broadcast, a cell broadcast entity and a cell broadcast cen- ter are used to send the weather forecast or other broadcast SMs to multiple BSCs for delivery. The broadcasts contain the data and identities of MSs that .ire to receive the message. The cell broadcast is on the cell broadcast channel (CBCH).

5.5 MOBILE APPLICATION PROTOCAL

Mobile applications are becoming very important in the age of the Internet. Data networks and dial-up services were mostly restricted to research laboratories and educational institutions in the early 1980s and became a household service by the late 1990s because of the emergence of applications such as email, e -cc)mmerce, and the World Wide Web. Recently, efforts provide similar applications on cellular networks. A major problem with providing such services on cellular networks has been the hick of resources such as bandwidth, processing power, memory, display sizes, interfaces like keypads, and so on that makes the service expensive. The con - straints are also larger such as more latency, less connection stability, and less pre- dictive availability. The wireless application protocol (WAP) and the i-mode service offered by NTT-DoCoMo of Japan are examples of how Internet leased ap- plications are being adapted to the cellular systems.

5.5.1 Wireless Application Protocol (WAP)

Initiated in 1997 by Nokia, Ericsson, Motorola and Phone.com, the WAP is an in- dustry standard developed by the WAP Forum [WAPweb] for integrating cellular telephony and the Internet by providing Web content and advanced services to mobile telephone users. The WAP protocol is expected to help implementation of a variety of applications that include Internet access, m-commerce, multimedia email, tele-medicine, and mobile geo-positioning. The WAP application frame- work can run over several transport frameworks that include SMS, GPRS, CDPD, IS-136, and circuit switched wireless data services. Using WAP the wireless net- work technology will allow development of variety of applications. WAP orients the display toward text and material suitable for very small screens, thereby reducing both the load on the network and on the mobile terminal. In a nutshell, WAP attempts to optimize the Web and existing tools for a wireless environment.

WAP provides an extensible and saleable platform for application development for mobile telephones. However, support for WAP on color PDA terminals is not very good. WAP also does not support seamless roaming between different link level bearer services such as CDPD and GSM, for example. Also, multimedia communications are not supported very well on WAP [FAS99]. For all these limitations, modifications to WAP will be necessary.

5.5.1.1 WAP Programming Architecture

How WAP does the extensions and modifications to the existing worldwide Web architecture is as follows. WAP introduces a gateway in between the wireless client and the rest of the Internet which manages the delivery of content to the mobile terminal. Such an architecture is shown in Figure 5.20.

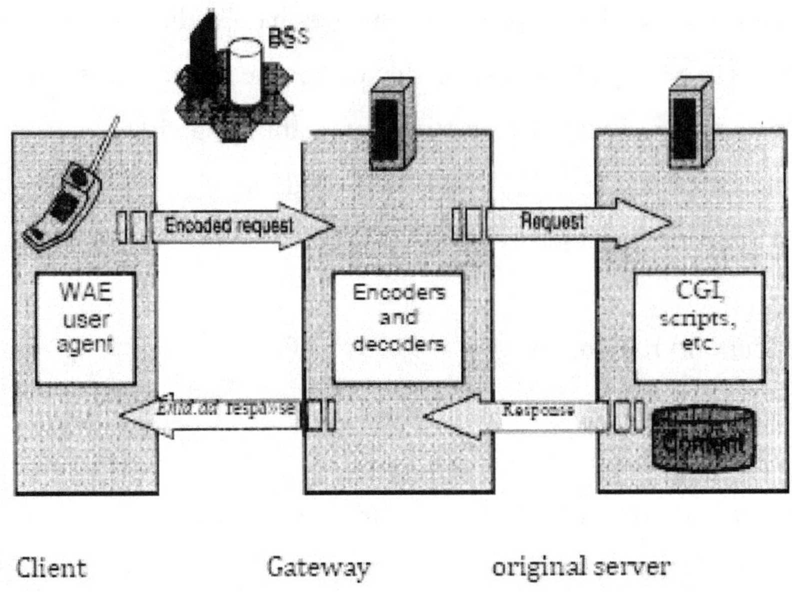

Most current Web content resides in Web servers and consists of as of material such as HTML pages, JavaScript interactive Web pages, images, and multimedia. These contents are developed for full -screen computer displays. A mobile terminal cannot access all this material because the screen size is smaller, the data rate for access is lower, and the cost of the access is higher than the wired acccss. To overcome this problem, the request for content is first matte to the WAP Gateway, shown in Figure 5.20. The WAP request is made using ‹i binary format of a wireless markup language (WML) that has some kind of a correspondence with HTML. That is, HTML pages can be converted into WML content. WM L was derived from the extensible markup language (XM L) and 0ascribes menu trees or decks through which a user can navigate with the micro browser. The binary request conserves bandwidth by compressing the data. The request is decoded by the gateway and transmitted to the original server as an HTTP re- quest. The server responds with the content in HTML. The content is filtered into WML, encoded into binary, and transmitted to the handset. A micro browser in the handset coordinates the user interface and is similar to the usual Web browser. In essence, the gateway acts as a proxy device within the network. An example of a WAP network is shown in Figure 5.21. The WTA stands for wireless telephony application that provides an interface to a wireless application environment for network related activities such as call control, access to local address box ks, net- work events, and so on.

5.5.1.2 Protocol Layers in WAP

The layered protocol architecture specified for WAP is shown in Figure 5.22. The wireless application environment (WAE) is an application development plat- form that combines aspects of the Web and mobile telephony. It includes a micro- browser, WML, a scripting language similar to JavaScript called WMLscript,

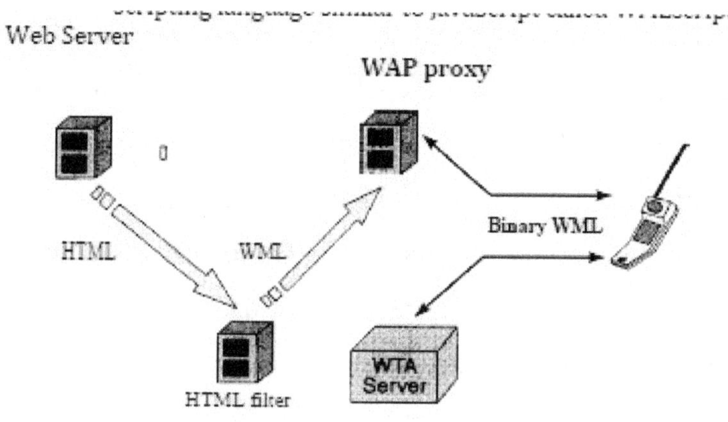

Figure 5.21 WAP example network.

Figure 5.21 WAP example network.

several data formats such as images, calendars, and records, and telephony applica-tions. The wireless session protocol (WSP) provides both a connection oriented and a connectionless service to the WAE. The connection-oriented service o(›erates on top of the wireless transport protocol (WTP) and the connectionless service on top of the wireless datagram protocol (WDP). These are similar to Internet's TCP and UDP, respectively. WSP can suspend or migrate sessions unlike protocols on the wired link, and it is optimized for low bandwidth links.

The wireless transport layer seCurit y (WTLS) is based on the IETF' standard transport layer security and the secure socket layer. It provides data integrity, privacy, authentication and techniques to reject replay attacks.

5.5.2 iMode

i-Mode is a service that tries to eliminate the use of a gateway and proc ide direct access to the Internet to the extent possible. With this goal in mind, Jap‹in's NTT- DoCoMo has introduced this extremely popular service in Japan in 1999. By November 2000 i-Mode had 14.9 million subscribers in Japan and Hong Kong. These terminals transmit data at 9,600 bps that allows graphics and small text mes- saging on a larger screen than the WAP. This display allows six to 10 lines of text at 16 to 20 characters per line that can be color or monochrome. i-Mode telephones can access HTML files across the web using C-HTML without a protocol like WAP. i-Mode is more similar to HTML which allows different computers to ex- change information. i-Mode extends this to communicate with PDAs and i-Mode enabled cellular phones. One of the major features of i-Mode is that its charging mechanism is based on packet transmission rather than connection time which makes it less expensive for most users applications. The next version of WAP is ex- pected to include CHTML as an alternative mechanism so as to include i-Mode as an option within itself.

5.6 Wireless ATM

Wireless ATM was first introduced in 1992 [RAY92], and it meant to pt ovide for an integrated broadband application programming interface (API) to the ATM network for a variety of mobile terminals. In 1996, a WATM working group was formed under the ATM forum that drew around a hundred participant s in their first meeting in Helsinki. Figure 12.1 illustrates the vision of the end-to-end ATM network that was used by the ATM forum. In the mid-1990s, a number of experi- mental projects at NEC Laboratories, Nokia, AT&T, Olivetti (now AT'&T), and other research labs developed prototypes for implementation of this concept, but in the late 1990s, the heat of the WATM cooled down significantly [PAH97], [RAY99]. In the year 2000, the ATM forum regrouped to pursue this mat ter by co- operating with other WLAN standards activities, in particular HIPE RLAN-2. However, research efforts for implementation of these testbeds discover‹:d a num- ber of interesting issues related to broadband wireless access that has had an im- pact on the development of new standards in this field. A comprehensive overview of WATM activities is available in [RAY99].

The first fundamental challenge for the implementation of a WATM system is that the ATM was designed for fast switches connecting extremely wid‹'laand and reliable fiber transmission channels. The wireless medium, however, is w'ry unreli- able and has serious limitations on wideband operations. This imposes problems in the basic transmission mechanism.

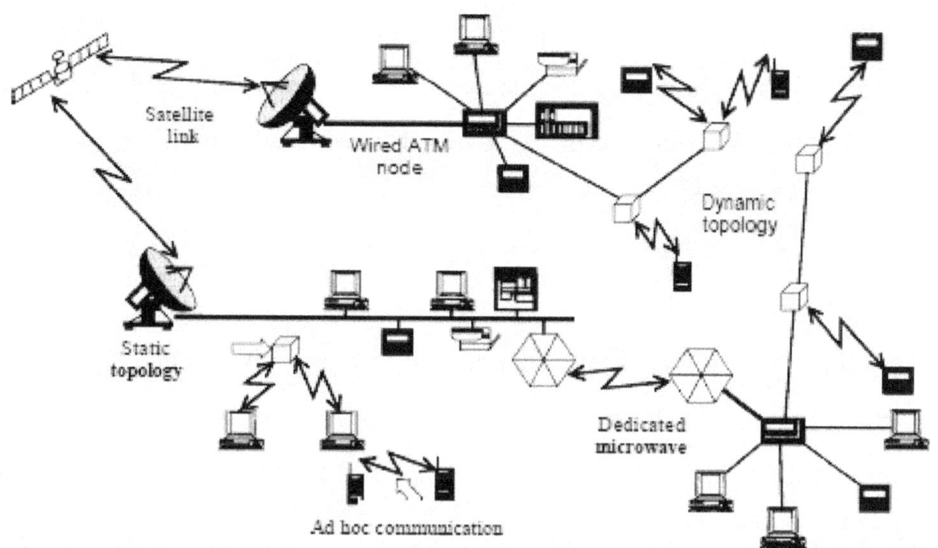

Figure 5.23 Vision of the ATM forum's Wireless ATM working group for an end-to-end ATM network [DEL96]

Wireless header	ATM header (5 bytes)	ATM payload (48 bytes)	Wireless trailer

Figure 5.24 Typical packet frame format for the WATM.

Figure 5.24 Typical packet frame format for the WATM.

Example : Format of WATM Packets

Consider the packet format for the WATM system shown in Figure 5.24. ATM packets (cells) have a fixed size of 53 bytes with a 48-byte payload. The benefit of the fixed packet size is that it facilitates fast switching in a multimedia environment. The ATM cells were considered for operation on reliable optical channels that do not need acknowledgment. When we use the same packet format in a wireless environment, for example, FHSS 802.11, we will have another additional 16 bytes for the PLCP header and a few more for a wireless MAC layer that makes the overhead so large that a 48-byte length of payload makes the transmission inefficient. On the other hand, with the unreliable fading environment in wireless channels, we need to add acknowledgment to ensure safe transmission of the packets. II' we change the packet format and add acknowledgments, then it is difficult to call this protocol wireless ATM. This would be a wireless method to interact with ATM switches. So the name WATM is not really appropriate. After all we don"t call 802.11 a wireless 802.3.

The second fundamental challenge is that the ATM switches are designed to support QoS based on a basic negotiation with the user terminal that is maintained throughout the session. In a wireless environment, because of the fluctuations in channel conditions, a continual support of a negotiated Quos is impossible. Besides, when a terminal roams from one AP to another, it needs to renegotiate its contract, anal the new AP may not be able to honor the old contract. Therefore, the basic promise of the ATM that is honoring a negotiated service would need a new definition.

Other challenges facing WATM are to find methods to provide faster and more reliable air-interfaces, to find a method to distribute the additional complexities of the network among the network elements, and to find an efficient way to cope with IP applications developed for connectionless environments.

5.6.1 Reference Model

The basic elements of the traditional ATM networks are ATM switches and ATM terminals. The ATM forum defines, among other things, two protocols, the user— network interface (UNI) protocol connecting user terminals to the switches, and the network—network interface (NNI) protocol connecting two switches to- gether [STA9Sb]. The elements of a WATM network are shown in Figure 5.24.

In the WATM environment, we have two new elements, the WATM-MS and the ATM-BS, and we need to upgrade the ATM switches to support mobility. The WATM environment needs to define a new UNI air-interface "W" for wireless op-eration and a new UNI-NNI interface protocol, "M" that connects the ATM-BS to the ATM switches. The WA TM-MS is physically implemented on a radio N lC (network interface card) hardware and mobility or radio enhanced UNI software for handling call initiation and traffic handling. The ATM-BS is a new small ATM switch with ports for wireless and wired connections. This switch also needs enhanced UNI-NNI software which supports mobility in the wireless medium. The A TM switch with mobility software is a normal switch with upgraded UNI-NNI software that handles mobility.

5.6.2 Protocol Entities

Figure 5 .25 represents a general description of the protocol entities in the ATM that includes the WATM entities. The PHY layer specifies the transmission medium and the signal encoding technique. In the wired part, the PHY layer standard specifies high-speed connection to SONET, TAXI, and UTP-3 [STAOO] media for optical and wired copper media. In the wireless part, the standard has not specified anything yet, but the experimental systems use variety of technologies commonly used in WLAN standards and products. The ATM network layer defines transmission in fixed-size cells and the use of connections for wired parts. Ad- ditional WATM data link control (DLC) and MAC layers are needed to adapt the system to the wireless environment. The ATM adaptation layer (AAL) is a service- dependent layer that maps higher-layer protocol packets (such as AppleTalk, IP, NetWare) into ATM cells. The ATM forum defines five different AAL specifica- tions, AAL-5 being the most popular in LAN applications that is also suitable for WATM operation. The user plane provides control (flow, error, etc.) over infor- mation transfer. The control plane provides for call establishment and control

Figure 5 .25 a Protocol entities in an ATM environment that supports wireless mobility.

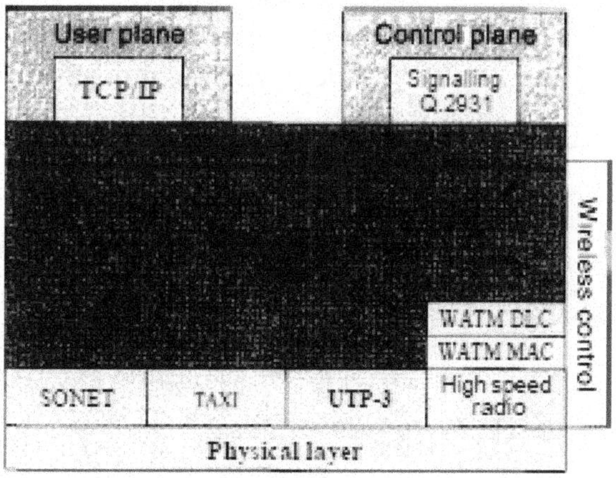

to support wireless mobile environments. In addition, a wireless control layer is needed to coordinate all the additional functionalities added to support wireless operation.

Figure 5.25 represents three possibilities for communication between a mo- bile terminal (MT) and a fixed terminal (FT). Figure 5.25(a) is a normal

WLAN- LAN communication. Two applications in the two terminals communicate through the TCP/IP protocol. The IP packets in the wireless terminal use the h4 AC and PHY layer of IEEE 802.11, and the IP packets at the wired terminal use the MAC and PHY layer of the IEEE 802.3. Protocol conversion takes place at the wireless AP. This situation is the same as normal WLAN operation described earlier .Figure 5.25(b) represents a case for communication between a WLAN and an ATM environment. The wireless side is the same as before, but the wired terminal applications run on top of the ATM protocol stack. The application on the ATM terminal could be a native ATM application or lP application. The AP in this case needs LANE software to interface the AAL- 5 packets to the 802.11 MAC. Figure 5.25(c) represents the third case when a WATM terminal communicates with an ATM terminal. The PHY and MAC layers of WATM are not yet specified, so the system is an experimental system using a proprietary design.

Figure 5 .25 clarifies the importance of two issues. Regardless of the technology for the air-interface, a local network works to run legacy applications over available backbones. If ATM switches move inside offices or homes and native ATM applications become popular, then there is a need for a full WATM service. If LANs, already installed in all offices and penetrating all homes, become the pre-dominant local access mechanisms, then WATM will not find any application. Today, as we discussed earlier, hopes for a WATM type of operation is in the pub-lic APs. At home and in offices, the existing legacy LANs appear to be adequate. One solution in this type of environment is to use the operation as in Figure 5.5(a) for the home and office and Figure 5.5(b) 1or public access.

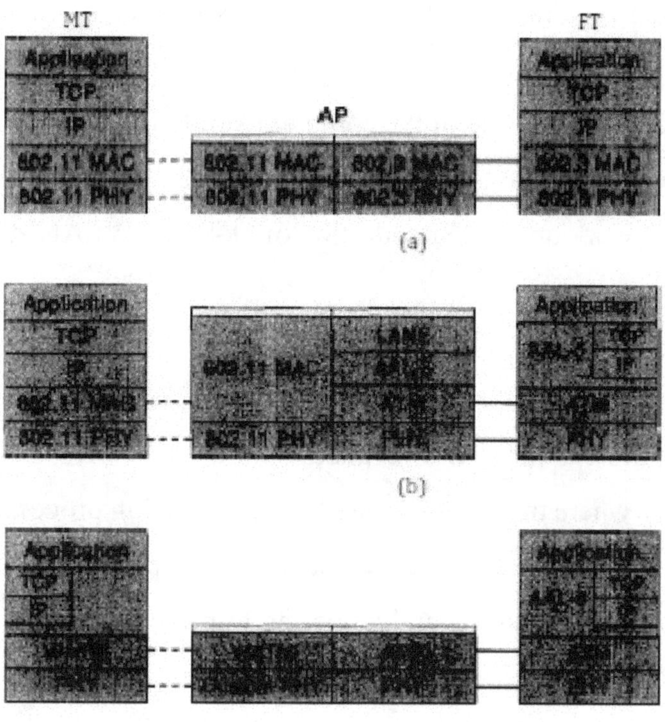

Figure 5.25 Different methods to run applications: (a) WLAN to LAN. (b) WLAN to ATM, and (c) WATM to ATM.

5.6.3 PHY and MAC Layer Alternatives

The ATM forum's WATM working group has not made any specification for a standard. To illustrate the PHY and MAC layer options for WATM, we provide a comparative overview of a few test beds used for implementation of the° WATM concept. summarizes various features of five major projects in this field [PAH97], [A GR96], [AYA96], [ENG95], [RAY97], [WAN96]. Of these, the SWAN and MII/BAHAMA were developed at AT&T/Lucent Research Labs, f)livetti in the United Kingdom, NEC was the leading project (in their laboratory in New Jer- sey), and the Magic WAND was supported by the ACTS research program in EC that involved a number of participants led by Nokia. These prototypes ot)erated in the ISM and U-NH bands. The data rates ranged from less than 1 Mbps to 24 Mbps. Transmission techniques included FH-SS, traditional QPSK with DFE, and OFDM. The access methods were token passing, reservation-slotted AL,OHA, or TDMA/TDD, all providing a controlled environment for the support of the QoS. Today, to support higher data rates of up to 54 Mbps, HIPERLAN-2 and IEEE 802.11a standards use OFDM modulation at 5 GHz. Prior to these stan‹)ards, the Magic WAND and MII/BAHAMA had adopted the same solution to prc>vide data rates around 20 Mbps. The access method of HIPERLAN-2 is s imilar to TDMA/TDD which was experimented in NEC's WATM prototype earlier. All these testbeds have tried different approaches to ensure certain levels of QoS. These efforts have helped the understanding of the complexity of QoS in ii wireless mobile environment, and have discovered partial solutions for this problem. These studies have laid a ground for the HI PERLAN-2 standard to work on implementa- tion of QoS in a WLAN standard.

5.6.3 Mobility Support

As we saw in previous examples of connection-oriented and connection less net- works, a wireless mobile operation requires a number of functionalities. The MS needs to support location management to identify where the MS is. It nee<ls a regis- tration process and a handoff procedure to register the terminal to an AP each time it is turned on and manage the switching of connections to other APs. It needs au- thentication and ciphering to provide security and power management to save in the life of the battery. We have provided detailed examples of these functionalities in connection-oriented (GSM and CDMA systems) as well as connection less net- works (WLAN and mobile data services). The overall structure of these functional- ities for WATM is very similar to the others. However, handling the connection in an environment where there is a contract for QoS is challenging. In the case of ATM, ATM cells must be received in sequence, and they all follow the same route (virtual circuit—VC). When an MS moves from one AP to another, the existing VC is broken. The VC should either be extended or reconstructed to satis Y the ne-gotiated OoS. This problem is quite challenging.

5.7 Hiperlan

The HIPERLAN stands for Hlgh Performance Radio LAN and was initiated by the RES-10 group of the ETSI as a pan-European standard for high-speet4 wireless local networks. The so-called HIPERLAN- 1, the first defined technolot'y by this standard group, started in 1992 and completed in 1997. Unlike IEEE 802.11, which was based on products, HIPERLAN-1 was based on certain functional requirements specified by ETSI. In 1993, CEPT released spectrum at 5 and 17 Gl4z for the implementation of the HIPERLAN. The HIPERLAN 5.15-5.35 GHz ban<) for unli- censed operation was the first band that was used by a WLAN standard tit 5 GHz.

These bands being assigned for HIPERLAN in the European Union was one of the motives for the FCC to release the U-NH bands in 1996, which stimulated a new wave of developments in the WLAN industry. During the standardization process, a couple of HIPERLAN-1 prototypes were developed; however, no manufacturer adopted this standard for product development.

For that reason, those involved in the EU standardization process consider this effort an unsuccessful attempt. Later on HIPERLAN standardization moved under the ETSI BRAN project with a new and more structured organization. Figure 12.6 [WIL96] shows the overall format of the HIPERLAN activities after completion of the HIPERLAN-1.

In addition to 5.7.1 HIPERLAN-I, we have HIPERLAN-2, which aims at higher data rates and intends to accommodate ATM as well as IP type access. This standardization process is under development. They have coordinated with the IEEE 802.11a in the PHY layer specification and current work on the MAC to support QoS is under progress. Other versions of HIPERLAN are HIPER-ACCESS for remote access and HIPER-LINK to interconnect switches in the backbone.

In the United States, these activities are under IEEE 5.16 for LMDS. Only HIPERLAN-1 and -2 are considered WLANs and will be discussed in this chapter. Most of the emphasis is on HI PERLA N-2 which has attracted significant support from cellular manufacturers such as Nokia and Ericsson.

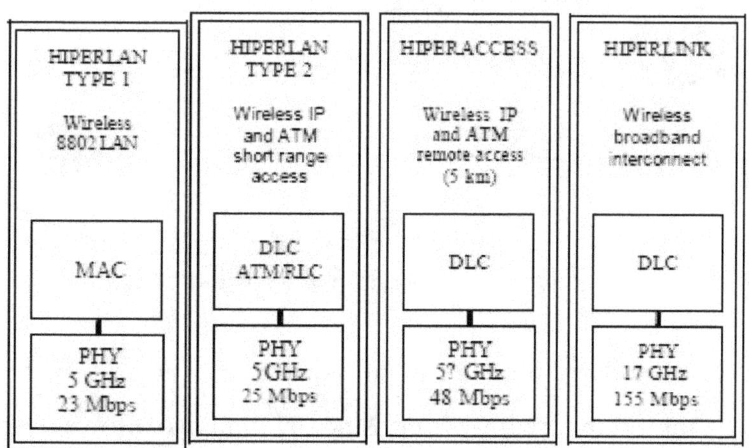

Figure 5.6 Divisions of the HIPERLAN activities.

Figure 5.6 Divisions of the HIPERLAN activities.

5.7.1.1 HIPERLAN-1 Requirements and Architecture

The original "functional requirements" for the HIPERLAN-1 were defined by ETSI. These requirements were

- Data rates of 23.529 Mbps
- Coverage of up to 100 m
- Multi-hop ad hoc networking capability
- Support of time-bounded services
- Support of power saving

The frequency of operation was 5.2 GHz unlicensed bands that were released by CEPT in 1993, several years before release of the U-Nil bands. The difference between this standard and the IEEE 802.11 was perceived to be the data rate, which was an order of magnitude higher than the original 802.11 and emphasis on ad hoc networking and time-bounded services.

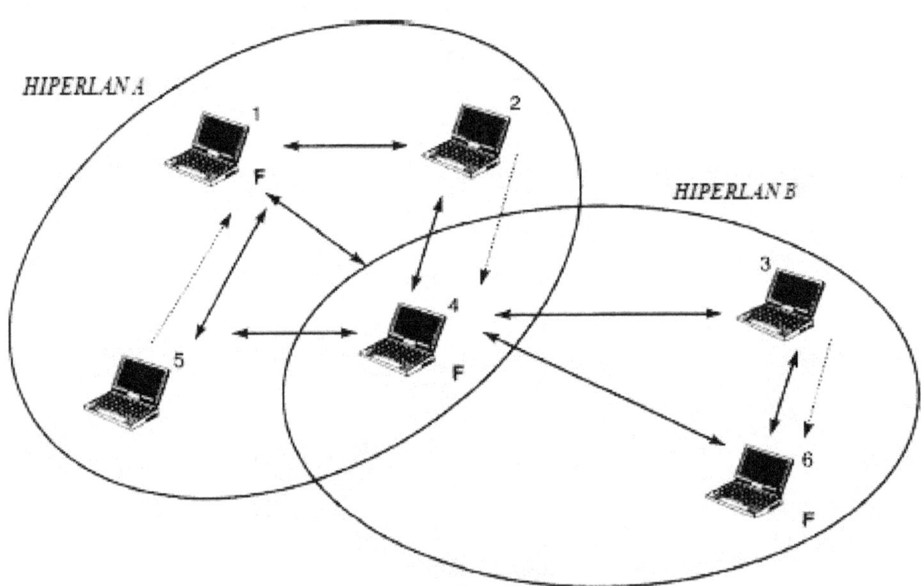

Figure 5.26 Ad hoc network architecture in the HIPERLAN-1.

Figure 5.26 shows the overall architecture of an ad hoc network. In HIPER- LAN-1's ad hoc network architecture, a multihub topology is considerecl that also allows overlay of two WLANs. As shown in this figure, the multihop routing ex- tends the HIPERLAN communication beyond the radio range of a single node. Each HIPERLAN node is either a forwarder, designated by "F," or a nonfor- warder. A nonforwarder node simply accepts the packet that is intendeifi for it. A forwarder node retransmits the received packet, if the packet does not have its own node address, to other terminals in its neighborhood. Each no forwarder node should select at least one of its neighbors as a forwarder. Inter-HIPER LAN for- warding needs bilateral cooperation and agreement between two HIPERLANs. To support routing and maintain the operation of a HIPERLAN, the form order and non forwarder nodes need to periodically update several databases. In Figure 5.26, solid lines represent peer-to-peer communications between two terminals and dashed lines represent the connections for forwarding. Three of the terminals, 1, 4, and 6, are designated by letter "F" indicating that they have forwarding connections. There are two overlapping HIPERLANs, A and B, and terminal 4 is a member of both WLANs which can also act as a bridge between the two. This architecture does not have an infrastructure, and it has a large coverage through the multichip operation.

As we mentioned earlier, HIPERLAN-1 did not generate any pro‹luct devel - opment, but it had some pioneering impact on other standards. The use of 5 GHz Figure 5.26 Ad hoc network architecture in the HIPERLAN-1. unlicensed bands, first considered in HIPERLAN-1, is used by IEEE 802.11a and HIPERLAN-2. The multihop feature of the HIPERLAN-1 is considered in the HIPERLAN-2 to be used in an environment with a connection to wired infrastructure.

5.7.1.2 HIPERLAN-1 PHY and MAC Layers

The PHY layer of the HIPERLAN-1 uses 200 MHz at 5.15-5.35 GHz, which is di-vided in 5 channels (40 MHz spacing) in the European Union and 6 channels (33 MHz spacing) in the United States. In the United States, there are 3 more channels at 5.725-5.b25 GHz bands. The transmission power can go as high as 1 W (30 dBm), and modulation is the single carrier GMSK that can support up to 23 Mbps. To support such high data rates receivers would include a DFE. As we discussed in Chapter 3, DFE consumes considerable electronic power. Using GMSK with the DFE is also challenging for the implementation of fallback data rates. The multi- symbol QAM modulation techniques embedded in the OFDM systems allow simple implementation of fallback data rates. In OAM systems fallback is implemented by simple reduction of the number of transmitted symbols per symbol interval while the symbol interval is kept constant. The PHY layer of the HIPERLAN-1 codes each 416 bits into 496 coded bits with a maximum of 47 codewords per packet and 450 bits per packet for training the equalizer.

The no preemptive multiple access (NPMA) protocol used in HIPERLAN is a listen before talk protocol, similar to CSMA/CA used in 802.11, which supports both asynchronous and isochronous (voice-oriented) transmissions. Carrier sensing in HIPERLAN-1 is active, rather than passive as in 502.11, and contention resolu- tion and ACKing is mandatory. The HIPERLAN MAC defines a priority scheme and a lifetime for each packet, which facilitates the control of QoS. In addition to the routing, the MAC layer also handles the encryption and power conservation. The MAC address of the HIPERLAN-1 uses six bytes to support IEEE 502.2 LLC and to be compatible with other 802 standards. Each packet has six address fields that identify source, destination, and immediate neighbor (for multihop implemen- tation) transmitters and receivers. IEEE 802.11 had four address fields because it does not support the multi hop operation.

Figure 5.27 shows the basic principles of the HIPERLAN-1 MAC protocol. If a terminal senses the medium to be free for at least 1,700 bit durations, it immediately transmits. If the channel is busy, the terminal access has three phases when the channel becomes available. These phases, shown in Figure 12.8, are prioritization phase, contention phase, and transmission phase. During the prioritization phase, competing terminals with the highest priority, among the five available priority levels, will survive, and the rest will wait for the next time that the channel is available. The combing algorithm that was described in Chapter 4 is used in five slots, each 256 bits long, to implement this phase. At the end of the prioritization period, all the terminals listen to the asserted highest priority to make sure that all terminals have understood the asserted priority level. This way MSs with the high-est priority survive and contend for the next phase, and others are eliminated from the contention. This prioritization mechanism is a counterpart of the three priority level mechanism that was implemented in the 802.11 using SIFS, PIFS, and DIFS interfacing intervals. The combing algorithm is more structured and active which

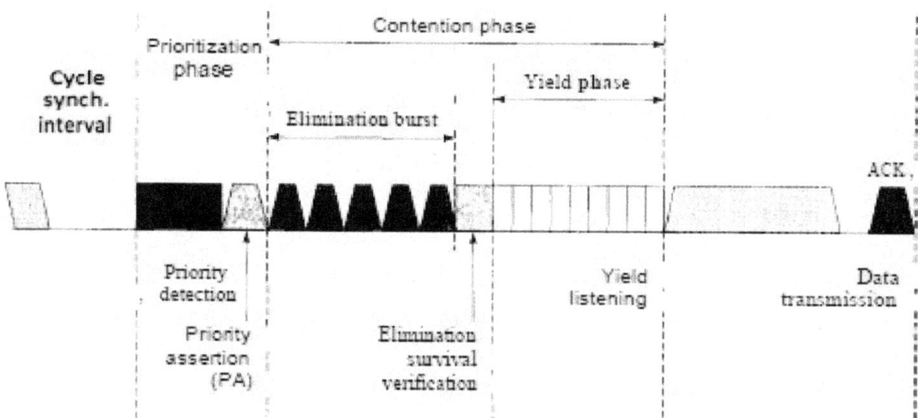

Figure 5.27 Channel access cycle in the HIPERLAN-I.

Figure 5.27 Channel access cycle in the HIPERLAN-I.

will provide for a more robust prioritization process. However, the realer should note that prioritization has not shown to be an important issue in the implementation of the WLAN products. All the existing 802.11 products don't implement PCF or any sort of prioritization.

The contention phase of the HIPERLAN-1 has two periods, elimination and yield. During the elimination period each terminal runs a random number generator to select one of the 12 available slots in which it sends a continuous burst of 256 bits. After sending a burst, an MS listens to the channel for 256-bit durations. If it does not hear any other burst after its transmission, it will send another burst after the twelfth slots in the elimination survival verification interval to ensure everyone that there are survivors. The terminals that hear a burst in this period eliminate themselves. The re- mainder of the terminals go to the so-called yield part of the contention interval. In the yield period, the remaining MSs have a random yield period that is similar to the 802.11 waiting counters. Each MS will "listen" to the channel for the dur:ition of its yield period which is determined from an exponentially distributed random variable, rather than a uniformly distributed random variable used in 802.11. The exponential distribution reduces the average waiting time for running the counter. If an MS senses the channel to be idle for the entire yield period, it has survived, and it will start transmitting data that automatically eliminates other MSs that are listening to the channel. Here the contention process is more complicated and has active as well as passive parts while contention in the 802.11 was entirely passive.

5.8 HIPERLAN -2

Today HIPERLAN-1 is not considered a successful standard by the European Union, but the HIPERLAN-2 project is very popular in and out of the European Union. The HIPERLAN-2 standardization process coordinated with IEEE 802.11 in While it is still under development, HIPERLAN-2 aims at IP and ATM type services at high data rates for indoor and possibly outdoor applications. It expects to support both connectionless and connection-oriented services which will make its MAC layer far more complicated than 802.11 and HIPERLAN-1 that supports only connectionless services. Connection-based services facilitate integration into the voice-oriented networks. The HIPERLAN -2 that started as a WATM type ac- tivity now aims at connecting to IP-based as well as UMTS and ATM networks.

In HIPERLAN-2 the ad hoc architecture of HIPERLAN-1 is expanded to support centralized access by using APs in a manner similar to IEEE 802.11. The TDMA/TDD-based MAC layer is similar to the PCS voice-oriented access meth- ods that were previously used in DECT, and this provides a comfortable environ- ment for traditional methods for support of QoS. This feature is carried from the WATM activities that we discussed earlier in this chapter. The OFDM modem operating at 5 GHz is the same as 802.11a. Support of data rates of up to 54 Mbps with this PHY layer opens an environment for innovative wireless video applications that is very crucial for development of integrated home networks. In the next few sections, we provide the details of the HIPERLAN-2 standard that are final- ized by the time of this writing. The HIPERLAN-2 standard activities group has four subgroups in interoperability, regulatory, application, and marketing. For more detailed and up-to-date information, the reader can refer to [HIPweb] or (JON99].

5.8.1 Architecture and Reference Model

The overall architecture of the HIPERLAN-2 is shown in Figure 5.9. Like IEEE 802.11, HIPERLAN-2 supports centralized and ad hoc topologies. In the central-ized topology of HIPERLAN, shown in Figure 5.9(a), connection between the MS and the AP is similar to that in 802.11, but communication between the APs are different. The IEEE 802.11 with IAPP protocol allows two AP connected to an IP-based subnet to communicate with one another. HIPERLAN-2 allows both handover in a subnet and IP-based handover in a nonhomogeneous network. This generic architecture allows seamless interoperation with Ethernet, point-to-point protocol connection (e.g., over dial-up modem connections), UMTS cellular net-works, IEEE 1394 (e.g., Firewire, i.LINK) for entertainment systems, and ATM-based networks. These features allow manufacturers to support vertical roaming capability over a number of networks. The ad hoc networking in the HIPERLAN-2 is expected to support multi hop topology that provides for a better coverage.

Features considered for HIPERLAN-2 are far more complex and detailed than the features of the data-oriented IEEE 802.11. As a result, HIPE.RLAN-2 uses a new protocol stack architecture that is similar to the voice-oriented cellular networks. Figure 5.10 illustrates the simplified protocol stack of the HIPERLAN-2.

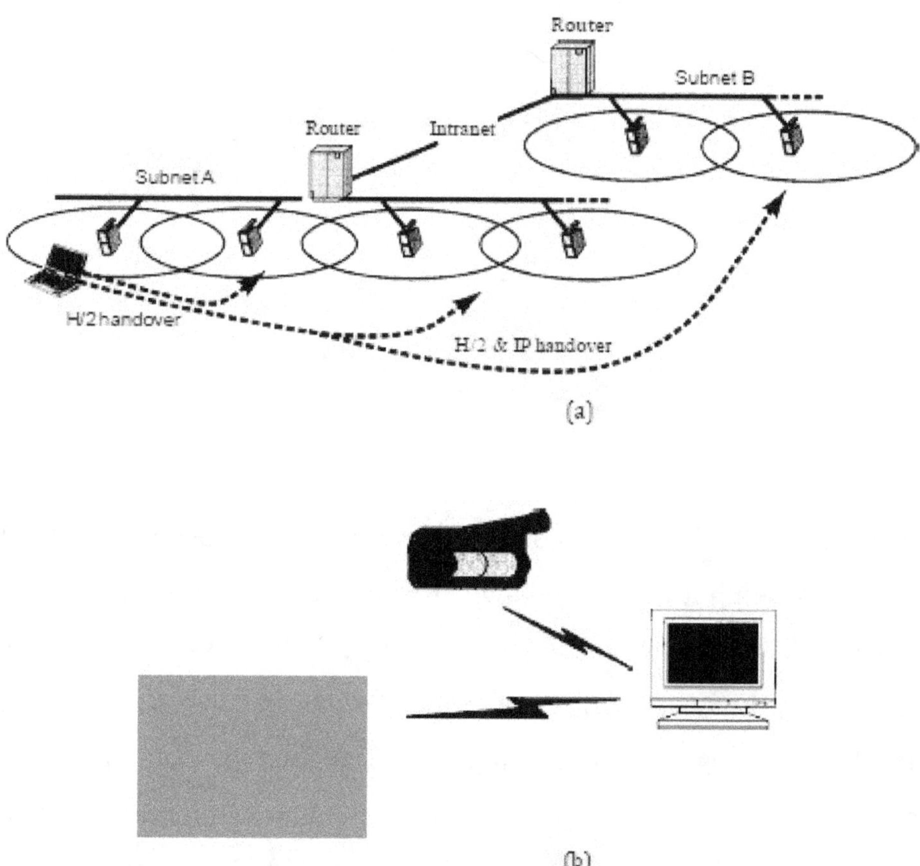

Figure 5.28 Topologies in the HIPERLAN-2: (a) infrastructure and (b) ad hoc.

Figure 5.28 Topologies in the HIPERLAN-2: (a) infrastructure and (b) ad hoc.

Basically there are three layers: PHY, DLC, and convergence. Multiple conver-gence layers, operating one at a time, map a number of higher layer protocol (PPP/IP, ATM, UMTS, Firewire, Ethernet) packets to DLC. The DLC layer pro-vides for the logical link between an AP and the MTs and includes functions for both medium access and communication management for connection handling. The DLC provides for a logical structure to map the convergence layer p‹ickets car- rying a number of different application protocols onto a single PHY layer .

5.8.2 PHY Layer

The PHY layer of the HIPERLAN-2 uses OFDM modulation that was described in Chapter 3. The specific details of the 802.11a/HIPERLAN-2 transmission system were illustrated in Example 3.12. The PHY layer of the HIPERLAN-i! standard

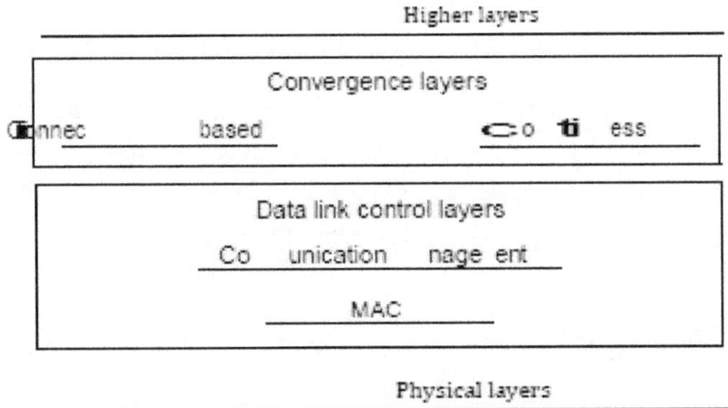

Figure 5.29 Protocol stack of the HIPERLAN-2.

adds the preamble of the DSSS IEEE 802.11, described in the previous chapter, to its own DLC packets. Then by defining a number of logical channels, similar to GSM or TDMA systems, transmits the packet as OFDM modulated bursts. Figure 5.30 shows the detailed block diagram of the modem. Like IEEE 502.11 FH-SS standard, the received data in HIPERLAN-2 is first scrambled for the whitening process. It is important to remind the reader that IEEE 802.11 DSSS does not go through the whitening process because the DS-SS process whitens the transmitted symbols when it turns the bits to chips. Like IEEE 802.11a, the scram- bled data in the HIPERLAN-2 is then passed through a convolutional coder that uses one of the rates—'/ , "h , or '/‹ that are used for different modulation techniques. The coded data is then interleaved to improve the reliability over temporal fading. The interleaved data is then modulated using BPSK, QPSK,

16-QAM, or G4-QAM, 20 MHz (64 carriers) Punctured code based on rate 1/2, constraint length 7 Figure 5.30 Block diagram of the OFDM modem to support a variety of data rates. Figure 5.31 shows all the data rates and corre- sponding modulation and coding schemes that are adopted by the IEEE: 802.11a and HIPERLAN-2 standards. As we explained in Example 3.8, there are 64 subcarriers in the OFDM modem of the IEEE 802.11/HIPERLAN-2 of which 48 are used for user data. To support multiple user data rates, modulation and coding in the subcarriers are changed, but the symbol transmission rate is kept at 250 ksps. By keeping the same symbol transmission rate for all data rates, lhe sam- pling rate of the signal and other signal processing filters at the receiver remain the same for all rates, but the coding of the bits and number of bits per symbol are changed digitally.

Example: Data Rates in HIPERLAN-2

For the 6 Mbps user data rate, each carrier carries 6 Mbps/48 = 125 kbps of data using rate convolutional encoder. The rate ? convolutional encoder requires a 250 kbps transmission rate to support 125 kbps user data. The 250 ksps user data is modulated over a BPSK modem that transmits one symbol per each coded bit. Therefore, the symbol or pulse transmission rate of the system is 250 ksps

Example: QAM and Rate / Convolution Coding

When we use 64-QAM modulation (six bits per symbol) with a rate / corivolutional coder the effective data rate will be 250 kbps/carrier X 4/3 X 6 bits/symbols x 48 carriers = 54 Mbps.

The symbol transmission rate of 250 ksps has a symbol transmission duration of 1/250 ksps = 4,000 ns. Therefore, each symbol is sent like a pulse of duration 4,000 ns with b00 ns time guard between two symbols. This time-gating process improves the resistance to multipath delay spread by preventing the inter symbol interference.

The standard also allows an optional 400 ns guard time for shorter distances where delay spread is smaller. Providing for a multirate transmission is a key feature of the 802.11a/HIPERLAN-2 transmissions. Multirate transmission provides for adaptation to the radio link quality and support of different DLC re- quests for transportation rates.

5.8.3 DLC Layer

The DLC layer provides for a logical link between an AP and the MTs over the OFDM PHY layer. Figure 12.32 illustrates the details of the DLC layer in the HIPERLAN-2. The MAC protocol and frame format for logical and transport channels are the major elements of the DLC layer. Using MAC protocol multiple users share the medium for information transmission and control signaling using transport channels. Using logical channels, similar to those used in voice-oriented networks, HIPERLAN-2 implements four protocols for proper operation of the network. These protocols are radio link control (RLC) protocol, DLC connection control (DCC), radio resource control (RRC), and association control function (ACF). DLC also supports the error control (EC) mechanism over logical channels to improve the reliability of the link.

The MAC layer protocol is dynamic TDMA/TDD, which was described in Chapter 4 under the voice-oriented fixed assignment access method, and it is similar to the access method used in DECT. This protocol supports AP to MT unicast and multicast communication, as well as MT-MT peer-to-peer transmissions. HIPERLAN-2 are mapped on to the SCH, LCH, and RCH transport channels. Figure 5.34 illustrates the relation between the logical and transport channels in HIPERLAN-2 standard. The SBCH is used only in downlink to broadcast control information related to the cell, whenever needed. It assists in handover, security, association, and radio link control functions. The DCCH conveys RLC sub layer signals between an MT and the AP. The UDCH carries DLC PDU for convergence layer data. The LCCH is used for error control functions for specific UDCH. The ASCH is used for association request and re association request messages.

Using the logical channels, HIPERLAN-2 implements the protocols for the proper operation of the network, shown in Figure 5.13. The RLC protocol gives a transport service for the signaling entities of the three other algorithms. These four entities provide for the DLC control plane to implement signaling messages. The ACF protocol handles association and dissociation to the network. To associate with the network, the MT listens to the BCH from different APs and selects the AP with the best radio link quality. The MT then continues with listening to the broad- cast of a globally unique network operator in the SBCH as to avoid association to a network, which is not able or allowed to offer services to the user of the h4T. If the MT decides to continue the association, the MT will request and be given a MAC- ID from the AP. This is followed by an exchange of link capabilities using the ASCH and establishing the PHY and convergence layer connection, as well as au- thentication and encryption procedures. After association, the MT can request for a DCCH that it uses to set up a DLC user connection with a unique support for QoS. For disassociation from the network, either MT notifies the AP that it no longer wants to communicate or AP realizes that the MT is no more active and it is out of the network. In either case, the AP will release all resources allocated for that MT. To implement the DCC algorithm, terminals request a DLC user connec- tion by transmitting signaling messages over the DCCH. The resource for the con- nection gets allocated, and after an ACK signal, the DLC connection is ready for traffic. The DCCH controls the resources for specific MAC entities. The algorithm also supports procedure for ending the connection or defining a new connection.

The RRC protocol handles handover, dynamic frequency seleclion, and sleeping mode and power saving operation. Like 802.11, the handover in HIPERLAN-2 starts with passive scanning that can be followed by an ‹ictive re- quest for handover. The difference between the 802.11 and HIPERLAN-2 is that HI PERLAN -2 provides two alternatives for passing the information for handover to the new AP. In the first approach, similar to 802.11, the new AP retrieves con- nection status and association information from the MT. In the second approach, MT provides the old AP address to the new AP, and the information is e: changed over the wire between the old and new APs. The second approach is faster, because the backbones always have higher bandwidth and capacity, and it does not add to the air traffic that is always desirable. The RRC in HIPERLAN-2 supports mecha- nism to measure the power and communicate with neighboring APs that allows d y- namic frequenc y selection (DFS). Similar to 802.11, the RRC of the HIPE RLAN -2 supports mechanisms for the AP to allow the MTs to go to sleeping mode to save in power consumption. The DLC layer of the HIPERLAN-2 also supports the error control mechanism to detect the errors in the arriving packets and arran *e the re- transmission through ACK/NACK signaling.

To support OoS HIPERLAN-2 recommends changing the periodicity of the transmitted messages that are illustrated in Figure 5.35. There are three! periodic operations shown in this figure, the longest belonging to the broadcast p‹eriod, the medium to Terminal A, and the shortest to Terminal B. Apparently, the delay as- sociated with the packets from Terminal B is the shortest and packets from Termi- nal A have medium delay as they are compared with the normal broadcast messages.

This mechanism allows a delay-controlled environment that is fertile for the implementation of the QoS control.

5.8.4 Convergence Layer

The main two responsibilities of the CL are adapting the service request from a higher layer to the DLC capabilities and to perform fragmentation and reassembly of different size packets from a variety of application protocols to HIPERLAN-2 packet format. Multiple convergence layers operate one at a time to map connection-based and connectionless higher layers such as PPP/IP, ATM, UMTS, Firewire, and Ethernet packets to HIPERLAN-2 DLC packets. To implement all these features, the CL of the HIPERLAN-2 provides a number of services. These services include segmentation and reassembly, priority mapping from 802.1p, ad-dress mapping from 802, multicast/broadcast handling, and flexible QoS classes [KHAOO].

5.8.5 Security

Comprehensive security mechanisms are seen for the first time in the HIPERLAN-2 system compared with other wireless standards. When contacted by an MT, the AP will respond with a subset of supported PHY modes, a selected convergence layer (only one), and a selected authentication and encryption procedure. As al-ways, there is an option not to use any authentication or encryption. If encryption is agreed upon, the MT will initiate the Diffie-Hellman key exchange to negotiate the secret session key for all unicast traffic between the MT and the AP. The Diffie-Hellman key exchange is discussed in Appendix 6A. In all other wireless systems, key management is a big issue. It is, however, not clear what the computational burden of the Diffie-Hellman key exchange is on wireless devices. Encryption is based on stream ciphers generated using a mechanism similar to the output feedback mode of DES [STI95].

HIPERLAN-2 supports both the use of DES and triple-DES (that is the de facto standard, while AES is in the standardization process) algorithms for strong encryption. Broadcast and multicast traffic can also be protected by encryption through the use of common keys distributed in an encrypted manner through the use of a unicast encryption key. All encryption keys must be periodically refreshed to avoid flaws in the security as discussed in Chapter 6.

Secret and public key algorithms can be employed for authentication. Au-thentication is possible using message authentication codes based c›n MD5, HMAC, and digital signatures based on RSA. Mutual authentication is supported for authentication of both the AP and the MT. HIPERLAN-2 supports a variety of identifiers for identification of the MS, via the network access identifier, JEEE ad-dress, and X.509 certificates. Challenge response mechanisms are also employed for identification.

5.8.6 Overall Comparison with 802.11

There are several hundreds MHz bands that are available for the 802.11a/ HIPERLAN-2 networks which can provide a comfortable multichannel operation for these standards. Availability of these bands and licensing conditions, however, is different in the United States, Europe, and Japan. Figure 12.17 shows the avail- able spectrum for the operation of the 802.11a/H1PERLAN-2 networks in typical countries around the world. There are 100 MHz unlicensed bands at 5,150— 5,250 MHz that are available in the United States, Europe, and Japan. Another 100 MHz of unlicensed bands at 5,250-5,350 MHz are also available in Europe and the United States. In the United States only, there is another 100 MHz of unlicensed bands at 5.725—5.825 MHz. Finally, there is 255 MHz of licensed hands at 5,470-5,725 MHz in Europe that are assigned for outdoor operation. As we dis- cussed in Chapter 11, the ISM bands in 2.4 GHz are only 84 MHz wide. For this reason, recently 5 GHz developments have dominated the attention of the wide- band wireless local access industry. However, the reader must note that I he pene-tration and consequently coverage at 2.4 GHz are better than at 5 GHz.

It provides an overall comparison between all aspects of the 832.11 and HIPERLAN-2 standards [JOH99]. The physical characteristics of HIPERLAN-2 and 502.11a are the same. The access method in HIPERLAN-2 is a voice-oriented access method that allows for better integration into voice-oriented b,ackbones such as UMTS and ATM networks. Connection-orientation, compulsory authenti-cation, link adaptation, dynamic frequency selection, and support of QoS make HIPERLAN-2 look like a next-generation cellular network that supports high data rates and provides IP services. The main distinction with a cellular system would be the use of unlicensed bands for which a service provider cannot predict the interference. The IEEE 802.11a is an IP-based network that draws from LAN backbone.

www.ingramcontent.com/pod-product-compliance
Lightning Source LLC
Chambersburg PA
CBHW081936160726
47999CB00008B/2408